The Wimbledon Synagogue Community Cookbook

Editor Liz Ison

The Wimbledon Synagogue Community Cookbook

wimshulcooks.wordpress.com

www.wimshul.org

Copyright © Wimshul Cooks 2015

978-1-909075-35-1

All Rights Reserved

No part of this book may be reproduced in any form,
by photocopying or by any electronic or mechanical means,
including information storage or retrieval systems,
without permission in writing from both the copyright
owner and the publisher of this book.

Published by Wimshul Cooks in association with Words by Design
Printed and bound by CPI Group (UK) Ltd, Croydon, CR0 4YY

Front cover: Rolling pin etched by Eleri Larkum. Photo by Libby Hipkins. Recipe for Eleri's gingerbread biscuits on page 135

Back cover: Photos by Libby Hipkins

CONTENTS

List of Articles	6
Acknowledgements and Credits	8
Foreword by Elisabeth Luard	9
Preface by Judith Ish-Horowicz	11
Welcome	13
Outline of the Book	15
A Note on Measurements	16
A Lettuce with Herbs	18
Don't Say Cheese	21
Community	25
The Jewish Year	109
Family Favourites	229
Cookie Gallery	319
Index of Contributors	329
Index of Recipes	337
Full Index	341

ARTICLES

Community

About the Wimshul Cooks Blog	Liz Ison	27
Kiddushim at Wimbledon	Judith Ish-Horowicz	30
Cakes, Care and Respect	Lynne Sidkin	33
Many Hands	Lynne Sidkin	39
Bread from the Earth and From Heaven	Rabbi S.A. Sheridan	41
Hallah and Sermon Preparation Plaited Together	Rabbi S. Rothschild	45
Shabbat Lunch with a French Twist	Josette Cohen	47
Abraham's Tent Confection	Eleri Larkum	49
Welsh Cakes and Strudel: A Bar Mitzvah Baking Tale	Renee Woolf	50
Hannah's Tzedakah Project	Hannah O'Keeffe	58
A Great Musician and a Great Cook	Sally-Ann Feldman	60
How the Bagel Arrived in SW19	Camilla McGill	65
Cooking and Learning at Apples and Honey Nursery	Claudia Camhi	72
Baking a Biblical Story at Playshul	Victoria Silverlock	88
Fairtrade at the Synagogue	Malcolm Clark	95
Cooking for the Wimbledon Night Shelter	Sally-Ann Feldman	96
Food and Community at Wimbledon & District Synagogue in the 1980s	Hilary Leek	103
A Mosaic Stew	Veena Vohora	107

The Jewish Year

Recipe for a Streatham Friday Night	Shoshi Ish-Horowicz	111
My Friday Evening	Julia Stanton	115
How to Break the Fast?	Carra Kane	127
Elucidating Latkes	Liz Ison	138
Time to Reinvent the Latke?	Alison Kelin	141

Reflections on Tu B'Shevat and a Date and Walnut Bread Recipe	Rabbi S. Rothschild	154
The Original Biblical Superfoods!	Y. Mason, S. Coussins & O. Kendler-Rhodes	159
Bazargan	Claudia Roden	167
Hamantaschen – Texas style!	Carra Kane	171
Baking Matzah in Ethiopia	Rabbi S.A. Sheridan	182
What to Eat on Pesach	Rabbi S.A. Sheridan	183
What Would I Put onto a Seder Plate?	Rabbi S. Rothschild	188
A Communal Seder	Camilla McGill & Carra Kane	191
Pesach Mornings by the Mersey	Mindi Ison	200
Recollections of Chilean Pesaj (Pesach)	Claudia Camhi	202
Matzah Pudding: A Victorian Odyssey?	Liz Ison	204
Memories of an East Ham Pesach	Heather Bieber	207
Old World Pesach Treats – Irish Style	Alison Kelin	208
Our Pesach "Plant"	Jo Freeman	210
My Mother's Pesach	Miriam Edelman	212
The Meaning of Matzah and a Short History of Bread	Rabbi S. Rothschild	220

Family Favourites

Soup, Beautiful Soup	Caroline Silver Lewis	234
Gooseberry Bushes and Gazpacho: Reminiscences and a Recipe	Diane Barnett	237
The Most Honest Recipe I Know	Rabbi Lionel Blue	257
My Dinner with Heston Blumenthal	Rabbi S.A. Sheridan	275
Flory Solomon's Indian Selection	Nina Portugal	280
Betty's Lockshen Pudding	Betty H. Burge	286
Middle Eastern Specialities	Gila Godsi	311
Marion's Recipes	Camilla McGill	316

Acknowledgements

A huge thank you to all those who contributed recipes and articles, to those who read and "follow" the Wimshul Cooks blog, and those who have attended cooking workshops and baking mornings.

> Grateful thanks to the support and contributions we have received from the following chefs and food writers:
>
> **Elisabeth Luard** (Foreword), **Claudia Roden** (Bazargan, p.167), **Heston Blumenthal** (Mushroom Spelt Risotto, p.278), **Rabbi Lionel Blue** (The Most Honest Recipe I Know: Arctic Chowder and Hummus Fit for Kings and Paupers, p.257), **Michael Leventhal** (Perfect Chocolate Brownies, p.294), **Silvia Nacamulli** (Pizza Romana - Candied Fruitcake, p.295), **Kim Kushner** (La Pasta - Orange Sponge Cake, p.297) and JC Food Editor **Victoria Prever** (Plum and Ginger Ice Cream with Crumble Topping and Roasted Nectarine Ice Cream, p.288).

Thank you to **Lotte Kramer** and **Jerry Markison** for permission to reproduce their poetry.

Thank you to the young artists who took part in a Wimshul Cooks Passover drawing competition. Their drawings, reproduced in this book, show how the Seder meal and its rituals continue to play such a central part in Jewish practice and identity.

Special thanks to those who **"bought a cookie"** and helped fund the printing costs as well as others who kindly made donations. The cookies appear in the Cookie Gallery. A big thank you to Josie Knox for proof reading, Liron Gilenberg and Nicki Howard for design advice and Tony Gray of Words by Design for publishing advice and assistance.

Credits

Cookbook design by **Liz Ison**. All photos (except those listed below) by **Libby Hipkins**.

Iced biscuits and etched woodwork were created by **Eleri Larkum**.

Liz Ison - Chocolate fridge biscuits, Girls making hallah, Friday hallah reveal, Hallah coming out of the oven, Hallah at the Isons, China cups of tea, Dreidel cookies, Latkes in the pan, Purim montage, Matzah making - Richmond, Falafel, Heston Blumenthal montage, Onion design cup and saucer.

Carra Kane - Communal seder; Veena & Mosaic lunch; **Judith Ish-Horowicz** - Savta making cake; **Eleri Larkum** - Abraham's Tent, Edible Sukkah and iced biscuits, House of Matzah in the making, Wimshul Cooks buns; **Rabbi Sybil Sheridan** - Matzah making in Ethiopia ; **Caroline Silver-Lewis** - Rabbi Blue and Rabbi Sheridan, Soup being served.

FOREWORD

What a magnificent record of love and care in edible form! Memories, images and personal recollections are the most unusual and valuable of all the contributions.

While the scent of good cooking rises from every page, the recipes have the ring of experience. There's no doubt that all are tried and tested, and there's no doubt of the generosity of the contributors in sharing their favourite dishes and the circumstances under which they were (and are) served.

I particularly enjoyed reading about the Polish Christmas at Wimbledon Synagogue since it pushes the boundaries of the collection right out into the wider community.

It would be a shame if this fabulous collection were not enjoyed by everyone of whatever religious or secular persuasion. We all need reminding of where we come from, as evidenced by the passion with which people, particularly those for whom the record is less visible (all of us whose ancestors are unrecorded in history books) go searching for their roots.

I once asked Claudia Roden why so many benchmark cookbooks were written by those of Jewish descent. She thought for a moment before giving her answer: "Diaspora – we need to remember who we are."

Congratulations to all involved.

Elisabeth Luard

Award-winning food writer, author and Trustee Director of the Oxford Symposium on Food and Cookery

PREFACE

"And you shall eat and be satisfied" (Deut 8:10)

Isn't it remarkable how a passing suggestion can grow beyond one's greatest imaginings and how, on the way, friendships are made, stories are told, laughter bubbles and innumerable cups of tea are drunk?

Liz Ison first mentioned the idea of a community cooking project to me a few years ago. Teaming up with Lynne Sidkin, our catering mensch, and the rest of the talented Wimshul Cooks group, a creative force was unleashed.

Recipes and stories have fallen like manna, each one delicious, filled with love and memories. I know you are tempted, and that's fine. You have the Wimshul Cooks' blessing to take your pick, have a bite and thoroughly enjoy every literary and culinary mouthful.

Kol Hakavod to Liz, Lynne and all the Wimshul Cooks team.

Judith Ish-Horowicz

WELCOME

Like many others before us, the group that set up Wimshul Cooks in June 2012 realised that food and community go hand in hand. We wanted to use the language of food to tell the story of the diverse, warm and inclusive environment that is Wimbledon Synagogue.

The blog that we set up, and this cookbook that grew out of the articles and recipes that we published online, shows how food helps our community and its families function and flourish. It includes recipes and stories gathered on many aspects of community life as well as many precious family recipes, a few "celebrity" guest recipes, poems and many warm personal memories.

We hope you enjoy reading the book and trying the recipes for yourself.

Liz Ison, Lynne Sidkin, Claudia Camhi, Libby Hipkins,
Eleri Larkum, Carra Kane, Alison Kelin, Miriam Edelman

OUTLINE OF THE BOOK

This book is in three sections: Community, The Jewish Year and Family Favourites.

Community - How food plays a part in our community life. Here you will find articles on Kiddushim, for ordinary Shabbats and for special occasions; on how cooking is the perfect way for children to learn about Judaism; on cooking for a Night Shelter and how the Ladies Guild of the 1980s produced the first Wimbledon Synagogue Cookbook…and much more.

The Jewish Year - We follow the festival year gathering together recipes that are both traditional and innovative, and feature reminiscences which reflect the importance of food in our memories of the past. For many, the experience of being Jewish has been shaped by the tastes and smells of the kitchen.

Family Favourites - Here is a large and diverse collection of recipes, many with a special story or meaning and reflecting the diverse and international culinary influences of the community.

A Note on Measurements

Our aim has been to modify recipes as little as possible from the original although, as well as careful checking and editing, we have made some changes so that recipes appear in similar formats. We have included metric and imperial measurements (i.e. grams, ounces, millilitres and fluid ounces). The exception to this are the recipes which use cup measurements (where adding in conversions distracts from the enjoyable simplicity of using cups) so we suggest you also use standard cups (available at cook shops) when making these recipes. However, if you wish to convert to metric or imperial measurements (or from metric/imperial to cup), you can use these tables as a guide.

When a recipe calls for a teaspoon or a tablespoon of an ingredient, use standard measuring spoons. One teaspoon is equivalent to 5ml; and one tablespoon is equivalent to 15ml.

Make sure you preheat the oven to the temperature specified in the recipes before putting your dish in the oven.

Oven Temperature

Gas Mark	°F	°C
1	275°F	140°C
2	300°F	150°C
3	325°F	170°C
4	350°F	180°C
5	375°F	190°C
6	400°F	200°C
7	425°F	220°C
8	450°F	230°C
9	475°F	240°C

If using a fan oven you will need to reduce the oven temperature in a recipe by 20 degrees.

Weights

Imperial	Metric
½ oz	10 g
¾ oz	20 g
1 oz	25 g
1½ oz	40 g
2 oz	50 g
2½ oz	60 g
3 oz	75 g
4 oz	110 g
4½ oz	125 g
5 oz	150 g
6 oz	175 g
7 oz	200 g
8 oz	225 g
9 oz	250 g
10 oz	275 g
12 oz	350 g
1 lb	450g
1 lb 1 oz	500 g
1 lb 8 oz	700 g
2 lb	900 g
3 lb	1.35 kg

Volume

Imperial	Metric
2 fl oz	55 ml
3 fl oz	75 ml
5 fl oz (¼ pint)	150 ml
10 fl oz (½ pint)	275 ml
1 pint	570 ml
1¼ pint	725 ml
1¾ pint	1 litre
2 pint	1.2 litres
2½ pint	1.5 litres
4 pint	2.25 litres

American Cup Conversions

American	Imperial	Metric
1 cup flour	5oz	150g
1 cup caster/ granulated sugar	8oz	225g
1 cup brown sugar	6oz	175g
1 cup butter/margarine	8oz	225g
1 cup sultanas/raisins	7oz	200g
1 cup currants	5oz	150g
1 cup ground almonds	4oz	110g
1 cup golden syrup	12oz	350g
1 cup uncooked rice	7oz	200g
1 cup grated cheese	4oz	110g
1 stick butter	4oz	110g

Liquid Conversions

Imperial	Metric	American
½ fl oz	15 ml	1 tbsp
1 fl oz	30 ml	⅛ cup
2 fl oz	60 ml	¼ cup
4 fl oz	120 ml	½ cup
8 fl oz	240 ml	1 cup
16 fl oz	480 ml	1 pint

A Lettuce with Herbs

Lotte Kramer

Lotte Kramer, mother of Wimbledon Synagogue member Stephen Kramer, was born in Mainz in 1923. She came to Britain in July 1939 at the age of 15 as part of the Kindertransport. Lotte and her husband were members of Wimbledon & District Synagogue for many years from the early 1950s until 2014.

In 1979 Lotte began to write poetry, compelled to articulate her experiences: "Memories of childhood in Nazi Germany, which I had buried for many years, came back and insisted on being written about*." She has gone on to publish many volumes of poetry.

A Lettuce With Herbs

I was sent down the hill
To the greengrocer shop
To buy a lettuce with herbs

That smell of freshness
Of chives, borage, dill,
As electric then as now

As I cut those couriers
In my garden bed
Filling my senses

With currents of joy.
Their fragrance invites
That dusty street

Snaking down the hill
And I skipping up
With a bundle of greenness.

*From Kramer's Introduction to her *New and Collected Poems*, Rockingham Press, 2011

Cherries

These cherries taste of summer streets to school,
Or rather of the walk there in the heat
When stumbling over melting tar the mile
Seemed endless. Pennies in my fist, the treat

Of shiny cherries waited. The corner
Shop was rich with fruit, all ripening juices
Cased in bumper beads from black to red, more
Like a feast of pregnant marbles than these

Perishable sights. I bought and clutched them
In a coarse brown paper bag. At the first
Break, their squashy sweetness shared our game:
We stained our faces, ears, our frocks, with thirst

For them, ignoring maggots that could lurk
Inside their flesh, a white curl in the dark.

An Old Woman Cooking Eggs

(Velazquez)

With wisdom she cradles the egg in her hand
And answers the questioning boy while her spoon
Is poised over sizzling eggs in the pot.
All is simple, the red terracotta is hot,
The knife is laid on the edge of the dish.
With her handsome old face she turns to the boy
Confirming her grandmother's hidden bond.

Reproduced with kind permission of the author

A Lettuce with Herbs (*Black over Red*, Rockingham Press, 2005); Cherries (*The Shoemaker's Wife*, Hippopotamus Press, 1987); An Old Woman Cooking Eggs (*Velazquez*), (*Turning the Key*, Rockingham Press, 2009)

Thea (Libby's daughter) and her great-grandmother Helen making hallah together.

Don't Say "Cheese"

Liz Ison

Libby Hipkins has been the Wimshul Cooks' photographer, capturing the project from the very beginning. When the Wimshul Cooks group first met, the youngest of Libby's three children Thea was a baby and was considered the most popular member of the committee, being passed round between us as enthusiastically as Lynne's chocolate tiffin.

Libby's photographic style is to act as witness, watching events unfold in a quiet and unobtrusive fashion while capturing the special moments and emotions as they arise. People rarely notice that Libby is taking photos, or even has a camera in her hand, helped by the fact that she prefers not to use flash. All the photos that Libby has taken were of real events, usually in the synagogue and never in a studio, always using natural light (of which there is not much in abundance in the middle of a synagogue).

The photographs of dishes that feature in these pages were made for events or meals such as the honey cake tasting morning or the spinach workshop. The food was of course all homemade with no food styling involved. Libby had to be quick too – the dishes needed to be snapped before they were gobbled!

At our first events, Libby would carry baby Thea around in a sling, "I would take off the lens cap with one hand, tuck it into my back pocket, while Thea would be sucking peacefully on a finger of my other hand. Many of the photos had to be taken one handed!" She doesn't like to stage shots, especially with children as they are rarely likely to co-operate, "I enjoy capturing children's expressions – their curiosity or reaction to something - moments when children are exploring, whether they are engaging with food and its texture or the outside world. A particular favourite were the trips to Garson Farm to pick fruit and vegetables for Sukkot and then capturing the beautiful synagogue Sukkah in the process of its transformation."

Libby started taking photos from the age of seven when she was given her first camera. "Since 2008, I've taken part in the "Photo-a-day" project which involves posting a photo online every day of the year. It has been a wonderful way of recording our family life." Libby and her husband Nick have sent their three children, Megan, Eli and Thea to Apples and Honey Nursery (based at Wimbledon Synagogue) and subsequently became members of the Synagogue, taking an active role in young family events.

About the Wimshul Cooks Blog

Liz Ison

There are so many food blogs out there – why did we create another one?

It is true that the internet is crowded with food blogs and cookery websites of all kinds, and there are many excellent sites covering Jewish food. What we feel is unique about WimShul Cooks is that it is a grassroots site, created for and by members of the community – a way to find out what your community friends are cooking and baking, and share what you are doing in turn. At the same time, it also shows the outside world what your community is like – or at least what it likes cooking and eating!

The Wimshul Cooks blog became a way of staying in touch with some of our members who don't come to the synagogue very often, or don't live nearby. It helps us engage with former members who have moved to other towns or countries. Families of members (whether they live here or abroad) are often our most regular readers and we have had submissions of recipes from people around the world. So, although the initial focus was local, our reach has, in fact, become global.

The interactive nature of the blog format is one of its greatest attractions. One idea leads to another ("Lynne, please give us your chocolate orange fudge cake recipe", wrote Lisa on the comments section of the blog. A couple of days later, Lynne had duly submitted the recipe and it was posted on the site). It wasn't long before people were coming up with their own ideas and articles.

Wimshul Cooks went on to develop a life of its own, moving seamlessly between the virtual and the real world. We organised tasting mornings ("Get innovative with Matzah" was one; honey cake tasting for Rosh Hashanah another), laid on some extra special Kiddushim (a Seven Species Kiddush for Tu B'Shevat and an artery-clogging cheesecake Kiddush for Shavuot) and organised workshops

on bagel making and pastry making. We encouraged people to write down their recipes and stories, took lots of photos and were thrilled to find more and more ways that food helps our community engage with family life, religion, culture, ritual and values.

Though we sought out specific articles, and cajoled people to part with precious family recipes, we found the project evolving in its own fashion. Some wanted to look back, with traditional recipes and a nostalgic glow, while other contributions are innovative and modern. We even have a few "celebrity" recipes submitted by Heston Blumenthal, Claudia Roden, Rabbi Lionel Blue and others and are very grateful for their support.

But at heart, we are carrying on the great tradition of our mothers and grandmothers who have shared their family recipes with friends or neighbours on handwritten pieces of paper, or passed on the knowledge mother-to-daughter in the kitchen – a blog is just the modern way of doing it.

Some highlights of the Wimshul Cooks blog

- Since we set up in 2012 we have published over 100 articles online.

- The blog has had over 22,000 views in over 70 countries from the UK to the USA, Sweden, Poland and Chile.

- Our blog has featured in the Jewish Chronicle and local newspapers.

- Our online survey on people's favourite Jewish foods asked such fundamental questions as whether people preferred traditional gefilte fish, sushi or fish and chips (gefilte fish is in third place). Asked who their favourite Jewish cook is, we're pleased to report that the most popular response has been "my mum", so Jewish mothers everywhere can give a sigh of relief.

34 LIFE/FOOD

LIFE FOOD

Wimbledon and District Reform Synagogue has hit upon a modern way of preserving and sharing recipes

Need a recipe? Check our blog

BY VICTORIA PREVER

Honey cakes at the synagogue's New Year tasting

What on earth would you cook Heston Blumenthal for dinner? This was the conundrum faced by Rabbi Sybil Sheridan which she recounted on a new food blog set up by members of Wimbledon and District Synagogue.

Rabbi Sheridan — one of the community's two female rabbis — told of her reaction after her husband, Maidenhead Synagogue's Rabbi Jonathan Romain — announced that he had invited the Michelin-starred chef to their home.

A group of synagogue members — all keen cooks — have inadvertently hit upon a very 21st-century way of engaging with their community while swapping their recipes and those of their mothers and grandmothers.

Last June, they launched a blog of recipes and articles about food and Jewish life. But they hadn't set out to be so innovative.

"We wanted to write a cookbook, to raise money for the synagogue. Not only recipes but also advice for community events, cooking for a crowd, how to use food to help children learn about celebrating Shabbat and festivals," says Liz Ison, the blog's editor.

She adds that they wanted to make the project a communal experience, with recipe and tips from synagogue members — "recipes from the diverse range of cooking traditions that make up our community".

In the planning stages, one of the group — keen baker Eleri Larkum — suggested they set up a blog as part of the cookery book project.

Ison admits she and the rest of the committee were not initially struck by the idea. "There were a lot of mystified looks. I thought what's the point of putting all of our recipes online? Who will buy the book if they can get them all free?"

But it only took a few days for Ison and the others to identify the immediate benefits.

Ison says she had already seen how useful food could be to engage people. "My three children all attended the Apples and Honey Nursery based at the synagogue. The nursery head, Judith Ish Horowicz, is an inspirational educator and I saw first hand from her how food and cooking can be a way of learning about Judaism and Jewish life. My children baked challah there very Friday — a highlight of their week — and I got involved in preparing the big bucket of dough for the weekly bake-in," she smiles.

"I realised a blog would be a great tool to share among ourselves — and the wider blogosphere — who we are and what we do, and writing about what we like to eat and cook."

She and the rest of the group were converted to the idea of transforming their plans from the fund-raising book to something that would benefit their lively community. And *Wimshulcooks* was born.

Nursery head Horowicz has played a pivotal role in the birth of the blog. "She's sort of like a saint — she knows everyone in the congregation and has brought most of the people involved in the blog committee to this project," says Ison.

The nine women on the team behind the blog reflect a wide range of talents and backgrounds within the synagogue's community. There are Sephardim and Ashkenazim, photographers, editors, nutritionists and educators, all with a passion for food and cooking.

Ison ensures that an entry is posted on average once a week. "Since we set up we have published over 30 articles and the blog has had over 2,500 views in more than 30 countries," she says proudly.

She is about to add rainbow biscuits (see recipe right) made by the children at Playshul — the pre-school section of the synagogue's cheder to learn about the story of Joseph.

Both of the synagogue's rabbis have embraced *Wimshulcooks*, adding their own foodie experiences. Rabbi Sheridan shared her Heston Blumenthal experience, while Rabbi Silvia Rothschild provided challah recipe, describing how she shapes her weekly sermon while waiting for the bread to rise and prove.

"The blog has become a way of staying in touch with members who don't come to synagogue often," explains Ison. "And it helps us engage with former members who have moved to other towns or countries."

The blog has also spawned events like their honey cake tasting for Rosh Hashanah. "Everyone baked two cakes — one to taste and a second to give to someone who was unable to cook their own," says Ison.

"One of our committee members, Claudia Camhi, bakes award-winning almond cakes professionally — and even created a recipe especially for the event." (See the recipe below.)

Nursery children and staff, synagogue office staff, the adult learning group and baby and toddler group all came along and shared the experience together.

"We think we've stumbled upon a great tool for increasing community engagement," smiles Ison, who says they still plan to produce their book in the future.

Find out what the Rabbi fed Heston, read a recipe from Claudia Roden and join the synagogue's hamentaschen bake-in only at Wimshulcooks.wordpress.com

Liz Ison (left) and Lynne Sidkin, two of the women behind the food blog

Rainbow coat cookies

- WE made these coat-shaped biscuits to celebrate the story of Joseph with the youngest children at the synagogue's cheder, using templates made of baking parchment, which they cut around with butter knives.

INGREDIENTS
225g softened butter
110g caster sugar
275g plain flour
Food colouring

METHOD
- Preheat your oven to 180°C and grease a baking tray.
- Cream together the butter and sugar to form a smooth, fluffy mixture.
- Sift in the flour a little at a time then knead into a ball of dough.
- Divide the dough into several smaller balls (we decided on 7 for the different colours of the rainbow).
- Take each ball and make a well in the centre. Add a few drops of your chosen food colouring.
- Work the colouring into the dough until the colour is bright and even. You can add a little more flour if the dough becomes too sticky.
- Roll out each different coloured ball flat and pile the different coloured doughs on top of each other. Roll the pile into a log shape.
- You can then cut slices off the log, each of which will have a rainbow of colours.
- Roll out a slice and cut out your shapes.
- Bake for 10–15 minutes until firm but not too browned.
- Cool on a wire rack.

Claudia Camhi's almond whisky honey cake

- THIS is my own recipe. It is a moist cake and the lemon zest makes it taste lighter. I use an 8-inch, non-stick in cling film, it can be frozen.

INGREDIENTS

METHOD
- Preheat oven to 180°C. Do not use fan setting.
- Place the mix into the tin and top it with the almond...
...in a baking...
...drizzle...

...foil marked in middle to form a pitched roof-like top. This will protect the top layer and will allow air to circulate without sticking to the mix.
- It is ready when you insert a cocktail stick at the centre of the cake and it comes out dry. It should look golden.
- Once cool, moisten by drizzling whisky over the cake with a spoon.

Jewish cookery group hope to publish book

A team of amateur Jewish cooks whose community blog has attracted the attention of celebrity chef Heston Blumenthal wants to publish its first book.

Wimshul Cooks was set up one year ago by members of the Wimbledon and District Synagogue in Queensmere Road.

The synagogue's community cookbook project began with the aim of creating a place where members could share their families' Jewish recipes, food memories and traditions.

Its success snowballed, attracting thousands of hits from as far flung locations as the Fiji Islands.

The Wimshul Cooks now hope to publish their 43 recipes, along with exclusive contributions from celebrity chefs Heston Blumenthal and Claudia Roden.

Judaism follows strict kosher practices that say only animals that both have "cloven hooves" and "chew the cud" can be eaten, such as cattle and game, but must be ritually slaughtered, while all dairy products must have come from kosher animals.

The book will be sold to raise funds for the synagogue and its chosen charities and will mark its 65th year.

Tasty treats: Kate and Liz sample some of the food

Synagogue's blog cooks up a storm with celebrity chef Heston Blumenthal

Kiddushim at Wimbledon

Judith Ish-Horowicz

> When you are asked in the world to come, "What was your work?" and you answer, "I fed the hungry," you will be told, "This is the gate of the Lord, enter into it, you who have fed the hungry."
>
> *Midrash Psalms 118:17*

I remember when I first came to Wimbledon, nearly 30 years ago, and the Ladies Guild, as it was then called, was struggling to find volunteers to prepare the weekly Kiddush table. The Guild, as it was renamed shortly afterwards, opened its doors to men but none of them seemed inclined to take up the challenge of organising the Kiddush rota.

Then along came Anne Bower, my mother-in-law, and in true Anne style, without fuss, she would ensure that the table was beautifully presented and that there would always be a welcoming smile and refreshments for both members and visitors.

When Anne became ill, Lynne Sidkin stepped in and continued the Wimbledon custom of hospitality which has now become a byword among synagogues across the length and breadth of the UK and, indeed, internationally!

Nobody tasting Lynne's famous lemon drizzle cake, coffee cake, chocolate brownies and fridge biscuits will forget their visit to Wimbledon. But it's not just the delicious cakes that feed and fill out our bodies; Lynne also nourishes our souls with her care and concern. If you are stressed over an upcoming simcha, Lynne knows how many glasses of juice you can get out of one carton, how many bridge rolls to order, where to get the best sushi – you name it, Lynne has the answer.

There is always soup or a cake in the freezer to take when visiting a sick friend and everything is prepared with such love and respect. I have on numerous occasions marvelled at the lightness of her baking but Lynne assures me that her cakes cannot be compared with those of her mother. She, says Lynne, is the true master baker!

At Rosh Hashanah, Lynne rustles up over 80 honey cakes for those who are alone, unwell, depressed or just to bring a smile to your face and help make the New Year even sweeter. At Simchat Torah, she ensures the Hatanim will be honoured with a truly delicious spread. We are strengthened with soup for our late night study session on Shavuot and there is always fruit cake to help concentration at the early morning Torah study sessions.

The schools of Rabbi Hillel and Rabbi Shammai were often divided but over Lynne there would have been no conflict.

Shammai said that one should "greet each person with a cheerful facial expression" (Pirke Avot 1:15) and Hillel said, "do not separate yourself from the community" (Pirke Avot 2:5).

Lynne creates community, ensuring that everyone feels welcomed, and we all love her.

Cakes, Care and Respect

Lynne Sidkin

Our son Sam was barmitzvah in 2002 and it was shortly afterwards that I became pulled into Synagogue community life. That was the year Rabbis Sybil Sheridan and Sylvia Rothschild arrived and I was asked by Hilary Leek to help organise the catering after the Induction Service. This was no gentle introduction – the number of guests expected was 400 and our task involved converting 28 loaves of bread into neat triangular sandwiches with no crusts!

Up until that time, Saturday Kiddushim were organised by Anne Bower, mother of Patrick and mother-in-law of Judith Ish-Horowicz. As she was becoming a little frail, I asked her one day if she would like me to take over the preparation of Kiddushim. She agreed with a warm, wide beam!

Initially, with the help of Alison Kelin, I introduced a system asking different families to take responsibility for organising Kiddushim, by bringing in three cakes, cutting them up and clearing away afterwards. However, this became increasingly difficult to manage: festivals sometimes fell on a Saturday or families wanted to host their own celebration Kiddush. A central co-ordinator was therefore needed and it was at this point that I took on the baking and running of Kiddushim myself.

Although we worry about dropping attendance at Saturday morning services, there is a core group of people who regularly attend, week in, week out. Over the years many of them have built up our community and deserve our care and respect. Several have their favourite seat in synagogue but sadly as the years pass some are no longer occupied. It is important to me that the Saturday morning stalwarts receive a warm welcome, a piece of home-made cake and perhaps a 'doggy bag' to take home.

Kiddush is a time when, at the end of a long week, the congregation can relax and chat and it also provides an opportunity for us to welcome visitors and encourage potential new members!

On a normal Saturday I usually provide three to four cakes. The most popular are the lemon drizzle cake and the infamous chocolate fridge biscuits. This recipe originally came from my mother's friend in Bristol and has now been passed far and wide. I find baking very therapeutic and most evenings during the week I bake between 5 and 7 pm. Output increased greatly when our son was away at university and I wanted to occupy the quiet hours!

On many Saturdays the community is treated to a special Kiddush by those celebrating a life-cycle event. On these occasions I speak to the host and discuss various options, menus and quantities. Over the years I have gained experience of caterers, costs and the best suppliers and I also advise and book waitresses through the Synagogue office. The content of fare varies considerably – there has been a definite move from the more traditional bridge rolls and bagels to platters of sushi. However, the fish ball still reigns supreme in its popularity.

My involvement with larger functions can prove both interesting and amusing. The most unusual request came from a host holding a pirate party who wanted a live parrot on site! Unfortunately this was not possible for health and safety reasons!

In addition to Kiddushim I 'don' my catering hat at Festivals and organise cheesecake, hamantaschen, fruit, doughnuts and honey cakes.

I also enjoy offering practical support to Shabbat Club and helping prepare food for the children following their services.

The single downside of the role has to be an increased calorie intake as a result of licking the cake bowls but it is a small price to pay for the pleasure I derive from what I do.

A Selection of Lynne's Kiddush Cakes

Honey Cake

Makes two loaf cakes.

450g (1lb) golden syrup

275ml (10 fl oz) cold water

200g (7oz) granulated sugar

240ml (8 fl oz) sunflower oil

3 eggs

450g (1lb) self-raising flour

1 level teaspoon each of ground ginger, mixed sweet spice and cinnamon

1 level teaspoon baking powder

1 level teaspoon bicarbonate of soda dissolved in 2 tablespoons plus 2 teaspoons Kiddush wine

Preheat the oven to 180°C (fan oven)/400°F/Gas Mark 6.

Lightly grease and line 2 x 2lb (900g) loaf tins. Heat the syrup, water, sugar and oil over a gentle heat until the sugar has dissolved. In a large bowl, whisk the eggs and then beat in the syrup mixture. Dissolve the bicarbonate of soda in the wine. Then add this as well as all the dry ingredients. Beat until smooth.

Pour into the two tins (about two-thirds full) and bang on surface to remove air. You should have enough mixture over to make about 10 fairy cakes!

Place tins in oven and immediately turn down heat to 140°C/325°F/Gas Mark 3. Bake for approximately 50 minutes until a rich brown.

This cake tastes best after it has been left to mature for two or three days.

Lemon Drizzle Cake

I think that alongside the chocolate fridge biscuits, this lemon drizzle cake is the most popular cake at Kiddush. I bake them in batches of four.

For the cake mixture

110g (4oz) margarine

170g (6oz) caster sugar

170g (6oz) self-raising flour

4 tablespoons milk

Grated rind of 1 lemon

2 large eggs

For the syrup

110g (4oz) icing sugar

Juice of 1 lemon

Preheat the oven to 160°C (fan oven)/350°F/Gas Mark 4. Grease and line a 2lb (900g) loaf tin. Put all the cake ingredients in a bowl and beat until smooth. Transfer to the tin and bake for 45 minutes. Remove cake from oven and stand on a cooling tray.

Mix the lemon juice and icing sugar together. Prick the top of the warm cake with a fork, then gently pour the syrup over.

The cake freezes very well and will stay fresh in an airtight container until it has all been devoured!

Chocolate Fridge Biscuits

These are one of my most popular bakes. The recipe originally came from my mother's friend in Bristol and has now been passed far and wide.

110g (4oz) margarine

2 tablespoons golden syrup

25g (1oz) caster sugar

1½ tablespoons drinking chocolate

225g (8oz) crushed digestives

225g (8oz) Cadbury's dairy milk chocolate for topping

1 tablespoon raisins

Melt margarine, syrup, sugar and drinking chocolate. Add biscuits to pan, followed by raisins and stir well.

Press mixture into 18 cm (7 inch) greased and lined square tray. Melt chocolate and spread over the top.

Refrigerate and enjoy!

Rocky Road

A newer addition to the repertoire.

100g (3½oz) butter or margarine

300g (10½oz) milk or dark chocolate

4 tablespoons golden syrup

200g (7oz) digestive biscuits

75g (3oz) vegetarian mini marshmallows

75g (3oz) raisins

75g (3oz) dried cranberries

If you wish you could substitute one of the fruits with chopped nuts.

Lightly grease and line a 20cm (8 inch) square tin, leaving an overhang so that the paper will cover the cake later. Melt the butter/margarine, chocolate and syrup in a bowl over hot water. Crush the biscuits and place in a bowl with the marshmallows and fruits. Pour in the chocolate mixture and mix well. Spoon the mixture into the tin and press down with a spatula. Fold the overhanging paper over the top of the cake and press down with your hands to compact the mixture. Place in fridge to set and then cut up into 25 squares.

Can be frozen. Enjoy and don't even think of the calorie content!

Chocolate Orange Loaf with Fudge Frosting

This is one of my favourite Kiddush cake recipes and I always make four at a time! My husband is delighted when I make a batch as it means he comes home to a large glass of freshly squeezed orange juice – the recipe requires only the orange zest!

For the cake

150g (5oz) self-raising flour

2 tablespoons cocoa powder

75g (3oz) drinking chocolate

125g (4½oz) caster sugar

125g (4½oz) butter or margarine

Finely grated zest of one orange

2 large eggs

2 tablespoons hot water

2 tablespoons cold milk

For the frosting

115g (4oz) icing sugar

25g (1oz) butter or margarine

1 level teaspoon instant coffee granules

1 tablespoon hot water

Preheat the oven to 180°C (160°C if fan oven) 350°F/Gas Mark 4. Grease and line a 2lb (900g) loaf tin.

Beat the eggs to blend. Combine the flour, cocoa powder and drinking chocolate in a bowl. Cream the butter or margarine until soft, then beat in the caster sugar a little at a time. Beat in the orange zest followed by the eggs then the hot water. Stir in the cocoa mixture, alternating with the cold milk.

Spoon into the tin and bake for 40-50 minutes or until firm to the touch. Leave to cool on a wire rack.

For the frosting

Sift the icing sugar into a bowl. Put the remaining ingredients into a small pan and heat gently, without boiling. Remove from the heat and pour over the icing sugar. Beat until smooth and spread over the top of the cake.

Tip: The cake cuts into ten slices and freezes well.

Dutch Apple Cake

I served this at last year's Shabbat Kiddush in the Sukkah.

Cake batter

175g (6oz) self-raising flour

175g (6oz) caster sugar

1 egg

125ml milk

40g (1½oz) melted butter

Topping

25g (1oz) melted butter

450g (1lb) baking apples

75g (3oz) granulated sugar

1 level teaspoon cinnamon

Preheat the oven to 180°C (fan oven)/400°F/Gas Mark 6. Grease and line a tin 30 x 17.5 x 2.5cm (12 x 7 x 1 inches).

Put the flour and sugar into a bowl and add the egg, milk and 40g of melted butter. Mix to smooth batter and pour into the tin. Brush with the 25g melted butter.

Peel and core apples and cut into slices. Lay slices in overlapping rows on the cake batter. Mix the sugar and cinnamon and sprinkle over the top.

Bake for 35 minutes.

Kiddush Chocolate Brownies

2 eggs

200g (7oz) golden caster sugar

150g (5oz) margarine

1 teaspoon vanilla essence

3 tablespoons boiling water

75g (3oz) self-raising flour

4 level tablespoons cocoa

70g (3oz) melted Cadbury's dairy milk chocolate

Preheat the oven to 180°C (fan oven 160°C)/340°F/Gas mark 4. Grease and line an 18-20cm (7-8 inch) square tin which is at least 2.5 cm (1 inch) deep.

In a food processor, process the eggs and sugar for 2 minutes. Divide the margarine into 4 pieces and drop in. Pulse for 2 minutes. Add the vanilla essence and boiling water and process until smooth. Add the melted chocolate, flour and cocoa and pulse until combined. Clean the sides of the bowl with a spatula.

Turn mixture into the tin and bake for 30 minutes.

Allow to cool and then sprinkle with caster sugar. Divide into squares and store in an airtight container when completely cold.

Many Hands...

Lynne Sidkin

A significant proportion of the 'activities' that take place at the Synagogue have a connection with food. Festivals, Kiddushim, talks, fundraisers, Havurah suppers and memorial services all involve food and on each occasion there is preparation, serving and clearing to be undertaken.

We truly could not manage without Ludmila, our head waitress and her current team: Kamila, Monika, Oksana, Sylwia and Danka. Ludmila has been involved with the Synagogue for 15 years and is responsible for organising waitresses to help at the various events.

She and her team, who mainly come from Poland, work incredibly hard, often for long hours and they have become an integral part of Wimbledon Shul. They put thought and care into the way they present the food which is noticed and appreciated by the Community, to the extent they are often asked if they will help at our members' home events.

This book provides a perfect opportunity to thank them for all they do for us. We're delighted that the team has contributed a typical Polish dish to this collection.

Polish Ryba Po Grecku ("Fish Greek Style")

Ludmila Gorna

We were really touched to be asked to contibute a recipe to this collection and to be considered part of the community. We enjoy the communal and inclusive atmosphere of the Synagogue, the generosity and good will of its members.

This recipe comes from Monika who is one of our team assisting at synagogue functions. It is one of her favourite recipes, cooked by her grandmother and mother and passed on to her. The fish is served with root vegetable sauce - it's simple, delicious and healthy. Traditionally cooked for Christmas Eve supper, it is good to eat at any time of the year.

1kg (2lb 3oz) cod or haddock

1 lemon

100g (3½ oz) all-purpose flour

Sunflower oil for frying

1 large onion

500g (1lb 1oz) carrots peeled and coarsely grated

2 parsnips peeled and coarsely grated

½ medium celeriac peeled and coarsely grated

2-3 tablespoons of tomato paste

500ml (3/4 pint) vegetable stock

1 or 2 bay leaves

4 allspice berries

Salt and pepper to taste

Rinse and pat dry fish fillets, season with salt and pepper and squeeze juice of half a lemon over the fish, leave to stand for 15 minutes. Dust in flour and sauté in oil until golden brown and cooked through. Remove from pan and drain on paper towels. Set aside.

Meanwhile, heat a large skillet over medium heat and add 2 tablespoons oil. Sauté onions for about 5 minutes and then add carrots, celeriac and parsnip and sauté for a few more minutes, then add the vegetable stock, allspice berries and bay leaf. Cook covered on low heat until vegetables are soft, stirring frequently for about 20 minutes, then add the tomato paste. Mix well and simmer until vegetables are very tender, stirring occasionally, and most of the liquid has evaporated (another 10-15 minutes). Remove the bay leaf and allspice berries. Season to taste with salt and pepper.

Lay the fried fish on a serving dish and cover completely with the tomato-vegetable mixture. Decorate with lemon slices.

Once cooled, cover and put in the fridge. Best served cold next day or after a couple of hours in the fridge. Usually served with a slice of sourdough bread as part of supper or brunch.

> ## "If there is no flour, there is no Torah"
> ### *(Pirkei Avot 3:17)*
>
> Two perspectives on Judaism and food from our two Rabbis, Sybil Sheridan and Sylvia Rothschild, who led our community from 2003 till 2014. Rabbi Sheridan's is an extract of the sermon that she gave to mark her retirement at a special Shabbat service followed by a fabulous Kiddush. Rabbi Rothschild gives her recipe for hallah together with a personal insight into the creative process of sermon writing.

Bread from the Earth and from Heaven

Rabbi Sybil A. Sheridan

In the Torah portion of Beshallach the Children of Israel were led by God towards the Red Sea. They saw the Egyptians coming after them and panicked. Moses stretched out his hand, the waters parted and the children crossed safely. But no sooner were they through, than they saw the Egyptians in hot pursuit. Moses stretched out his hand once more and the waters closed. On seeing the Egyptians drowned and washed up upon the shore, the people "feared God, and believed in God and in Moses" (Exodus 14:31).

But just three days later they were complaining: they had no water. What had happened to their faith?

What they saw at the sea was an event we still talk about - the one defining moment that transformed us - yet all they can think of is how thirsty they are.

The portion continues: they complain they have no food, so God provides manna and quails (Exodus 16). But soon they are thirsty again and then they are attacked by Amalek (Exodus 17).

How is it that so quickly their physical needs turned the spiritual experience into history?

"If there is no flour, there is no Torah," said Rabbi Eleazar ben Azariah (Pirkei Avot 3:17). No one can be sustained by visions alone. The Israelites could have continued singing and dancing and would have died in the desert in an ecstasy of faith, but what use would that have been? They needed to survive.

Yet, to quote another Jewish boy, "Man cannot live by bread alone" (Gospel of Matthew 4:4).

To live only for food and drink is to miss the point, we are so much more than our physical needs.

God instructs the people to gather a double portion of manna every Friday to sustain them over Shabbat. You cannot enjoy Shabbat without food. The term Oneg Shabbat - which we interpret today to mean singing and dancing, strumming a guitar and sitting in a circle - is based on Isaiah 58:13, "You shall call the Sabbath a delight." For the mediaeval Rabbis the meaning was very different. They said "delight" means enjoying three good meals on Shabbat – luxury few could afford the rest of the week.

The double portion of manna gave rise to our tradition of having two loaves of hallah on Shabbat. But Rabbi Yehudah Arie Leib Alter (1847-1905) the Chasidic Rabbi known as the S'fat Emet, suggests that the two loaves represent the two things needed to sustain us, bread from the earth, and bread of Heaven.

Without the one, we die. Without the other, we are barely alive. That is why he would recite two blessings over the hallah - hamotsi lechem min ha'aretz ("brings forth bread from the earth) over one - and hamotsi lechem min hashamayim ("brings forth bread from Heaven") over the other.

So when we go to synagogue and enjoy the Torah reading, and get into the spirit of the prayers, we are doing what God has commanded us. Then, when the service is concluded, and we enjoy the Kiddush, remember, that too is commanded by God.

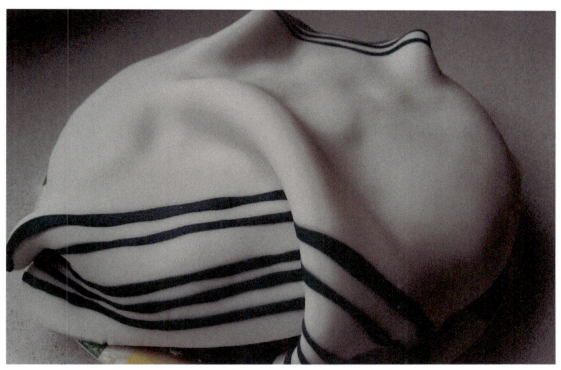

A cake in the shape of a tallit, made by Eleri Larkum
on the occasion of Rabbi Sheridan's retirement

Hallah and Sermon Preparation Plaited Together
Rabbi Sylvia Rothschild

Put in the bowl of your food mixer the following, in the order as given:

1 egg plus 1 cup warm water
1½ teaspoons of margarine or 3 teaspoons of olive oil
3 cups strong white bread flour
2 tablespoons sugar
2 teaspoons salt
2½ teaspoons dried yeast (or one sachet)

Now beat them together until you have a fairly firm ball. Put in a bowl, cover and leave in a warm place.

Next, take the mass of notes and ideas you have been making all week, and begin to assemble a sermon at your computer. By the time you have done a first draft (about an hour) the dough will have risen and it is time to beat it again.

After beating it, you have fifteen minutes to read and comment in pencil on how and where you will need to amend the draft of your sermon. By now the dough will have recovered from its severe beating, and will be beginning to rise.

Take it out of the bowl with floured hands and divide into two equal pieces.

On a clean surface take the first piece and divide it into six. Roll each sixth into a 'sausage' and place each of the strands alongside the other lengthwise, with their tops together.

Now, forget what you were going to change in your sermon and concentrate. You need to number each strand – one, two, three, four, five, six in that order, left to right.

Then, pick up strand number one (on the far left as you are looking) and pick up strand number four. Strand number one is now pulled across and over ALL the other strands EXCEPT strand number four (which it goes under), until it rests at the far right, and is now strand number six.

Renumber all the strands, from the left, one to six. Repeat the exercise, always lifting strand number four out of the way.

Eventually you will run out of length, your hallah will have magically turned from "portrait" to "landscape" and it will be plaited with six strands.

Now you can put it on a baking tray. Make the second hallah with the other piece of dough in your bowl, and then you have about an hour to let it rest, rise and grow while you get on with your sermon. Just as you are completely immersed in your argument, tear yourself away in order to put your hallah into a preheated oven 190°C/375°F/Gas Mark 5. But, before you do this, paint your hallah all over with some beaten egg as a glaze, or some runny honey.

Put in the oven and leave until the smell once more distracts you from your third sermon draft – about 25 minutes or so. If they look done, then they probably are done, and you can take them out to cool before setting them on your Shabbes table.

Get back to the fourth draft of your sermon, with the satisfying smell permeating the house…

Shabbat Lunch with a French Twist

Josette Cohen

I had an idea that was approved by the Synagogue Care Group to host a lunch for anyone who is alone on a Saturday lunchtime, whatever their age. The first lunch took place at the Synagogue after the service and was a great success.

We thought about menus and various choices. I did not want to have quiches, so I decided on salmon, cooked in the Synagogue kitchen the day before. It was a lot of work doing it for 25 guests, but I think it was worth the effort as everyone really seemed to enjoy it.

Saumon Poche

This is really more a French recipe than a Jewish one.

Serves 6

6 individual portions (boneless) of Scottish salmon

For the court bouillon (fish stock)

½ bottle of white wine (dry)

2 large carrots, peeled and cut up in round slices

1 large onion, peeled and cut into slices

Sprigs of parsley, dill and thyme (or a bouqet garni)

4 bay leaves (preferably fresh)

Salt

Peppercorns

Garnish

Wedges of lemon

Sprigs of fresh parsley and dill

First make court bouillon by putting all the court bouillon ingredients together in a large saucepan. Bring gently to the boil, then let it simmer for about 30 minutes. Leave to cool.

When cooled, put in the salmon. Bring back to boil, and then simmer. Poach for 10 minutes. Turn off the heat and let the salmon cool in the court bouillon.

Take fish out and put it on kitchen towel to get rid of excess liquid. Transfer to a dish.

Refrigerate till needed. Serve at room temperature.

Before serving, decorate with wedges of lemon, parsley and dill. Serve with mayonnaise, salad and new potatoes.

Tip: If, at some stage, there is not enough liquid, you can add a little water.

Alternative hot version with sauce

If you want to serve the fish hot with sauce, when cooked, take fish out and keep warm while you make the sauce.

Creamy sauce

50g (2oz) butter

50g (2oz) flour

½ pot of double cream

Yolk of one egg

Juice of ½ lemon

Melt butter. Then add flour and stir to combine. Add about ¾ pint (425ml) of stock slowly. Let cook for about 10 minutes until the sauce thickens. Add the cream and yolk and mix together. Then add the lemon juice.

Do not let it boil or it will curdle.

To serve

Arrange the fish in a dish and decorate with parsley and lemon wedges. Put the sauce in a separate jug to serve. Serve with new potatoes, spinach and peas.

Abraham's Tent Confection

Eleri Larkum came up with a unique Abraham's Tent Confection for the Kiddush following a "Welcome Shabbat", a Shabbat for all members, but especially in honour of those newer to the community.

The date was chosen because in that week's parashah we heard the first story of hospitality in the Torah. Abraham welcomes three strangers to his tent. What meal does he prepare them on a typical hot day? He asks Sarah to "make ready three measures of fine meal, knead it, and make cakes"; he chooses a calf and asks his servant to prepare it, and serves the meal – including butter and milk – to the strangers. Having been warmly welcomed, one of the guests tells the elderly Sarah the unlikely news that she will have a son – Sarah's response is to laugh.

Abraham's Tent Confection consisted of iced gingerbread carpets layered on top of shortbread sand, with a roof of fruit leather. There were gasps of delight at the unlikely sight, but not for long…eating a tent, carpets and the sand on which it stands is a serious business.

Welsh Cakes and Strudel: A Bar Mitzvah Baking Tale

Renee Woolf

At the Bar Mitzvah of Owen Woolf, we were treated to a really special Kiddush lovingly prepared and baked in Cardiff and personally delivered to Wimbledon Synagogue by Owen's grandmother, Renee Woolf. Wimshul Cooks' Liz Ison caught up with Renee afterwards.

How did you come to agree to bake for the Kiddush?

A few months before the Bar Mitzvah, my son Maurice asked me, "do you think you'd do the Kiddush for me?"

"Of course, I will," I replied. "How many people are coming?"

"About 230," he told me.

After I'd got over the initial shock, I got planning.

I have a lot of experience in catering for large numbers. I grew up in a big family of six children and we would always have guests over for meals, especially on Friday nights. I catered my own 70th birthday lunch for 100 and also prepared the dessert trolleys for my other grandson's Bar Mitzvah in Israel. My friends and I also made 500 scones in the kitchen of our Jewish old age home and served up a lovely cream tea to the residents.

How exactly do you go about baking for a Kiddush for 230 people at a London Synagogue when you live in Cardiff?

About a month before the Bar Mitzvah, I decided to get cracking and I planned to make something every day except for Fridays when I make my own hallah. Luckily my neighbour had a freezer he wasn't using so I stored everything in his and my freezers ready to be transported.

As I made progress, I would text Maurice messages like, "Keeping you informed – 120 scones made" or "Hello Maurice, 130 welsh cakes made today." After a while, he stopped replying to my texts.

So, without it being stressful, I made the following: 320 fish balls, 10 lemon cakes, 120 scones (to be served with cream and jam), 130 welsh cakes, 4 chocolate cakes, 100 pieces of apple strudel, 120 date squares, 120 rocky roads and 100 hazelnut biscuits. Oh, and 100 chocolate truffles. Just before, I also made marshmallows dipped in chocolate as I knew those would be popular with the children.

Everything fitted nicely into our car, though we did joke that the friend to whom we were giving a lift might have to sit on the roof. We delivered everything straight to the Synagogue. I also made some hallah which we had at our family meal on the Friday evening. When we got home I discovered we'd left a box of scones in the freezer.

Were you happy with how the Kiddush went?

Yes, I was.

I felt the Kiddush had a really nice family atmosphere and I think the fact that the cakes were home baked added to that feeling that we – family, friends and the congregation – were all one close community. Because there was plenty to eat, people stayed on, rather than rushing off. They stayed to chat and meet different people. It felt like an evening at home.

Owen told me it was a banquet, and I have been called the "fish ball lady" since! I made sure to walk round offering people more food – that's the Welsh way – I wanted everyone to eat well and feel welcomed. I love it when people have a second or third helping. That Kiddush, like so many other family parties and occasions over the years, will go down as what we call special family memory time.

Who has influenced your cooking?

I learnt a lot from my mother Leah Landy. She was one of 12 children, and she had six children of her own so she knew about cooking for a crowd. I don't know how she managed to do everything – she ran a business, brought up her family, contributed to community life and she was always entertaining – she really was an outstanding cook. She managed all that cooking without electric mixers or all the special equipment we have nowadays. I still follow her method of baking hallah, which involves letting the dough rise in a wicker basket, covered with a tea towel with two pillows on top.

I remember my mother's advice, "It's not always about how it looks. It's about how it tastes in the mouth." I think that's right: it's best to aim for something that tastes delicious, and something you know people like. My mother also taught me to lay a table with plenty of food for everyone. If there is some left over, that is much better than there not being enough.

I often repeat the same recipes because my friends ask for a particular cake or even expect particular dishes when they come over. So I aim to keep things simple but tasty. Things don't always go to plan. I couldn't lift the first cake I made off the table! But my sister encouraged me, telling me to never give up, and try again.

My signed copy of Evelyn Rose's cookbook is my Bible. I swear by her! My copy is virtually in shreds I've used it so much. Her recipes always work. Many years ago, our local WIZO group (of which I have been chairman for the last 10 years) invited Evelyn Rose to be a guest speaker. We prepared her and the group a dinner – the recipes were all out of her cookbook, of course. She said it was the best meal she'd ever had cooked for her. We modestly said, well it was all from your book. But she replied that we should take credit as we had cooked it. A while later, she was interviewed on Woman's Hour and was asked whether she found it hard to be cooked for. She replied that the best food she'd tasted was in Cardiff – she was referring to our WIZO meeting!

This isn't just about cake, is it?

I have learnt from my parents. They had a large family to bring up and they had to work hard all their lives. However busy they were, they would always keep the Jewish holidays. We have such lovely traditions and they are so often about food. I saw my parents change the dishes for Passover, and put out another table on Fridays for extra guests. My parents believed in giving to the community, not taking. I would recommend entertaining, even if it's just inviting people round for bagels or some cake. It's what life is about.

Renee, how do you do it?

I'm 72 years old but in my mind I think of myself as 56 and that seems to work! I work 2½ days a week, I'm very busy with the United Synagogue in Cardiff, with the old people's home, and with WIZO. It is about making an effort and being busy but I do it because I enjoy it and I just try to do my best.

What next?

I'm starting to think about Jenny's Bat Mitzvah (Owen's sister)… I'm planning to make florentines – they're always very popular. Hmm, and my roulade pavlova usually goes down well…

Finally, we asked for some feedback on the Kiddush…

"It was the biggest and most delicious I have ever seen… I especially liked the bagels, rocky roads, marshmallows, salmon, crisps, cupcakes, rice Krispy cakes, honey cake, chocolate cake and popcorn." **The Barmitzvah Boy**

"The strudel was the best I ever tasted." **Judy Weleminsky**

"When I arrived in the morning every inch of surface in the kitchen was covered with boxes of Renee's amazing 'productions'. She had thought of everything, from forks for the cheesecake to the icing sugar sifter for the strudel. At Kiddush everyone ate with real gusto and there really wasn't that much left." **Lynne Sidkin**

Renee's top tips

- Make what people like. You don't need to make complicated things. Stick with recipes that are simple and tasty.

- Freeze cakes or biscuits in small plastic boxes with non-stick parchment between each layer. They freeze much better this way, and can be defrosted in the box.

- You can't hurry cooking.

- Plan ahead and write down your plan.

- For a Kiddush or buffet, make small sized portions – it makes it easier for people to pick up with their fingers, and they don't necessarily need a plate.

- Make sure there is plenty to eat.

- Invite people over – get entertaining.

Strudel (My Way!)

Pastry

225g (8oz) plain flour

Pinch of salt

2 level tablespoons icing sugar

110g (4oz) hard Tomor margarine

1 egg yolk

Juice of ½ lemon or 1½ tablespoons lemon juice

2 tablespoons cold water

Filling

1 jar pineapple or apricot jam

225g (8oz) mixed dried fruit

2 grated cooking apples

Mix the egg yolk, lemon juice and water together.

Put all dry ingredients and margarine in the Magimix or food processor and process till mixed, then add the liquid mix until it forms a ball of pastry. Take the pastry, wrap in cling film and chill for at least 2 hours or overnight.

Roll out the pastry on a floured board. Cover with jam, mixed dried fruit and grated apples. Fold 2 ends in and roll up into a cylinder. Cut slits across the top at 2.5cm (1 inch) intervals and paint with egg. Refrigerate for 1 hour.

Cook at 180°C/350°F/Gas Mark 4 for about 45 minutes or until golden brown. Leave to cool, cut into slices and sprinkle with icing sugar.

Delicious warm or cold.

Scones

225g (8oz) self-raising flour

1 heaped tablespoon baking powder

25g (1oz) caster sugar

½ teaspoon salt

40g (1½oz) butter

150ml (5 fl oz) semi-skimmed milk

25g (1oz) sultanas if desired

Mix dry ingredients and butter in a Kenwood or food mixer, then add milk. Mix to a dough, adding more milk if needed. Roll out and use a 5cm (2 inch) round cutter to make individual scones. Put them well separated on non-stick parchment and brush with milk. Preheat oven and cook at 220°C/350°F/Gas Mark 4 for 10 to 15 minutes.

Slice when cold and serve with butter, cream and strawberry jam. Yum!

Grandma's Welsh Cakes

You need a bake stone or a heavy frying pan. Smear the base liberally with butter and heat on a high flame.

225g (8oz) self-raising flour

75g (3oz) butter

Pinch salt

75g (3oz) caster sugar

75g (3oz) currants

1 egg

Semi-skimmed milk

Mix dry ingredients and butter to form a crumble then add egg and mix. Then add milk until it forms a soft dough. Turn onto a floured board and roll out not too thick. Use a 5-6cm (2-2½ inch) cutter and cook on the bake stone or in the frying pan, turning until brown both sides.

Happy baking!

Hannah's Tzedakah Project

At Wimbledon Synagogue, there are great bakers and foodies of all ages. Hannah O'Keeffe, when preparing for her Bat Mitzvah, decided to write a cookbook for her Tzedakah project (carried out as part of her Bat Mitzvah preparations focusing on the mitzvah of charity). It is called "Baking with Hannah" and raised money for her chosen charity. Here is why Hannah did it:

I decided to put together a book with all the yummy things I love to make and to eat so that I could raise funds to support research into PANS/PANDAS. Those are paediatric neurological syndromes that cause acute and debilitating symptoms and are extremely disruptive to the health and lives of children and their families, especially as they are often misdiagnosed and treatment is costly and frequently not covered by insurance.

My first cousin has PANS and it is really difficult for her, so I wanted to do something to help her and other children with this illness. I am hoping lots of people will buy this cookbook and support my efforts on their behalf. If you would like to find out more about PANS/PANDAS, or get an idea of the ongoing research, please have a look at http://pandasnetwork.org which also serves the PANS community.

Hannah's Most Dangerous Cake

The reason for this being called Most Dangerous Cake is because now we are only ever five minutes away from chocolate cake at any time of the day! The recipe is from my aunt and I tried it as soon as I saw it.

Makes one chocolate mug cake

4 tablespoons flour

4 tablespoons sugar

2 tablespoons cocoa

1 egg

3 tablespoons milk

3 tablespoons oil

3 tablespoons chocolate chips (optional)

A small splash of vanilla extract

1 large coffee mug (the bigger the better)

Add the dry ingredients into the mug and mix well. Add the egg and mix thoroughly. Pour in the milk and oil and mix once again. Add the chocolate chips (if using) and vanilla extract and keep mixing.

Place the mug into the microwave and cook for 3 minutes on high. The cake will probably rise over the top of the mug but don't be too alarmed.

Allow to cool and tip on to plate if desired, then…eat!

A Great Musician and a Great Cook

In Memory of Raph Gonley
Sally-Ann Feldman

Many of us remember Raph Gonley, a member of our Community and Director of Music for over 12 years. He very sadly died at the end of 2012 and is greatly missed by all who knew him.

Raph's musical contribution

Raph contributed hugely to the musical life of the Synagogue and the many compositions that he wrote for the Synagogue Choir will keep his memory alive in their great beauty. Anyone who has attended a service on a Shabbat morning or the High Holy Days will have listened to or sung along with 'Nishmat'. Raph wrote the wonderful continuation music after the very well-known first few lines. This has become so much a part of the service that it has been taken up by Reform Synagogues throughout Britain.

Raph's culinary expertise

Raph was a man of many interests as well as music. He supported many charitable ventures but a very important hobby of his was food. He was an extremely good cook, and specialised in cakes. This member of the Choir remembers the refreshments that he and his wife Rosalind provided for us whenever we gathered at their home in Wimbledon. Raph always baked us a cake!

Combining charity and cooking, Raph was one of the founder volunteers from the Synagogue at the Merton Drop-In Centre for the Homeless. He was one of the first cooks to produce really excellent lunches on a large scale for all the visitors to the Drop-In. I believe the numbers to cook for could be 70 or 80.

A celebration of Raph

It was decided to hold a Memorial concert in the Synagogue in memory of Raph – not only of his music but of the man. There were musical offerings, including memorably one by Rosalind, Rosalind and Raph's three daughters and one of their sons-in-law. The entire family are talented musicians!

Catering tips from Sally-Ann

- Having refreshments for the interval was really important for the success of the event, and by asking people to bring a contribution, the event felt even more of a communal event.

- I decided to offer both savoury and sweet finger food, with more savoury than sweet. I've put on quite a few concerts and the like over the years and in my experience savouries go down better than cakes – though cakes are always required!

- One of the many joys of being a part of the Community of Wimbledon Synagogue is that it didn't take me more than the metaphorical five minutes to get the agreement of everyone I asked to bring along a plate of something. (Mind you, maybe they were just too scared of me to say no!) I called on two groups of people. Those treasures who are known in the Synagogue for always being willing to produce some food when required, and those who may not usually get asked but who were participants in the evening. I asked people if they preferred to make savoury or sweet, most having no preference, and drew up a list in the ratio I wanted.

- For an estimated 100 people I needed 12 platters of savouries and eight cakes. People brought bagels, sandwiches, cheese puffs, mushroom tarts… I advised people to make sandwiches from a loaf estimating that was enough for roughly 10 people. Others brought fresh fruit, water and juice. Tea and coffee were served by the waitresses, of which we had asked for three for the evening.

Here are two of Raph's favourite recipes kindly provided by Rosalind

Chilli Con Carne for Fifty
Rosalind Gonley

Raph did pretty well all our home entertaining. The chilli con carne actually resulted from the catering organised by Sharon Coussins at a Quiz Night fundraiser.

12 x 400g packets mince

10 large onions - chopped

1.5kg (3lb 4oz) chopped carrots

7 x 400g (14oz) tins chopped tomatoes

8 x 400g (14oz) tins kidney beans

1 teaspoon cumin

1 teaspoon curry powder

1 teaspoon cinnamon

1 teaspoon nutmeg

Salt and pepper

6 cloves garlic - chopped

2.5kg (5lb 8oz) rice

Brown the mince, stirring well. Add onions and garlic. Add tinned tomatoes. Season with cumin, curry powder, cinnamon, nutmeg, salt and pepper.

After half an hour add carrots and beans and bring to simmering point. Simmer gently for one and a half hours.

2.5 kg rice will need 5 litres of water to cook.

Tunisian Almond and Orange Cake
Rosalind Gonley

45g (1½oz) slightly stale breadcrumbs

200g (7oz) caster sugar

100g (3½oz) ground almonds

1½ teaspoons baking powder

200ml (6¾ fl oz) sunflower oil

4 eggs

Finely grated zest of 1 large orange

Finely grated zest of 1 lemon

Syrup:

Juice of 1 orange

Juice of ½ a lemon

85g (3oz) caster sugar

1 cinnamon stick

Mix the breadcrumbs with the sugar, almonds and baking powder. Add the oil and eggs and beat well. Stir in the orange and lemon zest. Pour the mixture into a lined and greased 20cm (8 inch) tin.

Place tin in a cold oven and set heat to 160°C (fan oven)/350°F/Gas Mark 4. Bake for 45 minutes until the cake is a rich brown and a skewer inserted in the centre comes out clean.

While the cake cooks, prepare the syrup. Bring all the ingredients gently to the boil in a pan, stirring well until the sugar has dissolved. Simmer for three minutes. Pierce holes in the cake with a skewer while still warm and pour the syrup over it. Leave to cool, spooning the syrup over the cake every now and then, until it is all soaked up. Serve with whipped cream or thick Greek yoghurt.

The cake tastes best a day after it is made and will keep in the fridge, covered in foil, for three or four days.

How the Bagel Arrived in SW19
Camilla McGill

The idea of the Parent Teacher Association (PTA) providing bagels at the Heder (Sunday school) came from Yvonne Mason. When I started to get involved a few years ago we were buying them from the Polish deli in Streatham who sold them to us in large paper sacks of 50 bagels which we froze. I noticed that once you got below half-way down the bagels started to get freezer burn. I also did a little investigation and realised that we could buy them at less than half the price by going direct to the supplier *The Beigel Bake* in Brick Lane in the East End. I managed to persuade my father, who is very familiar with the East End, to schlepp down there to pick up 10 sacks of bagels (500) and he now does this about once every 7 weeks. The production line is that he delivers them to my house, I re-bag them in plastic bags, 10 per bag (as they keep much fresher this way), and I take them to the shul freezer.

Parents from the Heder are encouraged to volunteer once or twice a term for 'Bagel duty' on a Sunday morning. We have two in the kitchen and one in the hall making cappuccinos using our Nespresso machine. It is so nice for teachers and any other adults who are around on a Sunday morning to get a lovely caffeine kick. A coffee at £1.50 a cup including a free biscuit we think is a bargain (especially compared to Starbucks) and is made with love by a Heder parent with all profits going to the Heder PTA for all kinds of expenditures.

Volunteers tell us that they really enjoy coming along. We have some great chats over slicing and buttering bagels - we make about 70 a week and it is so nice to serve the children at break.

The children come along clutching their pound coins (£1 for butter or cream cheese and £2 salmon and cream cheese). They are always polite and appreciative and we are so glad to give them a filling, non-sugary snack for break. Ok, so maybe a bagel made with white flour isn't the healthiest form of bread but the cream cheese and salmon are good protein so we think we're not doing so badly and, as sales show, the children love them.

In Autumn 2013 we started a really successful series of coffee mornings where each week the parents of one or two classes were invited to come for a coffee and to meet the other parents from their children's class. Complimentary Nespresso was served and although we announced that the event would last for an hour, most parents stayed for the whole morning chatting and getting to know each other.

The PTA feels that the coffee and bagel production has so many great functions. It means that Heder isn't seen as a place where parents simply drop and run - they frequently come in, sit and read the paper with a coffee and a bagel and have a relaxing morning. It gives parents an opportunity to get involved when they help, children feel taken care of and I'm sure reassured at break time that they are being served by other parents. No child goes hungry and even if they have come without money we are always happy to make a note of any debts and provide the bagel. Funds raised have bought the three sofas and coffee tables used so frequently in the hallway, and we regularly contribute to events for the youth club as well as for equipment and teacher training.

Bagels

Eleri Larkum

Dough

250g (9oz) strong bread flour

1 teaspoon quick yeast

½ teaspoon salt

1-2 teaspoons sugar

150ml (5 fl oz) warm water

Poaching

1 tablespoon bicarbonate of soda

1 tablespoon malt extract (or 3 tablespoons brown sugar)

Semolina

Toppings (poppy seeds or sesame seeds)

Put all the ingredients into a bowl and mix together (if using normal dry yeast, you'll need to start it off with the sugar and some of the water five minutes or so ahead of time).

Tip out onto a floured surface and knead until smooth and springy - about 10 minutes. Put the dough into a lightly oiled bowl, cover and let rise for about an hour or until doubled in size.

Divide the dough into six equal pieces (or more for smaller bagels). Shape the pieces into a smooth ball, and rest for about 10 minutes under a damp tea towel on an oiled surface.

Use a floured finger to make a hole in the middle of the ball, then roll it between one or two fingers on each hand to widen it out to a decent sized hole - it will close up again as it proves. Back under the towel for another 10-15 minutes rest.

Preheat the oven to 250°C/475°F/Gas Mark 9, and sprinkle your baking trays with semolina.

Fill a large pan with water, add the bicarbonate of soda, and the malt or sugar, and bring to the boil, then keep it at a strong simmer.

Lower the bagels into the water - as many as will float comfortably together - 3 or 4 probably. (Tip: if you put them in upside-down, they'll end up with their best foot forwards, so to speak). Boil for 1-2 minutes, flip them over, and same again on the other side (a longer boiling time is meant to result in a chewier texture - possibly, but I wouldn't worry if you're in a hurry). Take them out, draining any excess water, and put straight on the semolina covered baking sheet. Add any toppings whilst still damp.

Bake at 250°C/475°F/Gas Mark 9 for 5 minutes, then rotate the trays and reduce the heat to 220°C/425°F/Gas Mark 7 and bake for another 10 minutes or so (depending on size). They should be golden brown and firm.

Bagel workshop held at Wimbledon

Bagelology

The bagel's no ordinary roll.

It's more than baked dough with a hole.

It shows with its ring

Life's a cyclical thing.

Ain't it great eating bread with a soul!

Jerry Markison, The Jewish Limerick Book

Cooking and Learning at Apples and Honey Nursery

Claudia Camhi

Baking and sharing food is a hands-on way to build a sense of community and learn about Jewish values and traditions. At Apples and Honey Nursery, based at Wimbledon Synagogue, children follow the seasons and Jewish festivals through cooking.

Believe it or not these recipes are tricky to devise as they require engaging and involving children between two and four years old, integrating cooking with all areas of the curriculum and most importantly being able to eat the fruits of their hard labour quickly! Our experts at Apples and Honey suggest that assembling components is the best way for groups of young children to 'learn as they do'.

Daily and Weekly Routines

Mid-morning snack

There are daily and weekly routines around food. The mid-morning snack is set up to be a communal experience. The children busily cut and plate seasonal fruit and vegetables and sit around the table together to share the snack which is laid out attractively on colourful plates. They are encouraged to think about where the fruits come from (do they grow on the ground, vines, trees, bushes…?) before reciting the appropriate blessings in Hebrew. Taking a piece for themselves, each child must pass the plate on to the child sitting next to them. Reciting the blessing, offering the snack to others and remembering not to keep their favourite foods all to themselves… that's a pretty tough ask for such young children.

They are also given a choice of milk (halav) or water (mayim) to drink and then are allowed to pour it themselves. A few spillages here or there are mopped up without fuss: it's the only way to learn. Finally each child takes their cup and plate over to the sink to wash up, all part of learning to take responsibility for the whole process.

Shabbat

The smell of freshly baked hallah surrounds all on a Friday.

Welcoming in Shabbat on a Friday is the highlight of the week for the children as it is the day that they each make their own mini-hallah and two larger ones for the nursery Kabbalat Shabbat celebrated at the end of the morning.

The children punch, pull, plait and decorate hallah dough which is made and brought in by parents in a rota system. Once every half term the children make the hallah dough themselves. This gives them an opportunity to see how it expands overnight.

Whilst kneading the dough the children talk about their feelings. Sometimes they can choose to punch out all their 'bad feelings' and get rid of them before Shabbat. At other times they think about all their 'good feelings' and knead them into the hallah to make it taste more delicious.

The shape of the hallah is usually in the traditional three strand plait but this is varied during the year with lovely round and sweet hallot for Rosh Hashanah, Sukkot and Simchat Torah; a dreidel shaped hallah for Hanukkah; a ladder shape when learning about Jacob's dream and even six plaited hallot on other occasions.

By Kate Parsons

The parents are invited to join the children to celebrate Shabbat towards the end of the morning where everyone has an opportunity to learn and reinforce the customs and rituals of Shabbat. They sing songs, recite blessings and share all this together in a family atmosphere. Each week a different child gets to be the Shabbat host who sits at the head table and invites all his/her friends to share Shabbat with them.

> "Fridays were my favourite day of the nursery week. It is just so special to enjoy Shabbat together and really helps with the bonding together of the nursery community." Libby

> "It was a family event. Other nurseries keep families at 'arms-length', prioritising separation and autonomy over community and connection. The concept of being Shabbat host was very special for each child. It was about them, their stories and interests, with all that was exciting and daunting about being centre stage." Claudia

> "Celebrating Shabbat at nursery really enabled us as a family to celebrate together at home. The kids love being able to say the blessings." Carra

"Luke Skywalker is the Shabbat Host. Darth Vader is helping him light the candles with his lightsaber. Me and my nursery friends are watching"

THE JEWISH FESTIVAL CYCLE

Apple wedges dipped in runny honey, honey glazed hallah and honey cake are a must for Rosh Hashanah. If you visit at this time of the year, you will find many little sticky fingers getting ready to celebrate the Jewish New Year.

During Sukkot children learn, amongst other things, about the last harvests before winter. They usually have a visit to a local pick-your-own farm, Garson's Farm in Surrey to pick fruit and vegetables which they use to decorate the community Sukkah.

A Simchat Torah favourite is the preparation of an edible Torah. Wraps are carefully spread with cream cheese placed in a 'squeezy' bag to allow children to do their own writing. A bread stick is placed at each side of the wrap and rolled to resemble a Torah Scroll. The writing can also be done with jam or fruit laces.

Did you know that Hanukkah candles can be eaten? At the nursery, children make their edible Hanukkiot with a pitta bread base, bread sticks for the candles and satsumas or carrot sticks for the flames.

Tu B'Shevat isn't just a tree hugging festival. We celebrate with all our senses, enjoying the textures, smells and tastes of 15 different fruits as we make fruit kebabs, whilst also working on pattern making and sequencing. We talk about our feelings when the children create self-portraits out of fruit. A satsuma segment can be both a smile and a sad face, raisins can represent curly hair or tears.

Noisy Purim is tons of fun and lots of noise. At Apples and Honey all join in making popcorn, watching it pop and imitating its popping sounds whilst jumping up and down. Facilitating physical development has never been so much fun. The sweet hallah, full of raisins and chocolate drops, is not to be missed. The children also prepare Mishloach Manot baskets to give away, often to their friends at Nightingale House, a Jewish old people's home in Wandsworth.

For Passover the timer is on. Children busily make Matzot in less than 18 minutes. They also squeeze a mixture of coconut, sugar and egg into pyramid shapes and get them ready for baking. They try fresh parsley as part of the Seder meal that they themselves had planted as seeds during the earlier festival of Tu B'Shevat.

Another way to experience the bittersweet taste of the Israelite experiences in Egypt is through a "Moses in the bulrushes" activity. Having modelled a plasticine Baby Moses, wrapped him in a small blanket and placed him on a bed of damp cotton wool, the children sprinkle cress seeds around him and then wait to watch the 'bulrushes' grow, hiding Baby Moses from view. When the children harvest the mustard and cress a week later they can explore the sharpness of the mustard leaves alongside the sweetness of the cress, as well as revealing the figure of Moses to be discovered by Pharaoh's daughter.

How better to experience the Land of Milk and Honey than to create an edible Map of Israel for Yom Ha'Atzmaut? On oval pitta bread or home-made dough, the children can outline the shape of the map with tomato sauce and add its colours and flavours. Basil leaves or pesto can represent the sea and rivers, grated cheese mountains can sprout herb trees, rock salt can denote the Dead Sea and the children can use the seven species to mark places of interest. The

figure of King David can be cut, crown and all, and placed on the map in Jerusalem. Then we sprinkle him with olive oil – what a royal feast!

Lag B'Omer means picnic time. At Apples and Honey it means the nursery students preparing a picnic for a friend. This requires them to listen, wait and try to take another child's point of view. They need to ask their friend if they would prefer cream cheese or butter, if they would like it with or without cucumber. Then the little chefs prepare the sandwich having to keep in mind that this is not one for them to eat but for their friend to enjoy. Finally, they have to give their creation away and wait for their own sandwich to arrive. This is much harder to do when the friend has marked differences in their food preferences… certainly food for thought and a lesson for life!

Milk and honey are Shavuot's special ingredients. Children at nursery make fruit milk shakes with ice cream and love, blending them themselves. The way the milk, fruit and ice cream transform in front of their eyes captures their attention and gives way to all sorts of questions and explanations. They also make individual cheesecakes using a biscuit as a base, then they top it with cream cheese and maybe some jam or fruit. Squeezing fresh oranges is a holistic experience. What pride when the children manage to produce juice from their physical exertions! They can drink all those vitamins themselves or share with a friend.

FESTIVALS OF OTHER FAITHS AND CULTURES

At Apples and Honey, cooking is used as a medium for teaching the children about other faiths and cultures too and it is amazing how often rice features in these celebrations. For the Chinese New Year the children prepare rice with soy sauce comparing the textures of dry and cooked rice and then attempting to eat it with chopsticks.

Rice pudding is made for the Muslim feast of Eid-al Adha, flavoured with cardamom and rose water; a delicious treat for children and adults alike. Rice is also central to Norooz, the Persian New Year celebrations when it is cooked with green vegetables and is seasoned with parsley, coriander, chives, dill and fenugreek. These exotic dishes expand the children's horizons and help the children to literally taste and enjoy the flavour of various cultures.

Bible Stories

The Biblical story of Creation has an edible version too. Children use iceberg lettuce to represent clouds; raisins take the place of birds and breadsticks for trees. At times, slices of banana appear, resembling the sun, but that's dependent on the weather!

For the Genesis story of Esau, who sells his birthright to his brother Jacob for a 'mess of pottage' prepared by Jacob, the children prepare and eat some 'red soup' made from carrots and red lentils.

Recently we have had a wonderful new development at the nursery, the Biblical Garden. In their very own playground, the children can find the herbs, bushes and trees that are described in Biblical stories. They realise these plants and trees not only exist nowadays but also grew in a long gone era. The children get to know what a fig or olive tree looks like as well as find out what kind of care it needs. They see the grapevine changing around the calendar year and learn about the celebrations involving grapes, raisins and or wine. Even though the pomegranate is a Mediterranean bush it has managed to grow and even fruit in South West London and so have herbs like coriander, sage, hyssop, garlic and dill.

Children can harvest these herbs and use them for a festival: parsley at Pesach, coriander for Havdalah.

Plant Cycle

The children also experience the full cycle of plant life from planting a seed, to caring and nurturing its growth, to eating it. Finally, the leftovers are composted in the nursery's very own wormery. The wormery produces a good amount of liquid compost that is sold at nursery and Synagogue fairs to raise funds for the nursery.

So the use of this garden helps connect horticulture, history, Jewish traditions and learning, as well as responsibility towards the community and the environment. Wow!

Judith's Hallah Dough Recipe

Judith Ish-Horowicz

Judith Ish-Horowicz, her teachers at Apples and Honey Nursery, and lately some of the parents of the nursery children take it in turns every Thursday to make a batch – or double batch – of this dough at home. They leave it to rise over night and then, on a Friday morning, the swelling dough is carefully transported to the nursery in a very large plastic container. The children all take a small piece. They knead it, divide it, plait it, paint it with egg wash and sprinkle it with poppy seeds. Later, the air filled with the smell of freshly baked hallah, they sing some Shabbat songs and recite the blessing over some larger hallot also made from the same batch of dough. Finally, their week of nursery at an end, they take their little hallah home to eat – and many of these three and four year olds can restrain themselves that long because they want to show off their achievement to their family.

Makes 2 large hallot or many small ones

A 1.5 kg (3lb 5oz) bag strong white bread flour

Two 7g (¼oz) sachets of fast action dried yeast (14g – ½oz in total)

¾-1 cup sugar

3 heaped teaspoons of salt

3 eggs (medium free range)

¾ cup oil

2 cups luke-warm water (generous)

Extra flour for handling the dough

For glaze

1 egg

Poppy seeds

Equipment

Large food Mixer with a dough hook e.g. Kenwood Chef

Bowl for checking each egg separately

1 cup measure

¾ cup measure

1 teaspoon measure

2 cup measure Pyrex jug

1 knife for cutting the mixture

Bowl for poppy seeds

Pastry brush for glaze

Baking tray

Oven preheated to 180°C/350°F/Gas Mark 4.

Place all ingredients into bowl of mixer, dry ingredients first and then wet ones. Switch mixer on gently to prevent flour flying or water spraying. As the mixture becomes better blended, increase the speed gradually until the machine is dancing on the work top.

Stop machine at least once during the process to stir in any of the mixture that is not mixing well.

When the dough appears to be well blended and elastic it is ready. (It is better to have a sticky dough as the cooked hallah will be lighter.)

Remove dough hook from mixture and cover bowl with cling film to prevent the top from crusting over. Leave it overnight to rise. If you have the chance, pummel the dough mixture once it has risen and leave it to rise again as it improves the flavour.

Sprinkle flour onto prepared surface and tip the risen dough onto it. Knead the dough firmly but gently until it feels smooth and velvety, about 5 minutes using the palm of your hand and your fingers. Do not pull at it. If the dough starts to stick to your fingers sprinkle them with flour but don't let the dough become dry and crumbly.

Now is the time to add any extra ingredients, if you so wish (e.g. raisins, chocolate chips).

After braiding, glaze the surface of the hallot with beaten egg and sprinkle with poppy or sesame seeds. Bake for approximately 40 minutes (shorter baking time for smaller hallot) till base sounds hollow when tapped.

Homebrewed ale made by one of the nursery fathers for a sponsored walk and lunch

Baking a Biblical Story at Playshul

Victoria Silverlock

We were studying the story of Joseph's Splendid, Absolutely Magnificent, Rainbow-Coloured Coat on a Sunday morning at Playshul (for the under-5s and their parents) and made these truly colourful biscuits to go with the story. Our recipe was featured in the Jewish Chronicle!

Joseph Biscuits

225g (8oz) softened butter

110g (4oz) caster sugar

275g (10oz) plain flour

Food colouring

Cream together the butter and sugar to form a smooth, fluffy mixture. Sift in the flour a little at a time. Knead into a ball of dough.

Divide the dough into several smaller balls (we decided on seven for the different colours of the rainbow). Take each ball and make a well in the centre. Add a few drops of your chosen food colouring. Work the colouring into the dough until the colour is bright and even. You can add a little more flour if the dough becomes too sticky.

We gave each child a different coloured ball of dough to roll out flat on a floured surface. We then piled the different layers on top of each other.

The whole pile was rolled up into a log. When slices were cut we saw rainbows in each slice!

Each child rolled out the rainbow slice and with a butter knife cut around coat-shaped templates made of baking parchment.

The rainbow coats were placed onto a greased baking tray and baked in a moderate oven (180°C) for 10-15 minutes until firm but not too browned.

We let them cool for a few minutes while we finished Joseph's story. The children were very excited at seeing the finished colourful coat cookies!

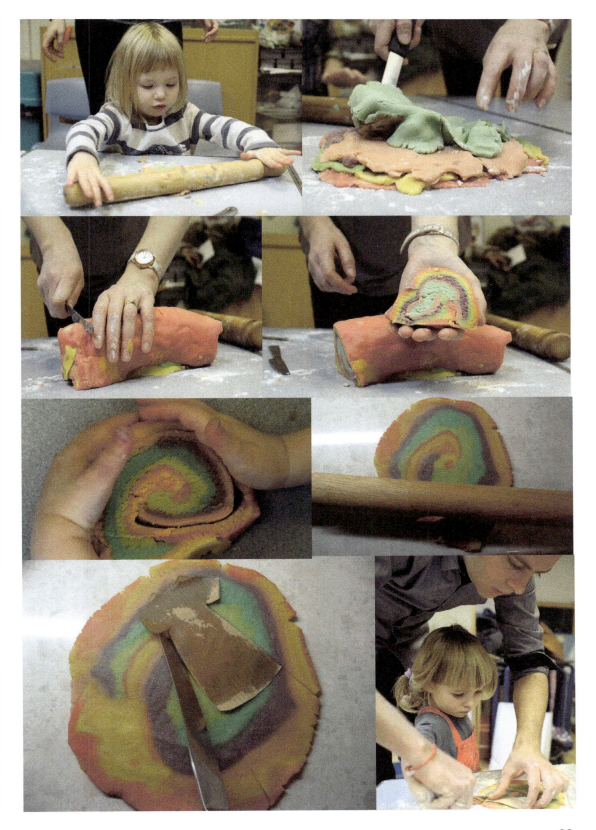

Twelve Tribes Cake

Eleri Larkum

Created for the Kiddush following a "Technicolour Shabbat", a communal Shabbat service run by the Shabbat Club (children's services) leaders. The Joseph story was the parasha that week.

Imprinted on the icing on the top of the cake are the names of each of Joseph's brothers. Joseph, of course, is represented by the inside of the cake.

The Jewish Home Corner in Playshul

Fairtrade at the Synagogue

Malcolm Clark

Here at Wimbledon we have been a Fairtrade Synagogue for several years and use Fairtrade tea, coffee and sugar throughout the year.

There are now thousands of Fairtrade products on sale in the UK, a good chunk of them available in a high street or cafe near you, and many others just a mouse click away. You'll find the Fairtrade Mark on one in three bananas, 10% of tea and coffee, and some of the most well-known chocolate bars. From flowers to fashion, and wine to wedding rings, an ever-increasing number of products bear the instantly recognisable Fairtrade Mark – the guarantee of fair prices, decent working conditions and an investment in the livelihoods and communities of the 1.24 million farmers and workers behind the products.

It is really important that we not only think about these issues as individuals, but that we also take greater collective action – as a school, a workplace, a Synagogue, a borough, a community – both to source more sustainably and to ensure that our voices are heard by those with power as well as those behind the till.

Every year my mother Anne Clark co-ordinates Fairtrade Fortnight at Wimbledon as well as running a stall at the Hanukkah Fair and other events.

Cooking for the Wimbledon Night Shelter

Sally-Ann Feldman

We have now completed several years at the Synagogue in providing food and shelter to 12 or 13 homeless 'guests' weekly for 14 weeks over the winter, giving them respite from the cold streets of Merton. The project is divided into two blocks of seven weeks, and a different faith venue takes responsibility for one night each week. The Synagogue is in the first block of venues and our night for hosting the Shelter has always been Monday.

We try to give our guests support in various ways, including talking to them about their individual predicaments with a view to helping them to find their way off the streets – Nikki Zisman, under the auspices of Merton Winter Night Shelter (co-ordinated by the YMCA), has been most active in this aspect of the Shelter. Whilst the guests are with us they are able to choose clothing and toiletries from the vast pile of donations we have been given each year, as well as benefitting from the services of translators if they need this.

But as we are Jewish and as this is a cookbook, I'm going to focus on the food!

Plan for the Evening's Food

The guests start arriving each evening from about 6 and from then until 8, when their evening meal is served, we provide tea, coffee and biscuits. The structure of the meal we provide is a tried and tested one – nothing extraordinary! Our major limitation is that we are of course a meat-free zone so, though this makes it easier for the milk/meat problems, we have to find interesting fish recipes for the seven weeks.

Two points – our brief on the Cooking Team is to provide food for the guests and the volunteers, who sit and eat with the guests. So this last year, the number of volunteers being legion, we have been cooking for 24 as a rule of thumb, the numbers varying from week to week, leaving more or less for second helpings. The second point is that the vast majority of our guests each year until now have been foreign, usually Polish, with a few Sri Lankans, so we try to think about this a little bit.

First Course

Our first course is always a bowl of home-made soup. We have been extremely fortunate each year to have had our freezer stocked with soups made by Polly Conn and her family, the trainee chefs. All sorts of delicious varieties: Vichyssoise, carrot and lentil, parsnip and lots more. We are immensely grateful to Polly. When we've used up all Polly's soups we've asked volunteers to make more.

We always serve sliced bread and butter with the soup, and Anne Clark also had the excellent idea of providing naan bread as well – largely for the Sri Lankan guests but eaten by everyone – which we cut into fingers and heat up for a few minutes in the oven.

Main Course

Next the main course. I like to always provide a separate 'interesting' vegetable, for example, ratatouille, or any kind of roasted vegetables, all highly nutritious and making the plate look prettier. However, we do frozen peas on one evening! The main course is ideally 'one-dish' so the carbohydrate element is included in the dish, but we have had one or two volunteers bring in potatoes separately. The dishes we have provided over the years have included pasta bakes (salmon, tuna), baked fish in a sauce, fish pies and fish cakes.

One year we had a memorable occasion when I was going for the easy option of fish in breadcrumbs with oven chips and peas. So what happens? The oven breaks down. The ovens in the upstairs kitchen are too small and too slow to be much use, so Annalise Zisman decided she would go to her local 'chippie' and buy everyone fish and chips – mushy peas included, although these were treated with some suspicion by our guests. I have to report that this was the most popular meal with our guests of the whole seven weeks (I can handle it – I'm not sensitive!) so much so that we are going to treat our guests to such a meal every year.

The Polish influence is that we always cut up real Polish pickled cucumbers from my local Polish delicatessen with every meal. The table is never complete without ketchup – often a Polish brand, and salt and pepper. And there are always plenty of jugs of water and squash.

We learned from another venue that a bowl of fresh salad is very popular with the main course. We did a simple salad – lettuce, baby tomatoes, cucumber, sometimes radish and a dressing.

Dessert

Not too much to say about puds except that we've found that Polish people aren't hugely interested in puddings. The volunteers are though and I don't see why they shouldn't be pampered. So we always have ice-cream around and I ask the volunteers to perhaps make a bit fewer than 24 portions of what they are making. Though having said that, we had an apple and mincemeat crumble brought in this year in and it all went! The answer is, I think, that you never know quite what's going to be successful on any one night.

We always lay out two large platters of fresh fruit – being winter there's not so much choice so it's usually satsumas, bananas, apples and pears. What is left of the fruit after breakfast is given to the guests to take with them for the day ahead.

I think I'm right in saying that we've never not had enough food – this is a Jewish kitchen and second helpings must be offered.

Yomtovim!

We celebrate Hanukkah every year during the Night Shelter period so we get to give our guests a bit of traditional Jewish cuisine. We are lucky to have latke-king extraordinaire Michael Freedman on our team and every year he has produced around 100 savoury potato latkes to complement our main course. He brings them on trays already cooked and we just heat them up in the oven. This year we served them with baked salmon pieces that had been marinated in garlic, spring onions and soy sauce. Anne Clark provided the traditional apple sauce.

Doughnuts are, of course, a necessity.

One year we had the problem of Christmas.

Because all but one of our guests was Polish one year, and Christmas Eve fell on a Monday that year, we felt we would like to give them a traditional Polish festive meal. Christmas Eve is when Poles eat their main Christmas meal, rather than Christmas Day.

So, what to do? Our lovely Polish translator Danka gave me the lowdown. Apparently traditionally Poles will serve 12 vegetarian dishes – relating to the 12 Apostles. We didn't provide all of them but gave them a table groaning with lots of bowls of some of the others. I sourced all the traditional dishes from my local Polish Deli, who gave me quite a bit of advice.

Soup was borsht of course. It comes with special dumplings filled with cabbage and mushrooms, and sour cream served separately. We also offered another more familiar soup for those who don't like borsht.

The vegetarian dishes are usually served with carp but we made salmon garnished with parsley and radish. The accompaniments to the salmon were:

Potato salad – made by my husband to his mother's German Jewish recipe

Hard-boiled egg halves smothered in mayonnaise (mixed with some yoghurt to lighten it), topped with spring onions and cooked peas, sprinkled with parsley and small pieces of red pepper. It looked very pretty and was one thing that I could make very easily!

Sauerkraut

Dumplings – these appeared to be a larger version of the ones put into the soup

A Polish diced vegetable salad in mayonnaise

Two types of herring – Polish rollmops and special ones in oil and onion

Pickled cucumbers and bread and butter as usual

The meal finished off with poppy seed and cheese cakes – special ones from the deli and a Christmas cake made by our volunteer from a local Church.

We were told afterwards that though the meal was enjoyed by all our guests – including the one Englishman – it was an all-too-poignant reminder to some of them that they were a long way from home. I'm undecided now as to whether it was the right thing to do.

We laid on some cars later in the evening to drive whichever guests wanted to go the Polish Church for Midnight Mass and they were all given a proper English Christmas lunch the following day at their next venue which, luckily for them, was a Church!

Co-ordinating the Food

It's far too much to ask one person, or a small band of helpers, to provide these large meals, and since we have so many lovely generous people in our Synagogue who would like to help us, we have been able to produce a delicious and varied meal every week with relative ease.

We create rotas for the four teams required each week to run the Shelter successfully. Evening 'welcoming' team, who stay till 10 or 11pm; night team, who arrive then and stay all night; and the morning team who arrive at 6am and provide breakfast, send the guests on their way at about 8am and clean and clear up. And then there's the Cooking team who come in at around 6 the evening before, and prepare, cook and serve the meal, then clear up the kitchen before we go.

The Evening team lay the table and are responsible for the teas and coffees. The Cooking team are always helped by the Evening team, who pop in and out of the kitchen all evening, so that no-one seems to have to do too much.

Our regular tasks each week are: butter bread, prepare naan, cut up two jars of pickled cucumbers, make sure salt and pepper sets are filled up, make two bowls of salad, and lay out two fruit platters.

If the soup provided by a volunteer has been frozen in our freezer, Helen Bramsted or someone else in the Synagogue Office takes it out of the freezer in the morning for us and puts it in one of the giant saucepans. Thanks Helen! We start warming it up around 7pm, very slowly. Often the food is made by one of the Cooking team so it comes in with them, ready for the oven. We don't do any actual food preparation for the meals on the evening. It would all become too fraught if we did that – at least I would become too fraught!

We also get a lot of dishes brought in for us by people who are not helping on the night so I ask them to put them in the fridge or freezer for us beforehand.

I keep a menu plan for every week and chat to the volunteers about what they would like to make. Obviously, we want to keep things interesting, not too repetitive. It's useful to keep this menu plan for ideas for the next year. I do the shopping for the 'regulars' on the preceding Sunday at Asda or Tesco and my Polish deli. I can get the free Polish papers and magazines from there as well, which is nice.

I think I can say that being on the Cooking team isn't too bad – and volunteers are always welcome.

Polly Conn's soup recipes that she regularly prepared with her granddaughter Gabby in vast quantities can be found in the Family Favourites section.

"EAT WITH US"

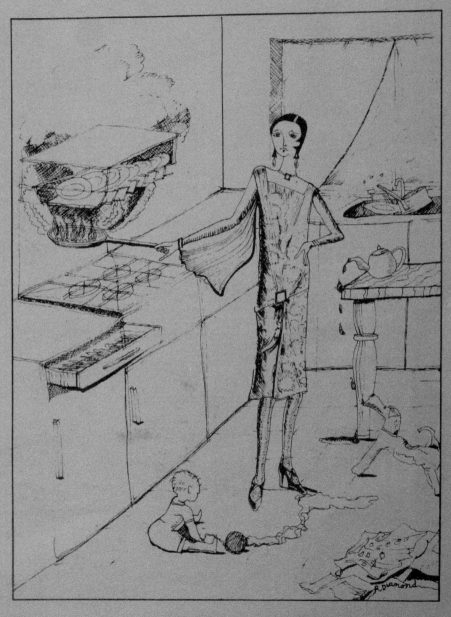

The Ladies of Wimbledon Synagogue
invite you to try their favourite dishes

Food and Community at Wimbledon & District Synagogue in the 1980s

Hilary Leek

I was on the Ladies Guild of Wimbledon Synagogue from the 1970s, a young mother when I joined, and a bit of a 'mascot' of the group as most of the other women were elderly. They would tut when my baby son Ben – who I brought along to meetings – made noises during proceedings. But they were fantastic.

A cookbook, *Eat with Us*, was written over thirty years ago by members of that Guild. It was a beautifully produced black and white booklet of typed recipes interspersed with lively line drawings.

Unfortunately, many of the wonderful ladies of the Guild have now passed away. I contributed a recipe to the book, and so did Stella Mason – we both had young children at the time of its publication in the late 70s/early 80s. Rosamund Diamond – whose parents were members of the community, and who is the sister-in-law of Judith Ish-Horowicz – did all the artwork and has kindly given us permission to reproduce some of it here.

Looking through its pages today, many of the recipes look wonderfully old fashioned. We must have thought some of them were really smart in the 1970s, but I'm not sure I'd be serving up sardine and spinach pâté next Friday night. The recipe I submitted – cucumber and cream cheese mousse – is something I'd never make these days – so high in fat! Now I tend not to follow set recipes, but produce fish dishes or lamb casserole according to my own formula which turns out slightly different each time, but always good.

When my children were growing up, our Friday night meal would be chicken soup followed by roast chicken: always popular and reassuringly predictable. When my husband James put the key in the door on his way in from work, at the end of a busy week, the smell that greeted him was almost as good as the meal to come.

```
CUCUMBER AND CREAM CHEESE MOUSSE      Hilary Leek

Serves 6

1 large cucumber                    2 level teaspoons castor
2 (8 oz) cartons of Cottage            sugar
   cheese                           ½ oz vegetarian gelatine
¼ lb mayonnaise                     ¼ pint double cream
¼ pint cold water
½ level teaspoon salt               Watercress

Peel the cucumber, cut lengthwise and remove seeds.
Chop the cucumber flesh finely. Blend the Cottage
cheese until soft, in a mixing basin; add the
mayonnaise and mix well.
Meanwhile, measure the water into a saucepan, add
the salt and the vegetarian gelatine. When soaked,
place over a low heat. Do not boil. Draw off heat
and cool.
Stir the cooled gelatine mixture into the mayonnaise
and cheese, add the chopped cucumber and fold in
the lightly-whipped cream. Mix thoroughly and then
pour into a 1½ pint ring mould. Chill until firm.
Turn out and garnish with watercress.

Serve with thinly-sliced brown bread and butter.
```

Worple Road, where the Synagogue was before we moved to Queensmere Road, was a vibrant community. It felt like one big family, with very few broiges. Many members were refugees from the war and, for them in particular, the Synagogue provided the sense of family and community that they craved.

There was no care group in those days, but the Rabbi would ask various members to make visits or cook meals for members of the community in need. I remember that as soon as I joined the Synagogue, the Rabbi asked me to visit an elderly person with dementia, and I visited her regularly with a friend.

It was always crowded for all the festival services, with standing room only. Simchat Torah was great fun, very lively and well attended. We would organise a Hanukkah Party for the whole community, and we would have 150 people along for whom we provided food, and a tombola and other fundraising activities. First night Seder was a very big event of the year, with 150 people attending, young and old. One of the members who was a caterer catered for it at cut price, and I remember making up Seder plates and mountains of haroset, in addition to what I needed to make for my own family Seder.

> **VERY QUICK CAKE FOR**   Stella Mason
> **VERY BUSY PEOPLE**
>
> 4 oz S.R. flour
> 4 oz castor sugar
> 4 oz soft margarine
> 2 eggs
> teaspoon of baking powder
> 2 - 3 drops vanilla essence
>
> Put all the ingredients together in electric mixer or blender and beat for two minutes.
> Put into 2 x 7" greased and floured cake tins and bake for 25 - 30 mins at $325°$ F or $160°$ C.
>
> *Variations:*
>
> 1 teaspoon strong coffee and 1 oz crushed walnuts; sandwich with coffee butter and cream.
>
> Add 2 oz currants and make into fairy cakes.
> Bake 15 min only.
>
> Substitute 1 oz of cocoa for 1 oz of the S.R. flour, add also a little more baking powder.

Kiddushim were organised by the administrator and two amazing waitresses, Dot and Vi, as well as Eileen on occasions. For a special Kiddush, the family or person hosting it would do all the shopping themselves, buying everything right down to the doilies, and then the team would arrive early, to get buttering the bridge rolls and to put out the fish balls. Dot and Vi were such characters and knew everything there was to know about the happenings and gossip at the Synagogue.

There were various clubs, committees and groups held at the Synagogue. The remarkable Friendship Club was held fortnightly for elderly people. Betty Lee and her husband ran the group for 18 years. Together with their helpers, they provided the attendees with a meal – which was cooked at Worple Road – followed by some form of entertainment.

Every committee or group had their own cupboard in the kitchen – which they kept locked – with their own supply of tea, coffee and biscuits. When I arranged the move to Queensmere Road, I had enormous difficulty trying to acquire the keys of these cupboards to get them emptied.

Sigi was Chairman of the Ladies Guild for many years. She had an awful time during the war and spent time in a concentration camp. When the war ended a young man named Sid Quick was one of the British soldiers (non-Jewish) who liberated the camp and found Sigi. They were later to marry though never had children. Sigi died many years ago and Sid – who continued to be a loyal friend of the Synagogue – died recently.

```
RECIPE FOR PRESERVING CHILDREN          Sigi Quick

1 grass-grown field
½ doz children, or more
Dogs, or puppies if available
1 brook
Pebbles

Pour children and dogs into field.  Allow to mix
well.  Pour brook over pebbles till slightly frothy.
When children are nicely brown, cool in warm bath.
When dry, serve with milk and freshly-baked
gingerbread.  Put to bed and cover well.
```

A Mosaic Stew

Veena Vohora

I work as a school cook at Mosaic Jewish Primary School, based temporarily at Wimbledon Synagogue since the school opened in 2013. Freshly prepared lunches are provided to the two classes of children every day and are all made in the synagogue kitchen. The menu is vegetarian.

Veena preparing wraps. Each child makes their own, choosing which vegetables they would like

I was born in Nakuru in Kenya and taught myself to cook when I was a student in London. At first I would end up with vast quantities of food as the pots and pans I used were so big. Remember in those days you couldn't just call your mother back home that easily for cooking tips! My husband and I later settled in the UK after he had been injured in the American Embassy bombing in Nairobi.

Working for Mosaic, I feel I have come full circle and am once again making food in large quantities. To keep cooking fun carry on experimenting and trying new recipes and ingredients.

Veggie Stew

When I went vegetarian, I created this recipe for veggie stew. It is one of my favourite dishes to make and children and adults love it too. One Mosaic student told me, "It's so good - I could have it for my breakfast, lunch and dinner!" I love seeing the children enjoy their healthy dinners.

Serves about 20 adults

6 onions, chopped

1 pack of celery, sliced

3 leeks (use less for children), sliced

1kg (2lb 3oz) carrots (cut long or in round discs)

1kg (2lb 3oz) potatoes, sliced into thin rounds

3 peppers (any colours), sliced

1kg (2lb 3oz) tomatoes (blended with 3-4 cloves of garlic)

A pinch of rosemary, thyme and parsley (preferably fresh)

Small amount of gluten-free flour

28g (1oz) butter

1 tablespoon olive oil

Salt (about 2 teaspoons) and pepper to taste

Prepare the vegetables as indicated. Blend the tomatoes with the cloves of garlic in a blender or food processor. In a large pot, melt the butter and oil. Gently sauté the onions, celery, leeks, carrots and potatoes. Then sprinkle lightly with gluten-free flour. Cook for a few minutes.

Then add the tomatoes (with garlic), peppers, and herbs. If there isn't sufficient liquid you can add some vegetable stock. Cover and simmer gently for about 20 minutes till all the vegetables are tender (don't overcook - you don't want a mushy stew). Season to taste.

Serve with fresh bread.

Tip: You can also add cooked beans and peas at the end.

The Jewish Year

SHABBAT

Recipe for a Streatham Friday Night

Shoshi Ish-Horowicz

Ingredients

- Three generations of one family
- A well rounded mixture of regular guests and people who haven't been invited before
- One kitchen and one table that, with additions, can seat nearly all invited guests
- Lots of singing
- Lots of chatting
- Vast quantities of food

Method

1. Take one big car and drive it to a supermarket to stock up on: nibbles, crisps, olives, pickles and crudités for before the meal, ingredients for at least two main dishes (see step 4) and fruit, ice-cream and sorbet (see step 4) for dessert. Collect the hallot from Korona's Polish Deli on Streatham High Road.

2. Remind Savta to make a vat of vegetable soup and her famous apple crumble or apple cake. If no Savta is available, another family member or guest can do this step. It works best, however, if this is completed by someone of a different generation to the person completing step 1.

3. Desperately try to clear enough space in a room for table, chairs, guests, nibbles, crisps, olives, pickles etc.

4. Start to cook. For the full Friday night experience there should be a large number of guests with different dietary requirements (gluten-free, lactose-free, vegetarian, vegan etc). To ensure everyone eats enough, make sure you cook at least two main courses to be served simultaneously e.g. salmon, new potatoes and green vegetables, cheesy pasta sauce and fusilli. Because there will be some guests who can eat everything, quantities should be sufficient for any combination of requests.

Of course, two dishes is the minimum, this stage can be as detailed and complex as time allows. The basic principle is inclusiveness, rather than individualisation though; even if you make every guest's favourite dish, each dish should be provided in quantities that allow all other guests to try it.

5. Be aware that guests will start to arrive before step 4 has been completed. Depending on space in the kitchen and how late you are now running, they can help with either stage 4 or move on to stage 5 – sitting around the table, chatting, getting to know each other and eating the nibbles, crisps, olives, pickles etc.

6. Make Shabbat. As many people should take leading roles in this as possible: different people lighting candles, making Kiddush etc.

   a. Light candles and sing Shalom Alecheim (this is a good way to prepare guests for the amount of singing which will follow)

   b. Make Kiddush and pass wine around the table

   c. Wash hands, singing a niggun (a song without words, or where the only words are lai, lai, lai).

   d. Bless the bread Apples and Honey Nursery style. This means that one person holds the two hallot. This is generally the youngest member of the family, or any nursery graduate. To allow everyone to take part and not get jealous, everyone else holds hands around the table, holding the elbows of the person with the hallot. It's like everybody is holding the bread!

   e. Walk around the table saying 'Shabbat Shalom' and kissing/ shaking hands. Imagine it's the end of a synagogue service and you want to greet everyone. This is also the time when children are blessed by parents or grandparents.

   f. In a traditional family, the husband praises his wife by singing or saying 'Eshet Chayl' (A woman of worth), the last lines in proverbs. To allow everyone to be praised and take part, the men and children sing Eshet Chayl to the women. Because this family believes in gender equality, the women and children then reply with the first verse of Psalm 1 ('Happy is the man'), praising the men.

7. Because of all the movement up until now, no one will have sat down. This is the time to allocate seating and lay the table. An Ish-Horowicz tradition from Poland is that the custom of knives being hidden during Shabbat blessings should be extended to all cutlery so all of the above has taken place without the table being laid. To the sound of additional singing (BimBam, Oseh Shalom), cutlery should be put out, any spoon fights that would have been inappropriate during blessings should take place and people should start to sit down.

8. Eat, drink, talk, repeat. At some point, a speech should be made thanking all the guests for attending and giving edited highlights from the past week.

9. When even Jewish mothers will concede that enough has been eaten, hot drinks should be made, chocolates brought out and grace after the meal (Bircat hamazon) sung.

10. Clear up the table in the knowledge that it's been a fitting start to Shabbat.

Tree of Life Hallah Cover, Eleri Larkum

Savta's Apple Cake

Hava Ish-Horowicz (known as Savta by her grandchildren)

This recipe is dairy free.

4 large cooking apples

2 tablespoons sugar

4 eggs

½ cup sugar

1½ cups self-raising flour

1 teaspoon baking powder

1 cup sunflower oil

Mixture of sugar and cinnamon (about 2 tablespoons sugar to 2 teaspoons cinnamon)

Preheat the oven to 190°C/375°F/Gas Mark 5.

Peel and slice the apples and place in pan with the sugar and cook till just soft. Add more sugar if apples are very tart. Leave to sit.

In a bowl, whisk the eggs together with the ½ cup of sugar till light and fluffy. Add the flour, baking powder and oil. Mix well.

Line a baking tin with baking paper. Layer the mixture in the tin: half the cake mixture, then apple slices, sprinkling a thin layer of the sugar and cinnamon mixture on top of the apples, then the remaining cake mixture to finish.

Bake in oven for about 45 minutes.

My Friday Evening
Julia Stanton

"Come down and light the candles, darling," says my husband and that is my Friday evening cue.

It signifies the end of a tiring week of work, chores and 'baked beans on toast'.

It opens the door to something that is spiritual, pleasurable and a slower pace. For me, Friday evenings are about family and friends. We frequently have guests and the Friday evening event is a very significant part of my Jewish identity. It is now an immense bonus if our grown up children are present.

It is a time to share weekly anecdotes, entertaining bits of gossip or simply to delight in the start of a fun weekend. I tend to make a big effort with the meal, to compensate for the weekday lapses in cooking and this is a great joy as I love cooking.

My husband blesses 'the kids' which never fails to be a moving experience and shortly after this, I am in the kitchen…mixing, putting the last touches to a recipe, and then, it is finally my turn to sit down and relax.

I invite you to try my late mother's recipe which can be done well in advance and is foolproof and delicious and, for me, a nostalgic reminder of my increasingly distant childhood home.

Lazy Chicken and Rice

Serves 6

5 tablespoons lime juice

2 teaspoons thyme (not fresh)

3 cloves garlic, crushed

¾ teaspoon chilli powder (or to taste)

Salt and pepper to taste

6 chicken legs (or thighs)

1 small onion, chopped finely

225g (8oz) mushrooms, sliced thinly

255g (9oz) basmati rice, rinsed and dried

3 tablespoons corn oil or sunflower oil

850 ml (1½ pint) boiling chicken stock

In a large bowl, combine the lime juice with the garlic, thyme, chilli powder, pepper and salt. Add the chicken portions and toss well to coat. Cover the bowl with cling film and marinate for 2 hours at room temperature or up to 24 hours in the fridge. Toss the chicken occasionally.

Preheat the oven to 200°C/400°F/Gas mark 6. Grease a shallow oven-proof dish and scatter the onion over the bottom. Cover with the mushrooms and then the rice. Remove the chicken from the marinade. Heat the oil in a large frying pan and fry the chicken over a low-medium heat for about 3-4 minutes on each side or until slightly browned. Arrange the chicken pieces in 1 layer, skin-side up, over the rice. Pour over any remaining marinade and the stock. Place uncovered in the oven and leave undisturbed for about 1 hour or until the chicken is cooked and all the stock has been absorbed by the rice.

ROSH HASHANAH

Apple Hallah

Liz Ison

This recipe is adapted from one in Marcy Goldman's *A Treasury of Jewish Holiday Baking*, a wonderful cookbook full of lovely ideas for festival and Shabbat celebrations.

Makes two loaves.

Dough

1 cup of warm water

½ cup of sugar

2 tablespoons dry yeast

½ cup vegetable oil

2 eggs

2 teaspoons of vanilla extract

2½ teaspoons salt

½ teaspoon ground cinnamon

5-6 cups strong white flour

Apple mixture

3 medium sized apples (red apples add a nice colour to the bread)

½ cup sugar

1 tablespoon fresh lemon juice

1 teaspoon ground cinnamon

Egg wash

1 egg, beaten

1 teaspoon sugar

To make the dough

In a large mixing bowl, whisk together the water, a pinch of the sugar and the yeast. Let the mixture stand for 5 minutes to allow the yeast to swell. Stir in the remaining sugar and the oil, eggs, vanilla, salt and cinnamon. Add most of the flour to form a soft but elastic bread dough. Add the remaining flour and knead for 8 to 10 minutes. You can do this in an electric mixer with a dough attachment.

Shape the dough into a ball, place it in a lightly greased bowl, place the bowl in a plastic bag – I use a big bin liner – and seal loosely (or cover with cling film). Let the dough rise until doubled (45 to 60 minutes). Alternatively, put the covered bowl in the fridge and let rise slowly overnight.

Apple filling

There is no need to peel the apples. Chop them coarsely. Put them in a bowl and toss with the sugar, lemon juice and cinnamon.

Egg wash

Whisk together the egg and sugar.

Next stage

(If you have left the dough to rise in the fridge, take it out and let it come back to room temperature before proceeding).

Oil two 900g (2lb) loaf tins (or a round 25 cm /10 inch springform pan).

Turn the dough onto a lightly floured surface. Pat it into a large round. Press in half the chopped apples. Fold the edges of the dough over the apples. Flatten again. Then press the remaining apples into the dough. Again, bring the edges of the dough over the apples,

pressing in any that may pop out. You want to try and incorporate the apples evenly throughout the dough. Don't worry if this is a messy process.

Let the dough rest for 5 minutes. Then using a sharp knife, cut into randomly shaped chunks – about 16 pieces. Lay the pieces of dough into the loaf tins, layering them up gently (they will expand and fuse during baking).

Brush on the egg wash to all exposed dough. Put the tins into the bin bag, seal loosely, and let the dough rise again until it is puffy and almost doubled (45-90 minutes).

Preheat the oven to 180°C/350°F/Gas Mark 4.

Bake for 40 to 45 minutes, until brown (cover with foil part way through if getting brown too quickly). Cool in the pan for 10 minutes before turning out to cool on a wire rack.

Tips

If you are fitting this into a busy day, and the dough has risen (first rising) but you're not ready to get on with the next stage, simply "punch" down, by pressing your fingers into the dough to deflate, and let it rise again.

Before putting in the oven, you could sprinkle with granulated or demerara sugar for an extra crunch. If you are making hamotzi with this on Rosh Hashanah, instead of sprinkling with salt, drizzle with honey before passing round.

Polly's 'Strudel' (Layered Apple and Plum Pie)

Marion Schindler

This is my late mother-in-law Polly Schindler's recipe for a dessert which she called strudel but is really a layered pie rather than a traditional rolled strudel. She always made it for Rosh Hashanah and I have continued the tradition: it is impossible for us to think of eating the festival meal without it. It was one of her family recipes brought from Poland to the UK in 1910.

Serves 10-12

For the pastry

500g (1lb 1oz) self-raising flour

250g (9oz) butter, cold and diced (or Tomor but better with butter!)

2 large eggs, beaten lightly (plus a drop of cold water if necessary)

125g (4½oz) golden caster sugar

For the filling

10 digestive biscuits

4-5 large cooking apples

750g (1lb 10oz) dark plums (not too sweet or ripe)

2 handfuls of mixed dried fruit (to include dried peel)

A little caster sugar

Crumb the flour and butter either by hand or in a food processor. When it looks like fine breadcrumbs, stir in the caster sugar and then the beaten eggs until the dough just comes together. Knead lightly and wrap in cling film and chill in fridge for about 30 minutes.

Preheat oven to 160°C/320°F/Gas Mark 2½.

Peel, core and slice the apples. Soften about half of the slices slightly in a saucepan over a gentle heat. Crush the digestive biscuits. Quarter and stone the plums.

Take the pastry out of the fridge and divide into two. Butter a deep pie dish (I use a rectangular one measuring 33cm x 25cm/13 inches x 10 inches). Roll out half the pastry and line the dish. Line the bottom with the crushed biscuits and then spread half the softened apple slices and half the raw ones over the biscuits, scatter some sugar over them, then a handful of dried fruit and half the plums. Roll out a thin slice of pastry just big enough to cover the fruit and lay on top. Repeat the layer of fruit omitting the biscuit crumbs. Then roll out remaining pastry and cover the dish, crimping the edges. Make a small cross in the centre with a sharp knife and I decorate it with a pastry apple and leaves. Brush with a little beaten egg or milk and scatter with caster sugar.

Bake for one hour, then raise temperature to 180°C/350°F/Gas Mark 4 for 15 minutes. Cover with foil if becoming too brown.

The pie keeps for several days in the fridge and freezes very well. Heat in the oven again after defrosting.

Tips

If you prefer a crisp middle layer of pastry prebake the pastry on a sheet for about 8 minutes till just golden before placing on top of the first layer of fruit.

This pastry is very good for making all sorts of pies and biscuits. I use it for all my sweet pies and to make plain and fruit biscuits.

Honey Cakes Galore

Think Rosh Hashanah. Think a slice of apple dipped in honey (and the sound of the shofar if you are not just thinking about food).

This section is less about the apple more about the honey in reflection of the tradition of baking and serving honey cake on the festival. Ashkenazim call the cake lekach in reference to the phrase "for a goodly lekach [portion] have I given you" (Proverbs 4;2). The sweetness of the honey is symbolic of the hope for a sweet new year. Did you know honey is also an ancient symbol of immortality and truth?

Lynne Sidkin's honey cake recipe is in the Community section.

Lekach (Honey Cake)

Helen Barnett

225g (8oz) plain flour
170g (6oz) caster sugar
1 teaspoon of cinnamon
1 teaspoon of mixed spice
170ml (5 fl oz) clear honey
115ml (4 fl oz) oil
2 eggs
1 level teaspoon bicarbonate of soda dissolved in 115ml orange juice
55g (2oz) chopped walnuts (optional)

Preheat the oven to 170°C/325°F/Gas Mark 3. Line a 25 x 20 x 5cm (10 x 8 x 2 inch) tin with baking paper.

Mix together flour, sugar and spices. Make a well in the centre of the bowl and add honey, oil and eggs. Beat well until smooth. Dissolve bicarbonate in orange juice and stir the fizzing liquid. Add to the mixture.

Pour into the tin. Bake for 1 – 1¼ hours.

When cold, foil wrap and leave if possible for one week before using as it improves with keeping. The cake can also be frozen.

Almond, Honey and Whisky Lemon Cake

Claudia Camhi

This is my own recipe. I wanted to create a new flourless honey cake for the Honey Cake Tasting organised by Wimshul Cooks.

Two years later my recipe and cake won a Great Taste Award from the Guild of Fine Food. It was a very sweet start indeed to the New Year.

It is a moist cake and the zing of the lemon zest makes it taste lighter.

3 tablespoons runny honey

80g (3oz) softened butter

3 eggs

120g (4oz) caster sugar

150g (5oz) ground almonds

Zest of 2 large lemons or a tablespoon of finely cut and caramelised lemon peel

Almond flakes for topping

4-5 tablespoons whisky

Preheat the oven to 180°C/350°F/Gas Mark 4. Do not use fan setting.

Prepare tin according to manufacturer's instructions. I use a 20cm (8 inch) non-stick loose base tin. It is a very moist cake so I do not recommend loaf tins as the cake may crumble when serving. Only fill the tin up to ¾ of its capacity to avoid sticky overflows.

Soften the butter and mix in the sugar, honey and lemon zest. Add the eggs and continue mixing until it looks homogenous. Now add the ground almonds and mix some more.

Place the mix in the tin and top with almond flakes. Bake on the middle rack for 45-60 minutes (baking times will vary depending on oven and tins). Don't worry: it will initially drip a bit. Honey cakes brown and burn quickly so half way through baking be sure to cover with a piece of aluminium foil marked in the middle to form a pitched roof-like top. This will protect the top layer from excessive heat and will allow air to circulate without sticking to the mix.

It is ready when you insert a cocktail stick in the centre of the cake and it comes out dry. It should look golden.

Once cool moisten by drizzling whisky over the cake with a spoon.

The cake should last for several weeks at room temperature as long as it is covered in cling film. It can be frozen.

Jamie's Apple and Honey Cake

Jamie Ryvchin

This recipe is adapted from a honey cake recipe of James Martin by adding a layer of caramelised apple slices on top. A winning combination. Too good just to make once a year.

Cake batter

170g (6oz) clear honey

140g (5oz) unsalted butter

85g (3oz) muscovado sugar

Water

2 eggs, beaten

200g (7oz) self-raising flour, sifted

Topping

2-3 apples, peeled, cored and sliced

2 tablespoons butter

2 tablespoons clear honey

Preheat the oven to 180°C/350°F/Gas Mark 4. Grease and line a 20cm (8 inch) cake tin.

Put the honey, butter and sugar into a saucepan with 1 tablespoon of water and heat gently until melted, shaking pan gently occasionally to mix. Remove from heat and add beaten egg and flour, whisk thoroughly until smooth. Pour mix into cake tin and bake for 40-45 minutes.

Topping

Heat butter and honey in a large frying pan until just melted. Add apple slices and toss to coat in the syrup (add more butter and honey if required to make sure everything is coated well).

Fry gently until apple just starts to colour then remove from heat. Gently place apple slices in a decorative pattern on the top of the cake whilst still warm. If there is any syrup left in the pan pour this over the top.

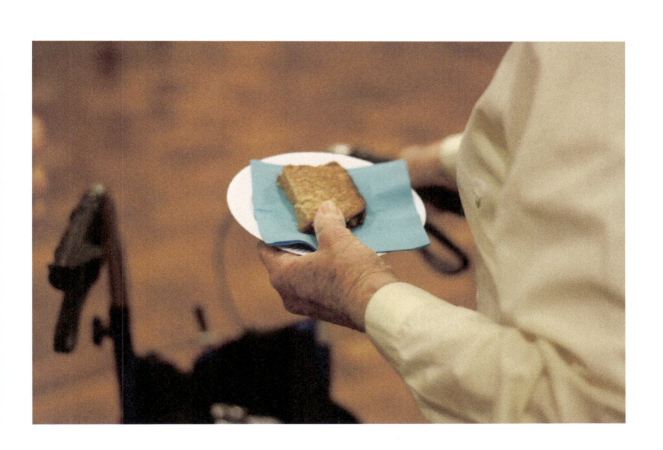

YOM KIPPUR

How to Break the Fast?

Carra Kane

When I decided to investigate how people in our community break the Yom Kippur Fast, I was amazed at the variety of responses I got, and the range of family traditions. One thing that became clear was that there is no "common" practice!

Whatever the traditions each family has, they hold a special place in our memories. As a parent I hope my children can look back at these years and remember the holidays with a special fondness that they wish to pass on.

Here are a few of the "traditions" within our community.

Carra Kane

My family is all American, and all from the South. I grew up in Houston, Texas. On my mother's side, her sister hosts Break Fast every year. When we arrive, there is an enormous breakfast buffet waiting! Blintzes, kugel, eggs, bagels, salmon, cream cheese, juice, chocolate milk, etc. Since our last meal was dinner - we have breakfast for Break Fast!

When I was growing up we alternated years going to each side of the family. My father's Aunt Virginia (who is now 98) always hosted on the Simon side. There was a slow cooker filled with Matzah Ball Soup, a huge bowl of chopped liver and crackers and we all helped ourselves when we were ready to break the fast. Then we ate an enormous dinner of meat, veg, sides and a huge assortment of desserts. I remember my brothers eating almost all the strawberries every year!

Amy Shocker

I grew up in Boston, MA. When I was growing up we always did breakfast for 'break fast'. We would eat eggs, bagels, lox, kugel and more. But over the past decade or so if I am back home, I go to the house of my rabbi friends (a couple, both rabbis) for Chinese takeaway!

Eva Azagury

I grew up in Morocco. Our tradition to break the fast is to drink egg yolk with sugar and rum (not that I ever had that)! Then for dinner, we would have meat, dates and cakes with fresh mint tea.

Claudia Camhi

I am from Chile. One side of my family breaks the fast with a sweet semolina pudding/flan, decorated with a magen david made with powdered cinnamon.

Yvonne Mason

My family always broke the fast with a cup of tea and a piece of challah with butter - then we went on to have a meal.

Liz Ison

When I talked to my late mother Rachel about her childhood memories of food and festivals, the Day of Atonement evoked as strong a culinary connection as Passover. She clearly remembered (this was the 1930s and 40s) that before the Fast her mother would cook a meal of roast beef followed by apple steffan, probably what she had eaten when she was a child. Apple steffan was only ever eaten on that occasion and was not remembered with great fondness! During the afternoon of Yom Kippur her mother would rush back home from Synagogue, so that she could start the evening meal preparations, then rush back again in time for the evening service. Baked custard and stewed fruit were always part of that meal.

When I was growing up in the 1970s and 80s, apart from apple mousse – a nod to the stewed fruit perhaps – these dishes were notably absent. The first ritual when we got home was for my mother to pour out cups of tea from the orange and brown teapot, and pass round slices of hallah (or chollah as we referred to it) thickly spread with butter, while the soup warmed up. I didn't drink tea then, but now, for me, that first cup of tea is the best cuppa of the year.

Miriam Edelman

In the small, no-rabbi, do-it-yourself synagogue in Kansas where I grew up, the community broke the Yom Kippur fast together. Everyone contributed a dish or two, and my mother always made the chicken soup. It was lovely to break your fast with a cup of hot soup, and it was our tradition. Everyone said Charlotte Edelman made the best chicken soup ever.

After Mom died, our friend Eileen wanted to take on the soup tradition in her name. She asked me to make it with her the first year, and to share the recipe.

Ah. The recipe.

Laughing, I confessed Mom's secret to Eileen. Her soup wasn't the slow cooked, home made wonder my grandmother would have made. Mom used soup powder. Cook the right vegetables (onions, a little garlic, carrots, celery, parsnip) in the made-up stock, and it tastes just like homemade - with less fuss and less grease. Particularly when cooking in a huge batch for a crowd, it was the only way to go. And if you use a powder like Telma's 'chicken', which is actually pareve (no meat or dairy), it's even vegetarian. This is what we do for the Wimbledon Seder. As my cousin Susan says, it's Happy Chicken Soup: even the chicken is happy.

Eileen wasn't having any of this. That first year, and ever after, she buys chickens, roasts them, and makes a proper chicken soup. And some congregants say it's almost as good as Charlotte's, which I guess is high praise indeed.

Naomi Glaser

I am originally from Toronto, Canada. We always broke the Fast with 'breakfast' style food. There were always a lot of sweets on the table such as cheese danishes, kuglohf (sweet yeast cake with chocolate running through it), hot chocolate...

Sharon Coussins

I grew up in a totally non-observant home, so all the Judaism we "do" now is what Ricky and I have started. We get together with close friends and take it in turns to host each year and do it pot luck!

SUKKOT

It is traditional to eat stuffed vegetables at Sukkot...

Aromatic Stuffed Peppers

Claudia Camhi

This is a vegetarian recipe with the delicate flavours and scents of Persian cuisine. My mother-in-law Monir Oroomchi has had the patience to introduce me to her cuisine and its subtle tastes.

150g (5oz) basmati rice washed in cold water 2-3 times and then drained

7 peppers (any colour)

Salt and pepper to taste

2 tablespoons crushed edible rose petals

4 teaspoons dry dill weed

1 teaspoon cinnamon

2 teaspoons turmeric

1 finely chopped onion

2 OXO vegetable stock cubes

2 tablespoons tomato puree

3 tablespoons sunflower oil

Find a medium-sized pot with a lid that can hold the 7 peppers upright. Heat 3 tablespoons of sunflower oil and stir fry the chopped onion until it is lightly golden. Set aside.

Rinse and dry the peppers. Carefully cut a top lid-like layer from each pepper (on the part that has the stem) and set aside, they will be used as a lid. Remove the white pith from the peppers.

Mix a cup of water with the tomato puree, one crushed OXO cube and half the stir fried onion and place in the bottom of the pan.

Rinse the rice in cold water until this comes out clear and then drain. Bring 4 cups of water and a tablespoon of salt to a rolling boil. Boil the rice for 5-7 minutes or until it is al dente. Drain, rinse with cold water and place in a bowl. Add the rose petals, turmeric, crushed OXO cube, the rest of the onion, the dry dill weed and gently mix using a fork.

Stuff the peppers with this mix, but be careful to not overfill as the rice will expand once completely cooked.

Sit the peppers upright in the pan and cover each one with its top.

Place the lid on the pan and cook/steam at a slow flame until the peppers are soft (20 minutes approximately). If the juices at the bottom of the pan look too thick add more water.

Stuffed Aubergines

Ella Raz-Rhodes

My grandson Aidan writes, "This recipe is a favourite of mine. When I come over to my grandparents' house after a particularly cold and dreary day at school, this really fills a spot. 'Comfort food' in every sense of the word."

Serves 6

3 large aubergines (½ per person)

400g tin of chopped tomatoes

50g (2oz) grated cheddar

Salt to taste

Freshly ground black pepper

Sweet paprika

Chilli powder (if liked)

1 tablespoon sugar

1 medium onion

2-3 cloves of garlic (chopped or mashed)

1 tablespoon rapeseed or olive oil

Cut the aubergines lengthways. With a sharp knife cut inside the rim of the aubergine so that all the inside flesh can be scooped out leaving the skin of the aubergine as an empty shell to be refilled later.

Cut the flesh into small pieces.

Chop the onion into small pieces and fry in the oil until soft (but not brown). Add the chopped aubergine to the pan and season with the salt, pepper, paprika, sugar and garlic. Add the tin of chopped tomatoes and cook on medium heat for 10-15 minutes until the aubergines are soft and the sauce thickens.

Taste to see if you wish to add anything. When cooked, fill the aubergine shells with the mixture and sprinkle with grated cheese and bake in the oven at 180°C/350°F/Gas Mark 4 until the cheese has melted.

Serve hot.

Best Ever Biscuits for Icing
aka Gingerbread Biscuits*

Eleri Larkum

Here is my recipe for best ever biscuits for icing. The baking time is approximate – I leave them in for as long as I can to get them nice and crispy. Don't worry if they are so crisp a trip to the dentist seems inevitable – they will soften up once iced.

For my apples and honey biscuits, I simply swapped honey for golden syrup. Possibly they don't get as crispy but they tasted beautifully of honey, and less intensely of ginger than when made with golden syrup.

130g (4½oz) butter

100g (4oz) soft brown sugar

8 tablespoons golden syrup or honey (120ml or 4 fl oz)

300g (10½oz) plain flour (sieved)

2 teaspoons ginger

1 teaspoon bicarbonate of soda

Beat the butter and sugar till pale. Mix in the syrup or honey, then add all the rest of the ingredients and beat till just mixed in.

Cover and chill dough for at least half an hour (it will sit happily in the fridge for a few days).

Roll out to about 5mm or less.

Bake in preheated oven at 180°C/350°F/Gas Mark 4 for 8-12 minutes.

*if you don't like gingerbread, leave out the ginger and have best ever treacle biscuits instead. They are also nice with nutmeg.

Eleri's Edible Sukkah

HANUKKAH

Elucidating Latkes

Liz Ison

"Although the potato latke has become the iconic Ashkenazic Hanukkah food, it is actually a relatively new innovation. The Maccabees never saw a potato, much less a potato pancake."

Gil Marks, Encyclopaedia of Jewish Food, 2010

So, how did potato latkes and Hanukkah become associated? Gil Marks, author of the *Encyclopaedia of Jewish Food* has done the research...

Let's start in twelfth century Spain. Rabbi Abraham Ibn Ezra (1089-1164) described (in his hymn Zemer Naeh) an idealised Hanukkah feast of wine, fine flour, doves, ducks and fatted geese. No latkes. No potatoes. No oil.

The tradition of eating fried food during Hanukkah – in recognition of the miracle of oil that is central to the Hanukkah story – appears to have originated two centuries later in 14th century Italy. The first recorded association between Hanukkah and pancakes was made by Rabbi Kalonymus ben Kalonymus (c.1286-1328), who was living in Rome. He included pancakes in a list of dishes to serve at Purim and Hanukkah. These would have been ricotta cheese pancakes and fried in olive oil.

Let's briefly stop off in the sixteenth century to observe that this was when the potato was brought over to Spain after its discovery in the Americas. The potato was very slow to catch on in Europe, having initially been greeted with hostility, and regarded as a source of leprosy or as poisonous.

By the nineteenth century, potatoes had become a staple of the eastern European diet, an integral part of Jewish cuisine – kugels, dumplings, knishes, kreplach, to name a few. The potato pancake, made from grated potato, had become common in many cuisines, German, Ukrainian, Swiss. So, at last, the Jewish version of this fried potato pancake – the kartofel latke – was prepared, especially for Hanukkah, when it was often served with braised brisket.

The origin of the word latke – basically "pancake" – is truly ancient – though we are talking Greek, not Hebrew. Latke is derived from the Ukrainian word for pancake and fritter, oladka, by way of the Greek eladia (little "oilies") which is derived from elaion (olive oil). Is there an irony here about having a Greek-derived word for one of the main culinary traditions of Hanukkah, the festival celebrating our fight against Greek assimilation?

Traditional Potato Latkes

1 kg (2lb 3oz) potatoes

2 eggs

1 teaspoon of salt

You can also add:

1 onion

4 tablespoons of matzah meal (binds the mixture better)

Oil for frying

Peel the potatoes and grate them using the grater disk of a food processor, by pushing them down the funnel (whilst giving thanks for the invention of electricity and grater attachments). Transfer to a bowl of cold water. Then drain and squeeze them in a colander – you can also put them in a clean tea towel and squeeze the liquid out. Finely chop the onion if using.

Beat the eggs lightly and add the salt. Stir together with the grated potato and optional chopped onion and matzah meal.

Heat the oil in a frying pan. Add oil to about 1cm depth. Take a tablespoon of the mixture, give it a further squeeze to remove any excess moisture, and drop into the hot oil. Press the latke down a little in the pan with a spatula or the back of a spoon. Fry till golden brown, then invert and finish off the other side.

Lift out and put on kitchen towel to remove excess oil. You can keep them warm in the oven till ready to eat.

A Woman of Substance

There was once a large lady called Sieff

Who loved latkes and brisket of beef.

This was no mere addiction

But deep-held conviction:

The core of her Jewish belief!

Jerry Markison, The Jewish Limerick Book

Time to Reinvent the Latke?

Alison Kelin

Hanukkah has always been a big deal in our house. When the girls were little they loved to decorate the house with paper dreidels and Hanukkah gelt and a huge paper chain Hanukkiah.

Latkes have also been important and over the years I have experimented with different varieties from carrot to broccoli. However it has only been in the last three years that I have completely changed how I make them. This is the controversial part – I bake them!

I can hear you all saying "but frying them is the whole point of Hanukkah" and I agree but when I realised just how much oil I was using every year (I usually make at least 500 latkes) I just couldn't continue. So now I just spray the tin with oil and bake them in the oven. Here are my favourite vegetable latkes.

Corn Latkes

4 cups fresh or frozen corn kernels, cooked, drained and cooled

Salt and pepper, to taste. I sometimes add cumin or coriander

2 large eggs

4 tablespoons flour

¼ cup vegetable oil, if frying

Sour cream

Parsley

Set the oven to 200°C/400°F/Gas Mark 6.

Puree ½ a cup of the corn and mix with salt, pepper (optional spice too) and egg. Stir in the flour and the remaining corn kernels.

Prepare a baking tray with greaseproof paper and then spray with fry light.

Then make the latkes by dropping tablespoons of the corn mixture onto the paper, leaving space for them to spread. Flatten slightly with the back of a spoon and bake for about 20 minutes, turning them after 10 minutes.

These are delicious served with sour cream mixed with chopped parsley.

Carrot Latkes

6 carrots

1 onion (or 4 spring onions)

3 eggs

Salt and pepper

50g (2oz) flour

½ teaspoon baking powder

Grate the carrots, chop the onion very finely and mix together. Add all the rest of the ingredients and mix well.

Cook in the same way as corn latkes.

Courgette Latkes

Exactly the same as the carrot latke recipe but use 3 courgettes instead. As they are so full of water you need to salt them lightly after grating and let them stand for about 15 minutes and squeeze to get rid of as much water as possible.

Green Bean Latkes

One packet of frozen green beans (about 350g or 12oz)

1 onion

3 eggs

50g (2oz) flour

Salt and pepper

Defrost the green beans, then blend in a food processor with the other ingredients and bake as above.

Cheese Latkes

250g (9oz) pot of ricotta cheese

75g (3oz) flour

3 eggs

2 tablespoons granulated sugar

½ teaspoon baking powder

A pinch of salt

Blend the ricotta cheese with the other ingredients and bake as above.

All these types of latkes freeze well.

Enjoy (You can enjoy many more, guilt and almost fat-free, if you bake them!)

Latke tasting morning

Baked Potato Latkes

Miriam Edelman

1 tablespoon and ½ teaspoon oil

2 medium onions, chopped

1 teaspoon paprika

1¾ baking potatoes

2 large eggs

1 teaspoon salt

½ teaspoon black pepper

1 tablespoon oil

More paprika to sprinkle

Preheat the oven to 200°C/400°F/Gas Mark 6.

Sauté onions in oil until softened, add paprika, let cool. Peel and grate potatoes, squeezing out excess liquid in strainer. Combine with the onions, eggs, salt and pepper.

Oil a 12 nonstick muffin pan. Add scant ⅓ cup to each cup. Spoon ¼ teaspoon of oil over each, then sprinkle with more paprika. Bake for 45 minutes or until brown at edges and firm. Run a spatula around edges to release.

Apple Latkes

Liz Ison

When we were planning the Wimshul Cooks latke tasting morning, I came across this recipe for apple latkes on the Smitten Kitchen website. It's fabulous.

3 Granny Smith apples

1 tablespoon lemon juice

6 tablespoons plain flour

1 tablespoon granulated sugar

¼ teaspoon cinnamon

1 teaspoon baking powder

2 eggs

Butter (about 2 tablespoons)

Peel and core the apples and then grate them in a food processor, using the grater attachment. Transfer to a clean tea towel and squeeze out the juice. You could save the juice in a small bowl, a chef's treat.

Transfer the grated apple to a bowl and stir in the lemon juice. In a small bowl, combine the flour, sugar, cinnamon and baking powder and then add to the apples, coating them evenly. Whisk eggs in the small bowl until lightly beaten and stir into the mixture.

Heat a large frying pan to medium with one tablespoon of the butter. Drop tablespoons of the batter into the pan, gently pressing them a bit flatter with the back of a spoon or a spatula. Fry until they are golden brown underneath, then flip to cook the other side. Transfer to kitchen paper.

You can keep them warm in the oven till ready to eat. Add a little more butter for each new batch in the pan.

Persian latkes

Claudia Camhi

My mother-in-law came up with this delicately flavoured recipe.

2 large courgettes

1 medium potato

2 eggs

2 level tablespoons plain flour

1 heaped teaspoon of crushed rose petals (do not use the ones in your garden you need to buy this from a Middle Eastern food shop)

½ teaspoon ground cinnamon

½ teaspoon turmeric

Salt and pepper to taste

¼ cup olive or sunflower oil

Grate the courgettes, one medium and one fine. Place them in a bowl and squeeze the water out.

Finely grate half a potato and medium grate the other half. Place in a bowl with the courgettes and mix in all the rest of the ingredients (except the oil).

Heat the oil in a non-stick pan. Place tablespoons of the batter into the hot oil and fry until one side is golden. Then turn over to fry the other side.

These are very aromatic little things and taste better immediately after frying. You can serve them with yoghurt and rice or just as finger food. This recipe should make 14 latkes.

Gluten-Free Latkes

Anne Clark

An inclusive recipe for a Hanukkah gathering.

500g (1lb 1oz) peeled, grated, raw potato (or 350g/12oz regular potato plus 150g/5oz grated onion and/or carrot and/or sweet potato)

2 large eggs

2 tablespoons buckwheat flour or gluten-free plain flour

Chopped parsley or coriander

Salt, pepper, paprika, ground nutmeg

Corn oil or rapeseed oil or sunflower oil for frying

Peel vegetables and grate coarsely. Squeeze off excess liquid by leaving them in a colander for at least half an hour with a weight, such as a heavy bowl, on top.

Add well-beaten eggs, flour and a generous amount of seasoning (salt, pepper, paprika, ground nutmeg, chopped parsley/coriander).

Heat a small amount of oil in a frying pan and drop in tablespoonfuls of mixture, flattening them as you do so. When golden on one side, turn and cook till golden on the other.

Drain on a metal rack rather than paper kitchen towels, if possible.

Makes about 20 small latkes. Important to use at least ⅔ regular potato to keep latkes from falling apart. You will probably need to add more oil to the pan from time to time while you are frying. Can be made in advance and reheated in the oven for 10 minutes at 200°C/400°F/Gas Mark 6. This actually enhances the taste and crispiness. Serve with apple sauce as a main course or with sugar and cinnamon as a dessert.

With thanks to Denise Phillips for helping me formalise the process.

Anne's Amazing Apple Sauce

Anne Clark

A family favourite, served with latkes on Hanukkah.

Makes 750ml (1⅓ pints) apple sauce.

1 kg (2lb 3oz) (cooking) apples (windfalls are fine)

150ml (5fl oz) orange juice (freshly squeezed or from a carton or bottle)

A handful of sultanas or raisins

Ground nuts: almonds, walnuts, hazelnuts (or a mixture) sprinkled to taste

¼ teaspoon ground cinnamon

A pinch of ground mixed spice

Date syrup (natural, sugar free – available from health food stores) to taste

Simmer peeled, cored, cut up apples in orange juice until soft. Mash with wooden spoon. Sweeten with dried fruit, ground nuts, spices and date syrup to taste.

Really easy to prepare. Can be cooked in advance – freezes well; allow plenty of time to defrost.

Pressure Cooker Apple Sauce

Liz Ison

1 kg (2lb 3oz) apples

1 cup of apple juice (or water)

Sugar to taste

Peel, core and cut the apples into quarters. Place the apples and juice in the pressure cooker. Lock the lid in place and bring the cooker to high pressure over a high heat. Then turn off the heat and leave the pressure to come down naturally.

You can then add sugar to taste. You can puree with a hand held blender or leave chunky.

This keeps well in the fridge and also freezes well.

Eleri Larkum's gingerbread dreidel

Dreidel Cookies

Victoria Silverlock

In preparation for Hanukkah, we made dreidel shaped gingerbread at playshul. The children had fun kneading, rolling and using the cutters to cut out dreidel shaped biscuits.

While the biscuits were baking, I read *Melly's Magic Dreidel* to the children. This story by Amye Rosenberg has been a real favourite with my own four children. It is about a little gopher called Melly who makes a clay dreidel for her family but asks a wizard to put a spell on it so her family will think it is special. The dreidel spins out of control causing chaos but is eventually stopped by the wizard himself dropping his magic hat on top of it. They all have hot chocolate and ginger dreidel cookies (which don't spin!) in the wizard's house at the end. As the story finished, we handed out the freshly baked gingerbread for the children to take home with them.

110g (4oz) butter

110g (4oz) sugar

275g (10oz) self-raising flour

2 teaspoons ground ginger

2-3 tablespoons syrup (warmed)

Cream the butter and sugar together until very soft. Sieve together the dry ingredients. Work into the creamed butter and sugar adding the warmed syrup a little at a time. Make into a pliable dough. Knead, then roll out on a floured board.

Cut out dreidel shapes with a cutter (or, if you don't have one, improvise) and place onto a lightly greased baking tray, not too close together as they spread when cooking.

Bake in preheated oven (180°C/350°F/Gas Mark 4) for 10-15 minutes.

Allow to cool slightly before lifting onto a wire rack. Sprinkle with sugar to look extra special.

A 1916 Plum Cake for Hanucah

Eleri Larkum recreated this recipe for Hanucah Plum Cake from a 1916 Anglo-Jewish cookbook, *Dainty Dinners and Dishes for Jewish Families* by May Henry and Kate Halford.

PLUM CAKE, RICH, FOR HANUCAH.—6 oz. butter, ½ lb. currants, ¼ lb. candied peel, ½ lb. flour, 1 tablespoonful treacle or golden syrup, a little mixed spice, 6 oz. brown sugar, ½ lb. sultanas, 2 oz. almonds, ¼ pint hot milk, 3 eggs, ¼ teaspoonful carbonate of soda.

Blanch and chop the almonds, cut the peel thinly, pick the sultanas, and clean the currants. Warm the butter slightly and cream it with the sugar; add the eggs, one at a time, and beat in the treacle. Mix in the fruit, then the flour, in which the spice has been mixed, and lastly, the soda dissolved in the warm milk. Mix all thoroughly and pour it into a cake-tin which has been lined with 3 thicknesses of kitchen-paper. Let the paper come 2 inches above the top of the tin. It need not be greased. Bake about 3½ hours in a slow oven. When quite cold, cover it with almond icing (page 114), and then with royal icing (page 115) (see illustration, page 89).

ALMOND ICING.—½ lb. ground almonds, 2 egg-whites, flavourings.

Mix the almonds and sugar together, th unbeaten egg-whites to make a stiff paste, fl out on to a sugared board. Work it with the paste. Form it into a round the shape of the top, and smooth it with a knife. If th may be covered at once with Royal icing; i to dry in the kitchen for a day before icing

ROYAL ICING.—½ lb. icing sugar, 1 or 2 egg-whites, a few drops of flavouring essence, colouring if desired.

Sieve the sugar, add the flavouring, stir in 1 unbeaten egg-white, and stir well. If too thick, add a little more egg-white, and stir till the mixture is very smooth. Beat it for at least 15 minutes, then cover the cake, smoothing it with a knife dipped in cold water. Colour the rest of the icing pink, yellow, or green, and decorate by pressing the sugar through an icing bag and fancy icing tubes.

Eleri: "I coloured the Royal icing pink and green, as suggested in the book, and I did 'press the sugar through an icing bag,' though not through any 'fancy tubes', as those were on the other side of the kitchen, and I was at that point, wishing I had been more faithful to the whole historical experience, and hired myself a kitchen of servants (I've seen Downton Abbey)."

TU B'SHEVAT

Reflections on Tu B'Shevat and a Date and Walnut Bread Recipe

Rabbi Sylvia Rothschild

In the first Mishnah of Rosh Hashanah we are told of four different New Years, and one of them is the New Year for trees, which falls on the 15th (Tet Vav) of the month of Shevat.

It sounds odd at first – why should trees have a new year? What do they do to celebrate it?

Well, sadly, the trees do nothing to celebrate. This is a date set for tax purposes – we are commanded to offer certain tithes from our grains and fruit trees, firstly to give 'Terumah' an offering to God in thanksgiving which was originally brought to the Temple, then to offer three different offerings in different agricultural years – one share given to the Levites, one share to be eaten in Jerusalem, and one share to be given to the poor. Also the age of a tree for the purposes of "orlah" (one is not allowed to eat the fruit from a tree in its first three years) was counted using Tu B'Shevat. The criteria as to which year a fruit fell into for tax purposes included which year it was formed in, and the critical date was the 15th of Shevat. Why this date? Because in Israel it was understood that the trees begin to grow on this date, coming out of their winter dormancy and beginning to form flowers and fruits.

While for a long time after the fall of the Temple the minor festival of Tu B'Shevat was effectively not much practised except in some liturgical amendments, it was not totally forgotten and there was an Ashkenazi custom to eat the different fruits and grains of Israel on the day "in honour of the significance of the day" and so grapes, figs, pomegranates, dates, olives, wheat and barley were all consumed especially on this day. In 16th Century Sfat in Northern Israel the Kabbalists who had gathered there connected the trees and fruit of the land with their own mystical tradition which used the idea of a Tree of Life with roots in the divine space and its branches in our world. They developed the kabbalistic Seder we know today. And of course return to the land and a renewed connection with the agricultural cycle has given Tu B'Shevat a new impetus in Jewish life today.

Trees have always been special in Jewish tradition, and fruit trees most of all. In the Bible the first thing that God does is to plant a garden within which are trees of all kinds and of course those two particularly special fruit trees – the Tree of the Knowledge of Good and Evil (the fruit of which was eaten by Adam and Eve) and the Tree of Life (whose fruit was specifically protected from being eaten by the expulsion from the garden of Adam and Eve). We are told that in order to imitate God, we too should plant our gardens and tend them well and planting trees in the Land of Israel is a mitzvah for us to this day.

Rav Kook, the first Ashkenazi Chief Rabbi of British Mandate Palestine wrote that agriculture has the power to unify the Jewish people, and that our ideal Jewish society should be based on agriculture rather than on commerce. Commenting on Mishnah Bikkurim 3:3 which tells us that, "All the professionals in Jerusalem would stand before them (the farmers) and inquire as to their welfare," Rabbi Kook wrote, "...When the nation is morally depraved, when individuals' eyes and heart are only upon money, these two types, those who engage in nature and those who engage in artifice become alienated from one another. The farmers, who dwell in villages close to nature, will be the object of disrespect on the part of the professionals who have learned how to live as a society divorced from nature." He worried that we would develop into a people who did not value the land and those who work it and who feed us all from it.

Fruit trees have a special place in our tradition – from the Biblical injunction not to cut down fruit trees in times of war and siege to the extraordinary blessing to be said on seeing for the first time that year a fruit tree in bloom, "Blessed are You, Eternal our God, King of the universe, Who has ensured there is nothing lacking in the world, and Who created in it good creatures and good trees in order to benefit and give pleasure to people." We are reminded that our lives are dependent on trees and plants, that we are nourished and sustained by them and would quickly die if they failed.

Tu B'Shevat comes to remind us to look again at how we value our trees and our land, and how we value those who work with the land in order to provide our food. It reminds us that we are all dependent on the natural world, that we must look after it and keep it in good order not only for our time but for the generations that follow. The Midrash in Kohelet Rabbah tells us that God took the first human being around the Garden of Eden and said, "See my works, how beautiful and praiseworthy they are, and everything that I created, I created for you. Be careful. Do not spoil or destroy my world, for if you do there will be nobody who will come after you to repair it."

My Mum's Date and Walnut Bread
Rabbi Sylvia Rothschild

½ cup roughly chopped walnuts
225g (½ lb) chopped dates
1 egg
1 teaspoon bicarbonate of soda
¾ cup boiling water
½ cup sugar
1½ cups self-raising flour
Large knob of butter

Preheat the oven to 180°C/350°F/Gas Mark 4. Put dates, bicarbonate of soda and butter into a bowl and pour on the water. Add beaten egg, flour and the other ingredients and mix together. Pour into a loaf tin and bake for one hour.

The Seven Biblical Species

On Tu B'shevat, it has become traditional to eat the seven types of fruits and grains named in the Torah as the main produce of the land of Israel. In Biblical times these foods were staples of the diet as well as being important from the perspective of religious observance because one of the Temple tithes derived from these seven foods.

> For the Lord your God is bringing you to a good land,
> A land with brooks of water, fountains and depths,
> That merge in valleys and mountains
> A land of wheat and barley, vines and figs and pomegranates,
> A land of oil producing olives and honey
> A land in which you will eat bread without scarcity.

Deuteronomy (8)

The Original Biblical Superfoods!

Yvonne Mason, Sharon Coussins and Orli Kendler-Rhodes

Let's look at the seven Biblical species: olives, wheat, barley, figs, dates, pomegranates, and grapes.

Not only are they delicious, and some may be included in our daily diet, it is also interesting to look at the health benefits of our ancient heritage…

Grapes

Commonly known in the liquid form as wine!

An occasional glass of wine helps to reduce cholesterol, something the French have also clocked onto. Not sure Palwin No 10 would qualify for this.

Olives

We all know that the olive branch represents peace. Also olive oil is healthy to use in salads and cooking as it is not a saturated fat.

Wheat and Barley

They are essential for our bread or hallah, breakfast cereals, and our lovely cakes, but also provide us with fibre, as will **figs** and **dates**.

New research is now going on in Israel to look at the various properties of **pomegranates** and **dates**. There is some evidence emerging about their ability to treat atherosclerosis (fatty deposits in the walls of arteries).

A Biblical Kiddush

Get your seven Biblical species into your baking! The recipes for hallah, muffins and cookies in this section incorporate the seven Biblical species (barley, wheat, olive (oil), grape, fig, pomegranate, date) and were created especially for a Tu B'Shevat Kiddush we held at Wimbledon.

The Kiddush included cakes and cookies containing the seven species, raisin and banana loaf, date and fig biscuits, chocolate and date loaf, wine and spice cake.

There was also a savoury platter of Persian aubergines, pine nuts and pomegranates served with a saffron and yoghurt dip.

To nibble there were chocolate raisins, figs, dates and pomegranate seeds. The Seven Species hallot was paired with a date butter. To drink there was pomegranate juice and orange barley water.

"Biblical" Hallah with Date Butter
Or...Hallah made with the Seven Biblical Species

Liz Ison

What better way to celebrate the two ancient grains and five fruits than combining them in a delicious hallah – a nod to the last line of the Biblical verse referring to the land where "you will eat bread without scarcity." It also includes orange juice and zest, so if you can find a Jaffa orange, you will be bringing the recipe into the modern era.

This recipe was inspired by a Fig, Olive Oil and Sea Salt Hallah recipe in Deb Perelman's *Smitten Kitchen Cookbook*. By throwing in a few extra ingredients, I came up with this hallah of the seven species. Perfect for Tu B'Shevat or Sukkot.

Dough (makes two loaves, or 16ish mini-hallot)

2 tablespoons dried yeast

1¾ cups warm water

⅓ cup granulated sugar

⅓ cup runny honey

3½ teaspoons salt

½ cup olive oil

3 eggs and 2 egg yolks

7½ cups strong white flour

1 cup golden raisins (first, soak in warm water for 5 minutes, before draining and drying the raisins)

½ cup chopped dates

Fig Filling

1 cup quartered dried figs, stems removed

¼ teaspoon freshly grated orange zest

½ cup water

¼ cup orange juice

Egg wash

1 egg, beaten

Topping

Barley flakes (available from health food shops)

Pomegranate seeds

Make the dough: In a large mixing bowl, stir together the yeast, water and a pinch of sugar. Leave for five minutes.

Stir in the remaining sugar, honey and salt. Add oil, eggs, yolks and flour. Stir. Leave to rest for 15 minutes, then knead by hand or with the dough hook of a food mixer for about 10 minutes. Add extra flour if it is too sticky.

Place the dough in an oiled bowl and cover the bowl with cling film, or a large bin bag. Leave to rise for about 1- 1 ½ hours, till doubled in size.

Make the fig filling: Put the chopped figs, zest, juice and water into a small saucepan. Simmer for about 10 minutes till the figs are soft. Leave in the saucepan to cool, and any remaining liquid will be absorbed. Blend to a paste in a food processor.

Prepare the loaves: Deflate the dough, and press the prepared raisins and dates into the dough, kneading and folding them in.

Leave to rest for 10 minutes before shaping. Divide the dough in half.

For a three-braid hallah, divide the dough into three, and roll with your hands into long ropes. Press the ropes flat and spoon a little fig mixture along the length of the rope. Then roll each rope up trying to "hide" the fig mixture within. Then plait the three braids together. At this point you can join the two ends into a round, if you wish. Repeat with the other half.

You can also make mini hallot. Make long ropes and fill with the fig paste as before. Then cut each rope into short sections, stretch again and tie into knots.

Put onto a baking tray that has been sprinkled with a little polenta. Brush with the beaten egg. Leave to prove again for about half an hour, loosely covered with the bin bag.

Bake: Preheat the oven to 200°C/400°F/Gas Mark 6. Brush the loaves again with egg wash, sprinkle with the barley flakes and put in the oven. After 10 minutes baking, turn the oven down to 180°C/350°F/Gas Mark 4. Bake for a further 25 minutes (10 minutes for small rolls). They are done if they sound hollow when you tap the bottoms.

Cool on a rack. Serve sprinkled with pomegranate seeds. If you are making hamotzi over the bread, why not have a bowl with extra pomegranate seeds that you can sprinkle over after the blessing, as you would normally do with salt.

This is delicious eaten with cheese – or serve it with some date butter.

Date Butter

Miriam Edelman

This is a 'butter' only in the sense that it is spreadable - there is no butter or other extra fat in it at all. I remembered American apple butter and so created a similar version out of dates.

Put 350g (12oz) pitted dried dates as flat as possible in a pot. Pour 400ml (¾ pint) boiling water over them. Leave to sit for at least an hour, probably better for longer.

Put on medium-low heat and simmer until very soft and water is absorbed; add more water if necessary and stir/smash with a wooden spoon occasionally. Cook for 20 minutes or until they are really soft. Cool.

Put the mixture through a food processor to puree. Push through a sieve and discard remaining husks. As the butter is quite thick, scrape the puree off the bottom of the sieve if necessary.

Add cinnamon and nutmeg, or other spices, to taste. Store in an airtight container in the refrigerator. Makes about 1 cup.

Seven Biblical Species Muffins

Carra Kane

I adapted this from a recipe on the blog *The Shiksa in the Kitchen*. The muffins contain almond milk, almonds being an unofficial eighth species as almond trees blossom in Israel at this time of year. The apple sauce makes it even more fruity and reminds us of that other New Year.

My daughter Jadyn ate one warm from the rack and approved. She liked the idea of all seven species being in one little muffin case. And my husband snaffled two when he got home from work but there were still plenty to take for the Tu B'shevat Kiddush.

I made double the quantity and made 24 muffins and a loaf cake.

¾ cup golden raisins

½ cup dates

½ cup dried figs

1 cup unsweetened almond milk

¼ cup apple sauce (from baby food aisle – I used Apple & Pear)

¼ cup pomegranate juice

1 teaspoon cinnamon

2 eggs

¼ cup olive oil

½ cup sugar

¼ cup brown sugar

1½ teaspoon vanilla

1½ cup all-purpose flour

½ cup barley flour (I used Country Grain Bread flour – which contains some barley flour)

2 teaspoon baking powder

½ teaspoon bicarbonate of soda

¼ teaspoon salt

Paper muffin tin liners and muffin tray

Topping

2 tablespoons granulated sugar

¼ teaspoon cinnamon

Cover the raisins with water and bring to a boil. As soon as the water boils, turn off the heat and leave for 10 minutes to plump. Drain and pat dry with a paper towel.

Preheat the oven to 200°C/400°F/Gas Mark 6. If your figs have tough stems on them, remove them and discard. Roughly chop dates and figs. Set aside.

Use a blender or food processor to blend together raisins, dates, figs, almond milk, applesauce, pomegranate juice, and cinnamon until smooth. Set mixture aside.

In a medium mixing bowl, whisk together eggs, olive oil, sugar, brown sugar, and vanilla extract.

In a large mixing bowl, sift together flour, barley flour (or a flour you can find with barley in it), baking powder, bicarbonate of soda, and salt.

Make a well in the middle of the dry ingredients (I used a cup/glass). Pour mixture from the blender into the well. Then add the egg mixture to the bowl.

Fold the dry mixture into the wet ingredients until the dry ingredients are just moistened and a lumpy batter forms. Do not over mix.

Mix the sugar and cinnamon together in a small bowl using a fork. Sprinkle about a ½ teaspoon of cinnamon sugar mixture evenly across the surface of each muffin.

Place muffins in the oven and immediately turn heat down to 190°C/375°F/Gas Mark 5. Bake for 25 minutes until the tops of the muffins are golden brown and a toothpick inserted in the centre comes out clean. Let muffins cool for 10 minutes before removing from the tin and cooling on a rack. Serve warm.

Seven Biblical Species Cookies

Miriam Edelman

Makes about 8 dozen medium cookies.

3 cups flour

1 teaspoon bicarbonate of soda

1 teaspoon cinnamon (possibly more of this and the other spices if you like a spicier cookie)

1 teaspoon ground ginger

1 teaspoon nutmeg

1 teaspoon allspice

½ teaspoon ground cloves

Mix all of the above together in a large bowl, then add:

2 eggs, slightly beaten

2 teaspoons vanilla

⅔ cup caster sugar

1 cup brown sugar, packed

⅔ cup butter, melted

⅔ cup vegetable fat (Stork, Trex), melted

¼ cup olive oil

2 tablespoons honey

½ cup pomegranate juice

Mix well with a wooden spoon until very well combined and brown sugar lumps are dissolved. Stir in:

3½ cups barley flakes

¾ cup chopped dates

¾ cup chopped figs

1 cup sultanas

Mix well. Drop tablespoonfuls onto ungreased baking sheets. Bake at 180°C/350°F/Gas Mark 4 for about ten minutes, until light golden brown. Cool 5 minutes then remove to rack to cool completely.

Barley Soup
Claudia Camhi

One of my mother-in-law's recipes that works so well for a snowy Tu B'Shevat.

150g (5oz) pearl barley

2 vegetable stock cubes

50g (2oz) butter

3 level tablespoons plain flour

350ml (12 fl oz) milk (semi or full fat)

Salt and pepper to taste

½ teaspoon ground nutmeg

Juice of 1 lemon

100ml (3½ fl oz) single cream

Rinse the barley in running water.

Place in a bowl and cover with boiling water for at least 3 hours or preferably overnight.

Drain, then place in a large pan and cover with boiling water and simmer until the barley is soft. This can take over an hour. Add the stock cubes and seasoning.

Make a béchamel sauce by:

Melting the butter in a small pot and then adding the flour. Use a low to mid flame. Whisk until it becomes golden (3 minutes approximately). Slowly add some milk and whisk until it is smoothly blended in.

Repeat this until all the milk has been used up. Add the nutmeg and seasoning to taste.

Once the barley is ready, dissolve the béchamel into the barley soup. This will thicken it up and make it creamy. Serve in small bowls with a few lemon juice drops, a dash of cream and freshly ground pepper.

Persian Aubergines
Claudia Camhi

A lovely and original vegetarian starter or a side for a buffet created by my friend Layli.

4 aubergines with skin

Plenty of olive oil, sea salt and pepper

A large onion

A handful of pine nuts

Grains of ½ a pomegranate fruit

For the sauce:

A pot of Greek yoghurt

Juice of ½ a lemon

Salt and pepper to taste

One crushed garlic clove

⅛ teaspoon ground saffron

Preheat the oven to 200°C/400°F/Gas Mark 6. Slice the aubergines lengthwise into 8 wedges (keep skin on). Toss aubergines in plenty of olive oil, sea salt and pepper. Roast well until very tender and browned for approximately 50 minutes.

Meanwhile chop and stir fry a large onion in olive oil until it is tender and add salt and pepper to taste and a handful of pine nuts.

Place the roasted aubergines on a serving plate and add the onions and pine nuts on top.

Sprinkle on them the grains of ½ a pomegranate fruit.

For the sauce

Mix a pot of Greek yoghurt with the the other ingredients and allow to rest in the fridge for half an hour.

The aubergines with yoghurt mix can be served with flat bread or rice.

Bazargan
Claudia Roden

Claudia Roden, author of *The Book of Jewish Food*, is a food writer and cultural anthropologist. As Simon Schama put it, "Claudia Roden is no more a simple cookbook writer than Marcel Proust was a biscuit baker." We are very grateful to her for submitting this flavoursome recipe to our collection.

This bulgur salad is of the Jews of Aleppo. The name implies it was made entirely from ingredients bought at the spice bazaar.

Sour pomegranate syrup and tamarind give the grain (burghul or bulgur) a delicious sweet-and-sour flavour and lovely brown colour. Use a coarsely ground cracked wheat if you can, but a fine ground one will do. Make it at least four hours before serving so that the wheat can properly absorb the dressing.

Serves 6 – 8

350g (12oz) bulgur

175ml (6 fl oz) extra virgin olive oil

4 tablespoons sour pomegranate concentrate or molasses (it is a syrup) or 2 tablespoons tamarind paste dissolved in 4 tablespoons boiling water

Juice of 1 lemon

5 tablespoons tomato paste

1 teaspoon ground cumin

1 teaspoon ground coriander

½ teaspoon ground allspice

½ teaspoon cayenne or chilli pepper, or more to taste

Salt

150g (5oz) walnuts, very coarsely chopped

100g (4oz) hazelnuts, very coarsely chopped

50g (2oz) pine nuts, lightly toasted

A large bunch of flat-leafed parsley (1 cup), finely chopped

Put the bulgur in a large bowl and cover with plenty of cold water. Leave to soak until it is tender. The time depends on how finely ground it is and how old. It can take from ½ – 2 hours. Drain in a colander with small holes and press the excess water out.

In a serving bowl, beat the olive oil with the pomegranate concentrate or molasses or dissolved tamarind paste. Add the lemon juice, tomato paste, cumin, coriander, allspice and cayenne pepper and salt and beat well. Pour over the cracked wheat and mix very well. Taste before you add more salt if necessary.

Before serving add the nuts and flat-leafed parsley and mix well.

Orange-Carrot Spice Muffins
Caroline Ingram

Makes 12 muffins

280g (10oz) plain flour

2 teaspoons baking powder

½ teaspoon bicarbonate of soda

½ teaspoon salt

½ teaspoon ground cinnamon

¼ teaspoon ground cloves

¼ teaspoon ground nutmeg

1 egg

85g (3oz) white granulated sugar

Finely grated rind of 1 large orange

180ml (6 fl oz) orange juice from the orange (can make up the remainder with water)

100g (4oz) grated carrot

90ml (3oz) vegetable oil

60g (2½oz) raisins (optional)

Topping

3 tablespoons light brown soft sugar

1 tablespoon melted butter

60g (2½oz) chopped walnuts or pecans

Prepare your muffin tray. Preheat the oven 190°C/375°F/Gas Mark 5.

In a large bowl, sift together the flour, baking powder, bicarbonate of soda, salt and spices. In a separate bowl, beat the egg with a fork. Stir in sugar, grated orange rind, juice plus water, carrot and oil. Pour all of the liquid ingredients into the dry mixture. Stir till just incorporated, adding dried fruit towards the end.

Spoon into the tin. Combine topping and spoon over the tops. Bake for 20 minutes until the tops spring back when pressed gently.

Banana and Raisin Loaf
Alison Kelin

Makes 1 full-sized loaf or 2 small loaves.

Preheat the oven to 180°C/350°F/Gas Mark 4.

In one bowl, combine:

90g (3¼oz) butter, softened

2 eggs

2 or 3 very ripe bananas

155g (5½oz) sugar

Use a potato masher, fork or spoon to squish the banana and mix the ingredients together. It is alright for there to be small (1cm) chunks of banana in the batter, but you want most of the banana to be reduced to mush.

In another bowl, combine:

155g (5½oz) self-raising flour

¾ teaspoon salt

½ teaspoon bicarbonate of soda

¼ teaspoon baking powder

½ teaspoon cinnamon (optional)

Combine the wet and dry ingredients and mix until the ingredients are blended together. Then add 50g (2oz) raisins.

If you like, stir in additional ingredients here as well as or instead of the raisins, such as chopped walnuts or pecans, dried cherries, cranberries or apricots, or chocolate chips. A handful (about 50g/2oz) is about right.

Pour the mixture into greased baking tins and bake until a toothpick inserted in the centre comes out clean. Small loaves take around 30 minutes; a normal-sized loaf takes around 50 minutes.

Remove from the oven. This loaf is great warm, but it is excellent cold too.

After they have cooled for 5 or 10 minutes the loaves can be removed from the pan to cool. Once they are cool they can be individually wrapped and frozen.

Iced Pomegranate Grains

Claudia Camhi

I learned this delicious way to use the pomegranate whilst strolling around a little town in Israel called Kyriat Tivon. The hedges between houses were in fact pomegranate bushes and it was beautiful to see the ripe fruit hanging from the branches. It was not frowned upon to take a fruit to eat from any hedge and carry on walking.

2- 3 pomegranates

Cut the fruit in horizontal halves.

Whilst holding the pomegranate facing over a bowl, beat each half on the outside (skin) using a wooden spoon. This should allow the seeds to come off without having to go through the painstaking task of fishing for each grain, squeezing them in the process and getting your fingers stained for days!

Place the grains in a freezer bag and pop it in the freezer for a few hours.

Eat these natural mini ice fruit lollies on their own, over ice cream, in drinks or sprinkled over other fruits (melons are a good combination).

PURIM

Hamantaschen – Texas style!
Carra Kane

Making hamantaschen is something I only started doing since becoming a parent. When Jadyn was in Reception, I knew the best way for the little ones to remember me and the Jewish stories I read to them, was through food! I pre-made the dough, rolled it out and made dozens of "pre-cut" circles, so each child only had to scoop their favourite flavoured jam into the centre, then I helped them pinch the corners. Instant success…

It seems I am always looking for a good dough to make and a friend in Houston (who briefly lived in Wimbledon) sent me the recipe that her Synagogue sisterhood used for their Annual Purim hamantaschen Fundraiser. Beth Israel is the oldest Synagogue in Texas and where my father's family has a long history. When I went to the Synagogue's website, I was reading about the history of the sisterhood and at the end of the article I discovered it was written just a few years ago by my Great Aunt Virginia. I was amazed to read the Synagogue membership is currently over 1700 households! I wonder how many hamantaschen they managed to bake?

Hamantaschen

454g (1lb) salted butter (room temperature or softened)

450g (2 cups) sugar

4 eggs

2 teaspoons (10ml) vanilla extract

¼ cup (60ml) milk

2 teaspoons baking powder

875g (7 cups) plain flour (sifted)

Combine butter and sugar. Add eggs, vanilla and milk. Combine baking powder with the pre-sifted flour and stir into batter. Divide into 2 or 3 "balls" and wrap them in cling film or wax paper and put them in a bag. Keep the dough refrigerated overnight or make a few days ahead and freeze it.

When you are ready to bake, preheat the oven to 180°C/350°F/Gas Mark 4. Be sure to roll out your dough to about ⅛ inch thick (or even thinner).

Use a 3 inch cookie cutter (or larger) or even the rim of a cup, to cut your circles out of the dough.

Place no more than a teaspoon of filling into the centre of each circle. Be careful not to overfill, or you risk them opening during baking.

Either pinch your corners or fold to make the 3 points.

If you would like professional looking hamantaschen, brush with egg just before baking.

Bake for 10-15 minutes (or until golden brown). If you are making large quantities, I recommend lining your trays with baking paper. This saves time when removing each tray from the oven. You can just slide the entire sheet off and put the next set in once the tray cools. Allow hamantaschen to cool before eating.

Hamantaschen – WimShul Style!

The Wimshul Cooks' Purim bake-in was a truly 'hands-on' and inter-generational event, enjoyed by the nursery, baby and toddler group, and adult education classes.

Two baking stations were set up – one for the adults, the other for the children – and both quickly turned into hives of industry. Wimshul Cooks had prepared batches of dough and the team brought in various fillings: apricot with syrup, apple, sultana and cinnamon, chocolate chips, jam and, a certain boy's special request, cream cheese with vanilla and chocolate!

To background music of Purim songs, the children from Apples and Honey Nursery came up in groups and with a little help each produced their own hamantaschen which they were able to eat later. Some chocolate chips didn't quite make it into the pre-cut dough circles but disappeared into little mouths – after all, Purim is about having fun!

Some interesting shapes were created, including crescents and some that reminded us fondly of kreplach, and the trays were then passed through to the kitchen where they were topped with sprinkles and mohn and baked.

Lekvár

Olin Sloan

Plums and apricots, peaches, almonds and cherries are all species of the widely cultivated genus Prunus, a member of the Rosaceae (rose) family. It is thought that plum trees first arrived in Europe from the Middle East during the 13th century with Frenchmen returning from the Fifth Crusade. However, they may have been introduced much earlier by the Romans.

Apparently there are now over 300 varieties of plum in Britain. They come into season around the time of Rosh Hashanah (late August to early October). However, at other times of the year when fresh fruit isn't available, Lekvár, an aromatic, delicious reduction of dried fruit (sometimes also referred to as fruit butter) is made. Of Slovakian origin Lekvár is particularly common in Hungarian cuisine.

Lekvár can be made from all the species of the Prunus family. It can also be made from apples, another member of the Rosaceae family (though not of the Prunus family).

As sugar was rare and expensive until modern times, Lekvár's sweetness was usually derived from the fruit itself, produced by the concentration of natural sugar during cooking. Traditionally it was used as jam by peasants who spread it on their bread. Today sugar is added both as a sweetener and as a thickener.

Lekvár has many uses. Apricot or prune lekvár is used to fill the Eastern European hamantaschen eaten at Purim and the Austrian krapfen (doughnuts) eaten at Hanukkah. It is also used as a filling for pastries (such as Danish, the Franco-German fluden eaten on Shabbos and at Rosh Hashanah and the Czech kolache eaten at Purim). It is used in dumplings made with an unleavened dough (such as the Polish pierógi and the Ukrainian vareniki) as well as in the kugels eaten on Shabbos. It is used to good effect with biscuits, the Austrian kipfel and croissants and it is used as a filling in crêpes (such as palatschinken, thin pancakes common in Eastern Europe). Lekvár is also used in pastries such as strudel.

500g (1lb 1oz) dried apricots or prunes, pitted

Water to just cover fruit

50g (2oz) caster sugar, or more, to taste

1½ tablespoons lemon juice

20g (1oz) ground nuts, almonds for apricots, walnuts for prunes, optional.

Cover fruit in saucepan with water. Simmer for 10-15 minutes without letting all the water evaporate or the lekvár will burn. Add more water if necessary. Once fruit is soft add sugar, lemon juice and ground nuts, if using, and cook until thick and has formed a puree. If the Lekvár is runny continue to cook a minute or two more.

PASSOVER

How to Make Matzah

Miriam Edelman

This is a fun activity to do with children.

Preheat the oven as hot as it will go (200°C/400°F/Gas Mark 6). Line baking trays with parchment paper.

Combine in large bowl, making a well in the centre:

2 cups unbleached kosher for Passover flour (NOT self-raising!)

Pinch of salt if desired

Make ready in a measuring cup 1 cup liquid:

>⅔ cup cold spring water
>
>⅓ cup olive oil (or use more water)

Set timer for 15 minutes. You have 18 minutes (the time prescribed for ensuring that the flour mixed with water does not begin to ferment), but this will make sure there is no error. Start the timer just before you add the liquid to the flour. Stir liquid into flour.

Turn out onto floured board to knead until smooth and elastic, adding more flour as necessary. You may wish to divide the dough into 3-4 parts for kneading, or after kneading and before rolling.

Roll as thin as possible and transfer to parchment-lined baking trays. With a fork, perforate dough all over the surface. Gently stretch the dough to enlarge the holes a little and ensure flatness.

Put in oven within the 15 minutes (really 18) deadline to prevent fermentation/rising.

Bake 15-20 minutes until lightly and thoroughly brown—if you take it out too soon it will taste like paste, and if you leave it too long it will burn, so pay attention. Allow to cool.

Heder Matzah Workshop held jointly with Richmond Synagogue

Baking Matzah in Ethiopia
Rabbi Sybil A. Sheridan

Photos taken by Rabbi Sybil Sheridan during her visit to Gondar

Matzah is hand-baked on open fires in the community compound in Gondar, Ethiopia to be shared amongst the community for Passover.

Many thousands of Ethiopian Jews (the Beta Israel) left Ethiopia for Israel in the 1980s and 90s. However, the Zera Israel are a group of Ethiopians of Jewish descent who are still living in Ethiopia. They follow a Jewish way of life, living in Gondar, having moved there from their villages hoping to seek a new life in Israel. Meketa is a UK-based charity founded by Rabbi Sybil Sheridan in 2012 which supports this community, through education and livelihood projects.

What to Eat on Pesach
Rabbi Sybil A. Sheridan

When Passover draws near, the annual anxiety over what to eat – or, more exactly, what not to eat begins.

The Bible is clear. No 'leaven.' But what is leaven? It is usually defined as fermented grain – specifically, fermented of the five species of grain that grow in the land of Israel. These are: wheat, rye, barley, oats, and spelt. So wine (fermented grape) is allowed but whisky (fermented rye) is not. Matzah, which can be made of wheat or rye or spelt baked quickly so it does not ferment and therefore does not rise when baking, is our staple food for the week; but cake, if made from the same ingredients, but requiring the fermentation process to make it rise, is strictly forbidden.

So far, so reasonably clear. We eat matzah; we eat cake made from potato flour or matzah meal, risen with an unhealthy lot of eggs. We drink wine, port and brandy and other fruit concoctions.

But then we get to the complicated bit. Ashkenazi communities (those that settled in Germany and parts north and east from there) developed other rules. No rice, no peas, beans or other pulses were allowed, kitniyot they are called in Hebrew. The reason for this is hard to fathom, as they are not grains. Some claim it is because they used to be stored in old flour sacks and so would have been coated in the forbidden stuff. Others reckon it is because if you grind pulses, they look exactly like wheat flour and so could easily be confused. Either way, the tradition is centuries old and as much part of the Seder tradition as the Exodus itself. However, if you are Sephardi (coming from Babylonia to Spain and then all parts west and south of there), you do not follow these traditions – and indeed, rice remains the staple (once carefully checked there are no hidden wheat grains among the seeds) in such communities as those in India and Pakistan.

Pesach by Zoe aged 9

So, what happens in a community like ours, where we have a mixture of Ashkenazi and Sephardi? Usually, where there is such a 'mixed marriage,' the couple is expected to observe the most stringent partner's set of practices, but not so in the case of Pesach. If an Ashkenazi woman marries a Sephardi man, she is expected to put her principles aside and cook him rice and beans, for heaven forbid that he suffer on Pesach! This suggests that the custom regarding kitniyot is not a law, or even a rule – unless it is a rule made to be broken. The first Reform Synagogue in this country was just like a mixed marriage since the founding families came from both Sephardi and Ashkenazi backgrounds. The Reform Movement has continued the tradition and so will allow for kitniyot at a Seder, so long as there is sufficient food for those who observe the Ashkenazi traditions not to feel short-changed or uncomfortable. So for example, at our Seder at home (we are a Sephardi family) we usually have fish, with potatoes, courgettes or a cucumber salad, any vegetable, possibly, but never peas – even though we could. However if we have vegetarian guests or if people offer to bring a salad, I have no hesitation in cooking up a nut roast with lentils, or having a bean salad on the table. I know the Ashkenazim will not be hungry.

So in short, these are the foods not to bring to a Seder:

- Bread, biscuits and cake made from the five species of grain mentioned above.

- Do not use any standard flour, or baking powder of any kind.

- You shouldn't eat couscous or polenta, semolina or pasta either.

These are the foods I consider a must have at a Seder: Matzah – of course – it's a mitzvah – but also cakes made of potato flour, ground almonds or matzah meal, meringues and puddings with fruit; pavlovas and trifles made with stale Pesach cake. Biscuits of all sorts using almonds and other ground nuts: cinnamon balls, macaroons, etc. Soups and sauces can be thickened with potato flour or arrowroot. Be careful of the oil you use for cooking. Avoid vegetable oil and corn oil, go for sunflower or olive oil instead. Go for wine vinegar rather than malt vinegar. Check out the ingredients in prepared sauces: mayonnaise, tomato ketchup, and the like – it's best to get a kosher brand or make it yourself, if you can.

If you eat kitniyot then any pulse, peas, beans or lentils are permissible as well as rice. Quinoa is all right. The ultra frum have declared it not kosher for Pesach but they are just being spoilsports. If you are coming to the communal Seder, and bringing along a salad, then dishes with kitniyot are quite acceptable, providing it is clear that they contain beans or peas, so those who do refrain from them can avoid them.

Of course the main protein sources are untouched by this. Meat, eggs, fish and cheese are fine – within the usual range of kashrut. However, I never go for kosher milk, butter, tea, coffee or jams. That is just a racket ensuring you are paying way over the odds for the security that no one with a ham sandwich in his breast pocket will have leant over your food and dropped crumbs in it. Firstly, this is so unlikely to happen; secondly, if it did happen, you would not be held responsible since it would not be your fault; thirdly, if it did indeed happen the proportion would be so tiny in comparison to the rest of the ingredients as to have no effect on the general kashrut.

But I am complicating things. The main thing is, enjoy your Seder and enjoy your food throughout the seven days of Pesach. It is a great time to experiment and to indulge. Make the most of it!

Passover by Hannah G aged 9

Seder Night by Tomer aged 12

Seder Plate by Ariella aged 8

Seder Plate by Sophia aged 8½

What Would I Put onto a Seder Plate?

Rabbi Sylvia Rothschild

It has become a "contemporary tradition" to place an extra item on the Seder plate in addition to the traditional items – here is my choice and the reasons why.

I would choose a pomegranate to be on my Seder plate as a reminder of the many different strands of my Judaism and the fact that I am free to have a complex layered understanding of tradition. The pomegranate is one of the seven species the Bible tells us about growing in the land of Israel, fruits which are traditionally eaten on Sukkot, a full half year from Pesach, a reminder of the connection to the Land to which I remain spiritually attached. It was said to be one of the fruits brought back by the spies to demonstrate the fertility of the land – a tempting luscious fruit that can only be eaten sensually, as the Song of Songs reminds us.

Tradition tells us that a pomegranate has 613 seeds – equivalent to the mitzvot, and I particularly like the chutzpah of such a statement and the fact that we remember it while knowing that it is not remotely true. I like that the mitzvot are likened to the jewelled seeds, and the implication of richness and nourishment within them, while remembering the hard pip within each seed that can be both irritation and pleasure, and that can stay with one long after the juicy flesh has been taken. And I like the way that pomegranates are so useful in so many ways – as health food, as astringent, as spice and decoration, as traditional remedy for any number of ailments, as drink and paste and marinade. It prompts me to think of the multi-faceted ways Judaism is expressed, from the traditional covenantal relationship and discipline of mitzvot, to the loose warmth of 'kitchen Judaism' as people respond to the remembered smells of the different festival foods through the year.

The Bible tells us that Aaron wore a special garment as high priest, and it was decorated with alternate bells and pomegranates on the hem, so that when he moved the sounds of these objects clashing would be heard and people would know he would be safe – indeed the Bible is starkly clear – "so that he will not die." This brings me from the sacrificial system of Biblical Judaism right into the modern world of Jewish community – people will pay attention to how others are, particularly those who are vulnerable. They will notice if they haven't seen or heard them, and do something so that their lives are sustained and preserved. The pomegranate is the standard bearer for communication in community.

Another tradition tells us that the forbidden fruit eaten by Eve in Eden was not the apple (a later pun on the Latin 'malum' to mean both bad and apple) but the pomegranate. If it is truly the fruit of the tree of knowledge of good and evil, it would be a potent reminder at Seder that we have choices in what we do, a freedom in our lives with consequent responsibilities. We cannot accuse others for our not having achieved what we know we should have, or take refuge in the modern day 'slavery' to routine. The pomegranate would challenge us –"know what is important, do what is right."

A pomegranate is similar in shape to a grenade (indeed its name in both English and Hebrew reflects this) and so it would be a salutary reminder that even that which is beautiful and health-giving could easily become dangerous and destructive in the wrong circumstances, another warning on the Seder table to remind us that our Judaism can either sustain us in living well or in living selfishly and without care or thought for the others among whom we live. Choose life, says the Bible, but both blessing and curse are set before us and it is our freedom to decide which way to go.

And finally – the best way to eat a pomegranate is to cut it into two pieces, turn each upside down in one hand and hit it with a wooden spoon so that the seeds fall into a waiting container. A satisfying if difficult thing to do well, a metaphor for much of the Jewish world, one might think. But the best bit comes last – once the Seder is over and a home must be found for the objects on the Seder plate, to eat a wonderful juicy fresh pomegranate must be the best end to the ritual I can think of!

A Communal Seder

Camilla McGill and Carra Kane

Rabbi Sheridan made an appeal for someone or a group of people to take on organising the second night Seder.

Carra and I both felt strongly that the Seder is so important for so many people - whether they are members or not, no matter what their connection is with the shul, we were determined to make it a great success. We really wanted to get the word out there to make sure that as many people as possible heard about it. Carra set to with the social networking side of things posting on various Facebook pages. We wrote several letters for the office to send via email and the Synagogue newsletter and we personally invited as many people as possible and, thanks to

Ricky Coussins, it was on the website with a form to register online.

We were astonished to see as time grew near that the numbers were creeping up and up. Our panic began rising and there were lots of phone calls, texts and emails back and forth. Ocado orders were amended, extra trips to Tony's and Asda were made and extra helpers were enlisted for the kitchen. By the time the big day came, we were up to 170 people booked. Armed with our spreadsheets, time-table and aprons we met at 10am and basically didn't stop till the guests started to arrive just before 6.

It was a fantastic team effort. All worked tirelessly making haroset and matzah balls for an army. Everyone had been asked to bring a dish and we supplied a basic menu. We made chicken-less soup which was a tasty vegetable broth flavoured with non-chicken stock, and some chopped up carrot and leek. We strained the broth and cooked the matzah balls separately then added them to the broth to serve. The main course was salmon fillets. These were marinaded in a mixture of freshly squeezed orange juice, tamari sauce (wheat-free) and grated fresh ginger. Then they were baked in foil in the oven for 10 minutes. For the children we just did the salmon in a little olive oil and butter. We also provided baked potatoes and baked sweet potatoes for those who didn't want fish and served them with a choice of grated cheese and baked beans. People brought a wonderful array of side dishes and desserts which we put out on the communal serving tables with the salmon and baked potatoes.

Crossing the Red Sea by Zoe aged 7

Seder by Alexandra aged 4

Seder Night by Ariela aged 6¾

Bitter Herbs by Bibi aged 6

The House of Matzah

Eleri Larkum

Eleri: "Obviously I knew matzahs aren't flat – I've tried to butter enough of them in my time to know that. But it was only when I started to assemble the house that I realised what this might mean…icing, piped into the gaps, and plenty of it. And string for the subsidence.

The roof is covered in white chocolate mixed with raspberry jam, then iced. The rest is all fruit and chocolate."

Ways with Matzah

Liz Ison

Matzah, delicious simply with butter, or homemade lemon curd. Here are some other ways you might like to try.

Chocolate and Orange Matzah

200g (7oz) dark chocolate

1 large orange

5 Matzah

50g (2oz) white chocolate

Lay the matzah side by side on a large baking tray lined with baking parchment. Zest the orange using a peeler or zester and set aside. Melt the dark chocolate either in the microwave or in a bowl over a pan of simmering water. Spoon the melted chocolate over the matzah and spread evenly to coat with a brush or spatula. Sprinkle the orange zest evenly over the matzah. Melt the white chocolate. Dip a fork into the melted chocolate and drizzle over the matzah in pretty patterns.

Once cooled and set, break into pieces.

Matzah Granola

The recipe, based on one by Martha Stewart, can be adapted by changing the type of nuts, using different dried fruit, perhaps substituting the butter for oil, or the honey for maple syrup.

Advanced warning: this is very moreish and may be difficult to keep to a once a year treat. Serve with yoghurt or milk for breakfast or dessert. Or just eat plain as a snack.

3 cups matzah, crumbled into small pieces (about 7 sheets)

2 ½ – 3 cups of roughly chopped pecans and almonds

85g butter or margarine

½ cup dark brown sugar

½ cup honey

1 teaspoon salt

4 teaspoons of ground cinnamon

1 cup raisins

Preheat the oven to 170°C/325°F/Gas Mark 3. Lightly grease a large baking tray.

In a large bowl, mix together the crumbled matzah and nuts. Spread them onto the baking tray. Bake for about 15 minutes, stirring every 5 minutes, watching they don't burn.

While they are toasting, put the butter, sugar, honey, salt and cinnamon in a saucepan and melt gently.

Transfer the matzah and nuts to a bowl and stir in the melted ingredients, combining well. Return the mixture to the baking tray. Bake in the oven for a further 10 to 15 minutes, stirring at 5 minute intervals. Finally, add the raisins and combine. Leave to cool. Once cool, break up into small pieces.

Store in an airtight container or transfer to transparent bags and give as gifts. Keeps for 1 to 2 weeks.

Toffee Matzah Crunch

This is adapted from a recipe by Marcy Goldman

6 sheets of matzah

230g (8oz) unsalted butter

215g (7½oz) light brown sugar

Pinch of salt

Preheat the oven to 190°C/375°F/Gas Mark 5. Line a baking sheet with foil and cover with baking parchment. Cover the sheets with the matzah, breaking the matzah to fill. Melt the butter and sugar in a saucepan over a medium heat stirring continuously. After about 4 minutes the mixture should start to boil. Boil for 3 minutes stirring continuously.

Remove from the heat, stir in a pinch of salt. Pour over the matzah and spread to cover with a spatula.

Turn the heat down to 175°C/325°F/Gas Mark 3 and bake for 15 minutes checking every 5 minutes to check it is not burning.

Cool, break into pieces and store in an airtight container.

Option: To make chocolate coated toffee matzah crunch, sprinkle 160g (5oz) of chocolate chips over the matzah as soon as you take it out of the oven. Leave for 5 minutes to melt, then spread the chocolate using the spatula.

Pesach Mornings by the Mersey

Mindi Ison

Unpacking the Pesach dishes is like greeting old friends you have not seen for a whole year. My children were always so excited to see their blue and white plates decorated with beautiful birds which are used for fried matzah. They were not so thrilled to see the small grey bowls from which they had to eat the obligatory breakfast compote. They would cheer up when we unearthed the special little pot for lemon curd. Every year they would ask me why I only made lemon curd on Pesach and I would tell them it was to make Pesach special.

My recipes are the old ones I learnt from my mother Tamara Applebaum and which I have continued to make for 55 years.

For breakfast we would have alternate days of matzah pancakes and fried matzah - only to be eaten after the compote or, as the children called it, compost.

Lemon Curd

100g (4oz) unsalted butter
225g (8oz) caster sugar
3 lemons
3 eggs

Grate the lemons and squeeze them. Place the grated rind and strained lemon juice into a thick bottomed saucepan together with the sugar and butter. Heat on a low light until the sugar is dissolved. Stir. Then whisk the eggs and add to the pan, stirring with a wooden spoon until the mixture thickens. Do not boil. Turn off the heat and continue stirring for a minute and then pour into 2 warm dry 340g glass jars. Cover, and when cold keep in the fridge.

I prefer to make the above amount and do not double up as it does not keep well and is so easy to make small fresh amounts during the week.

Matzah Pancakes

2 eggs

½ teaspoon salt

1 tablespoon caster sugar

125ml (4 fl oz) warm water

75g (3oz) fine matzah meal

Place the eggs in a jug and beat them with 2 tablespoons of water. Add the meal and sugar slowly and enough water to make a thick batter which drops from the spoon. Then heat some sunflower oil, about half an inch deep, in a frying pan and drop spoonfuls of the batter into the hot oil. They will puff up and when they become brown turn the pancakes over and cook the other side. Serve hot with a mixture of cinnamon and sugar or homemade apricot eingemachtes.

Fried Matzah

3 whole matzah

2 eggs plus a pinch of salt and pepper

Break the matzah into small pieces about 2 to 3 inches and place in a colander. Pour hot water over them. Whisk the eggs and add enough milk or water as if making an omelette and place in a bowl. Add the drained matzah and mix well. Fry in a mixture of heated sunflower oil and butter or oil alone.

I serve it with sugar or jam but many people, like my husband, prefer the fried matzah plain from the pan.

Compote

I use plain dried fruit and not the tenderised fruit. When cooked, a large casserole or bowl will keep in the fridge for four or more days. You can use all or just a mixture of the fruit I list depending on your family's preference.

250g (9oz) dried prunes

250g (9oz) dried apricots

250g (9oz) dried apple rings

125g (4½oz) dried figs

Handful of sultanas

Wash the fruit well and then place in a large bowl and cover with cold water. Leave overnight. The next day empty the soaked fruit together with the juice into a large saucepan and add a lemon cut up into slices and 150g sugar. Cover and simmer very gently till fork soft. When cold place in the fridge. It is delicious served with single cream, or plain or Greek Yoghurt.

Happy Pesach breakfast.

Recollections of Chilean Pesaj (Pesach)

Claudia Camhi

My mother Patricia Jacard went back in time to remember how Passover celebrations were like when she was around five years old (the 1950s) growing up in Santiago, Chile. Her memories are of quietly observing at home unusual and hurried activity and busyness, in the days running up to Passover, watching her mother and the house help get rid of traces of bread and all that was not kosher for Pesaj. Then, the special table layout, big family gatherings for the second Seder night and the long reading of the Hagaddah including a bit of a quibble over who was the youngest and had the right to ask "why is this night different from other nights?"

A traditional starter at her parents' David and Matilde's table was Pesaj Spinach Minna drizzled with grape syrup and to finish the meal off marruchinos (almond macaroons) to accompany the coffee.

After the Second Seder, school and working life would continue as usual with just a few differences. For breakfast, sheets of crunchy Matzot would be covered in homemade fruit jams, quince pâté or mashed ripe avocado pears with plenty of salt. This may sound strange to people growing up in cultures where cereal is the staple breakfast food, but in Chile the norm was toast and milk for the children. School snacks consisted of sandwiches made in the same way and many questions to answer from the non-Jewish classmates who were very interested both in the food and story of Pesaj.

Pesaj Spinach Minna Drizzled with Grape Syrup

500g (1lb 1oz) sturdy spinach leaves, washed, patted dry and sliced into 1 cm strips

250g (9oz) ricotta

3 large eggs

150g (5oz) grated cheddar cheese

8 matzah sheets briefly soaked in cold water

Salt and pepper to taste

3 large peeled and boiled potatoes

A little sunflower oil

Preheat the oven to 180°C/350°F/Gas Mark 4.

Make a potato puree by mashing the boiled potatoes and adding salt and pepper to mix. Set aside.

Place the spinach, ricotta, grated cheese (setting aside a little for the topping), eggs, salt and pepper in a large bowl. Work the ingredients with your hands as if it was dough in order to make sure the spinach is well covered with all the ingredients.

Oil the bottom and sides of a baking dish that is large enough to hold 4 matzah sheets. Soak the matzah sheets briefly in water. Place four matzahs covering the bottom of the baking dish. Then place the spinach mix and cover with the rest of the matzah sheets, a bit like a giant matzah sandwich.

Finally, cover the top matzahs with the potato puree, sprinkle with some grated cheese and bake for 45-60 minutes until it looks golden. Slice in squares and optionally drizzle with grape syrup before serving.

Matzah Pudding: A Victorian Odyssey?

Liz Ison

My late mother Rachel Nathan always made a batch of matzah pudding for our family each Passover. We often ate it for lunch after coming home from Synagogue on the first day of Pesach. To me, it is as symbolic of the festival as the horseradish, only a lot tastier. It is rather like a fruity bread pudding and transforms matzah into a tasty English-style pudding. The recipe was from Florence Greenberg's *Jewish Cookery Book*, first published in the 1930s. My mother's well-worn copy was the 6th edition published in 1958 and was probably given to her as a wedding present.

In fact, when my mother heard about our cookbook project, she handed me one of her own mother's cookbooks, *Dainty Dinners and Dishes for Jewish Families* (3rd edition) published in 1916 during the First World War. It was written by May Henry and Kate Halford.

Turning the pages of the little book was a revelation. It was filled with English dishes, followed by their French names. It was Victorian cuisine with a French outlook and an occasional nod to a Sephardic heritage with the inclusion of a Spanish dish, like bola (a Spanish cake) but little mention of what we might today consider traditional Jewish fare (in fact, there was a recipe for cold fried fish and "A modern luction"- lokshen pudding – nestled amongst "leg of mutton", "Empress Pudding" and "creams à la Duchesse Marie").

It was a moment of revelation because, growing up, I had always been slightly puzzled by my Anglo-Jewish culinary heritage. While others enjoyed chicken soup, fish balls and so on, we would be tucking in to lamb and mint sauce, apple charlotte, meringues filled with whipped cream and a great many steamed puddings. Delicious but not particularly exotic.

My grandmother's cookbook was of an era when, despite – or because of – the huge influx of Eastern European Jewish immigrants, the Anglo-Jewish community positioned itself as part of the English establishment. Rather like the cookbook, the community found a way of being discreetly Jewish and very English. It reminded me of some members of my family, who, after attending the Shabbat morning service, would stroll over to Lord's Cricket Ground in St John's Wood after lunch to watch a cricket match for the afternoon.

Dainty Dinners also has a baked or boiled "Motza Pudding" recipe, very similar to Florence Greenberg's, with the suggestion to use dripping for the baked version and chopped suet for the boiled version.

Was this cookbook the origin of the tasty Matzah pudding I eat? I decided to consult the seminal *Jewish Manual* published in 1846 by "a Lady", thought to be Lady Judith Montefiore, wife of Sir Moses Montefiore and considered the first major Jewish cookbook published in English.

Here was a similar recipe entitled "Passover Pudding", talking euphemistically of "biscuit powder" and with a rather more vague ingredients list and method but unmistakably, a Matzah Pudding circa 1846!

Florence Greenberg's Matzah Pudding

Serves 4

110g (4oz) sultanas or raisins

2 matzot

75g (3oz) margarine (original recipe called for suet)

50g (2oz) brown sugar

2 tablespoons matzah meal

2 eggs

50g (2oz) currants

½ teaspoon mixed spice

Topping: a tablespoon of demerara brown sugar

Soak the matzah in a bowl of cold water till it is soft. Then squeeze if very dry with your hands. Put it in a bowl and beat it up into small pieces with a fork. Add the remaining ingredients and mix thoroughly. Turn into a greased pie dish, sprinkle the top with the brown sugar, and bake at 190°C/375°F/Gas Mark 5 for about one hour.

A Lady's Passover Pudding

Mix equal quantities of biscuit powder and shred suet, half the quantity of currants and raisins, a little spice and sugar, with an ounce of candied peels, and five well beaten eggs; make these into a stiff batter, and boil well, and serve with a sweet sauce.

Some modern tips The dish is easy to prepare and can be made in advance. Serve with a dollop of cream, crème fraiche or vanilla ice cream. It freezes well.

Illustration from Dainty Dinners and Dishes for Jewish Families (3rd edition) by May Henry and Kate Halford (1916)

Memories of an East Ham Pesach
Heather Bieber

My memories of Pesach growing up in East Ham are of incredibly hard work. Even as a young child I was expected to help clean shelves and cupboards and schlep down all the china and cutlery that I hadn't seen for a whole year.

The highlight came on the afternoon before the Seder service when my father and I searched the room for chametz that my mother had hidden in the living room. This was rather like hide-and-seek, great fun for a child. I felt very important when we took the scraps of bread together with the feather we had used to sweep up the bread into the garden and burnt it all.

The Seder seemed interminably long and our family didn't possess musical voices, but this never stopped them "singing" all the songs. The meal was a welcome sight with all the familiar odd plates that reappeared having been packed away for a year. I never enjoyed the hard boiled eggs in salt water that were presented in my grandmother's old tureen (although over the years I have grown to enjoy them). Next we had chicken soup with Pesach Lochen which my sister now always makes every year. This is enjoyed by all my grandchildren.

Passover Lochen
Pinch of salt

3 eggs

3 tablespoons water

3 tablespoons fine matzah meal

Whisk all ingredients together until smooth. Heat a frying pan with oil and, when hot, pour in batter. Pour excess back and cook in a thin layer like a pancake. Then turn over and cook on the other side. Turn out onto greaseproof paper. Use up the rest of the batter to make more pancakes. When cool, roll up and cut into "lochen", strips of about 1 cm wide. Just before serving the soup add the lochen. Heat through for a short time and serve.

Old World Pesach Treats – Irish Style

Alison Kelin

Pesach always brings wonderful memories flooding back to me. Growing up in Dublin in the 1960s/70s, I can remember the excitement when the boxes of china and cutlery came out of the attic, when we went round the house with a candle and feather and when we had to have an afternoon nap before the Sedarim.

Best of all are the food memories: tables laden with so many goodies that we didn't have during the rest of the year. My mum had two aunts who were in the catering business and going to their homes was such a treat. Whenever we went to Aunty Bloomie she would open the door and say "Oh why didn't you tell me you were coming. I have nothing in the house to offer you." She would then proceed to bring in so much delicious food that the table was groaning.

Imberlach – Carrot Candy

900g (2lbs) carrots, grated
450g (1lb) sugar
450g (1lb) honey
1 lemon – juice and rind
2 teaspoons ginger
50g (2oz) chopped nuts (optional)

Put everything in a saucepan and simmer slowly until the liquid is all gone. Spread out on a lined tin (about ½ inch thick) and when it is dry cut into squares.

Teiglach

Little knotted pastries baked in a honeyed syrup. Really for Rosh Hashanah but we made it with matzah cake meal for Pesach.

3 eggs, beaten
2 teaspoons sugar
2 tablespoons oil
2 cups matzah cake meal
¼ teaspoon ginger
⅓ cup raisins
¼ cup chopped nuts
1 cup honey
1 cup sugar
2 teaspoons ginger

Combine the first 5 ingredients. This is the dough.

Divide it into two.

Roll each into a long strip about ⅛ inch thick and 5 inches wide.

Spread with raisins and nuts and press them into the dough with a rolling pin.

Roll up, pinching the open edge firmly to roll. Then cut into pieces about 3/8 inch.

Boil the honey and sugar in a deep saucepan.

Turn the heat down low and carefully drop in the strips of dough one at a time. When all are in, cover and continue to simmer for half an hour. Check it then and turn the strips round so that the ones on the bottom are now on top. Simmer until they are all golden brown and sound hollow. Test one. It should be dry and crisp inside. Sprinkle the ginger into the syrup and stir. Turn off the heat and add 2 tablespoons boiling water. Stir. Remove the teiglach with a slotted spoon and cool.

Eingemachts (Beetroot Jam)
Mel and Barry Angel

This recipe is an Angel family tradition. Each year my mother-in-law Audrey Angel made jars of Eingemachts for Pesach and it is a family favourite spread on matzah. For the last few years we have been growing a bed of beetroot on our allotment plot specifically for Barry to make this and we give jars away to family and friends over Pesach (but always keep a couple for ourselves).

The quantities given make approximately 4 jars

1800g (4lb) beetroot

130g (3lb) sugar

2 lemons

¾ tablespoon ginger

Glass jars/jam jars

Wax paper discs (optional)

You will need to start by sterilising the jars – you can do this in the oven but be careful when you take them out – they are HOT.

Peel and cut beetroot into strips. Put beetroot in cold water and soak overnight. Rinse beetroot and boil for 20 minutes. Take off heat and wash again. Boil beetroot in a pan with ½ to ¾ glass of water and sugar. Simmer for 15 minutes. Peel and slice lemons and add to the pan.

Continue to simmer (with no lid) for 2 hours. Add ginger. Keep stirring while simmering.

Let it cool a little then poor into the sterilised jars. Put a wax disc on top of the jam in the jars and leave to cool completely. Put on the lids and store in a cool place.

Tips: You don't need any special jam making equipment just a bit of patience. We use latex (or similar) gloves when handling the beetroot, or you will end up with purple hands. We use Douwe Egberts coffee jars. It is a good idea to get the wax paper for jams to keep the jam preserved until eaten. You can get these at Lakeland or other cooks shops. It lasts for ages. We make it in September/October when we harvest the beetroot and it is fine for the following Pesach.

Our Pesach "Plant"

Jo Freeman

Every Pesach these days I visualise my Grandma Dora watching my every move and despite my inner protestations as to "Why do I do this," Grandma I do it for you.

I was brought up in the 1950s in the Medway towns - Chatham to be precise. In my memory Pesach preparations began early.

Knives were stuck in the earth and the glassware was put in a baby bath and covered with water for several weeks before the festival to kosher them.

As Pesach approached we made the trips down to the cellar where the 'plant' as my grandmother called it, rested from year to year. Out came the pan that was bought in Mence Smith's, a hardware store of the time. This particular pan (still in use today) was bought in 1921 for sixpence (very expensive) and the fish service that was a wedding present in 1920 and so on.

Over the years my 'plant' has hand-me-downs from my husband's family too so our wine cups and matzah plates come from Granny Mona, along with a bone china tea set that was our wedding present from WIZO in the 1970s. We only use cups and saucers at Pesach in our house now!

Halibut Sweet and Sour

Jo Freeman

Adapted from Florence Greenberg

700g (1½ lbs) halibut or other white fish

2 onions

2 tablespoons oil

1 dessertspoon potato flour

Chopped parsley

2 egg yolks

2 lemons

852ml (1½ pints) water

Salt, pepper and powdered ginger to season

Cut the fish up into convenient-sized pieces for serving. Slice the onions and fry them in the oil in a pan until lightly browned. Then lay in the fish and season with salt, pepper and a pinch of ginger. Pour over the hot water, cover, and cook gently until the fish is done – about 15 minutes.

Remove the fish from the water, place on a serving dish, and reserve the cooking liquid. In a pan, pour the strained juice of the lemons on to the potato flour. Mix smoothly and add 425ml (¾ of a pint) of fish stock. Stir until boiling and simmer for five minutes, then cool. Beat up the egg yolks lightly and gradually pour the sauce on to them. Return to the saucepan and stir until it thickens. Do not reboil, or it will curdle.

Pour the egg and lemon sauce over the fish and refrigerate. Serve cold, sprinkled with finely chopped parsley.

Pesach Rolls

Judy Weleminsky

When an American friend first introduced me to Pesach rolls I thought they were such a cheat – surely something soft and fluffy with air in it couldn't be kosher unleavened bread? But when they taste this good – why not?

Delicious eaten on their own or with fillings, superb eaten warm and quite acceptable cold. Perfect for a school lunch box. Thirty minutes max from cupboard to table and in my house considerably less before the plate is cleared on day 1. Enthusiasm can wane by day 7!

Makes 12 to 16 rolls depending on the size.

2 cups water

1 cup oil

3 cups matzah meal (all types work – I like the medium meal best for texture)

2+ tablespoons sugar (depending on how sweet you want)

1 teaspoon salt

4 eggs

Preheat the oven to 180°C/350°F/Gas Mark 4. Bring water, sugar, salt and oil to a boil. Mix in the matzah meal and then the eggs. Form gently into rolls (the less you compact it the lighter they will be).

Bake on a baking tin for 15-20 minutes until the outside is getting a little golden.

Best eaten on the day but ok on the next day.

My Mother's Pesach

Miriam Edelman

We lost my mother Charlotte Edelman (z"l, may her memory be a blessing) some years ago, but I never remember her more than at Pesach. Mama loved Pesach. My grandmothers (zichranot livracha) had very similar china and silver, so Mama was proud to be able to lay a Seder for at least 30 with matching dishes and cutlery. She was a wonderful cook, and enjoyed both her own Pesach recipes and mine. She required my meringue macaroons and chocolate toffee matzah, and really loved it when I learned to make matzah. As my sisters and I became adults, this was a command performance: she wanted her chicks around her at Pesach.

She liked the cleaning less, even when, as she got older, I did it for her. She was a Depression baby and hated to throw anything away, unless I could demonstrate to her there were bugs in it, and living out in the country in Kansas, this wasn't infrequent – I have never needed any further incentive for the thoroughness of my Pesach purge. It got easier when I saw the light that we are all Sephardi now, so we no longer had the battle of the peanut butter with my dad – who has issues with Pesach, but that's another story.

Mom was a guiding light of the little no-rabbi Synagogue in the small university town where she raised us, and much of her work involved organising things to feed people: Shabbat dinners, onegs, speaker brunches, the communal Yom Kippur break-the-fast, and especially the community Seder. As she got older she reluctantly agreed to hire someone she knew to help with the catering for the Seder, but it was several more years before she trusted her to make the matzah balls.

Matzah balls, or knadels, or kneidlach, were a serious business to my mother, a keen partisan for the 'Fluffy' side in the Matzah Ball War. I have long been careful to use the more neutral words 'Fluffy' and 'Dense' to describe these factions, rather than the pejorative terms each side usually uses to describe the other. For my mother, and, as I have discovered, for many on both sides, there weren't two valid options: the other side just can't cook. I think Mom perceived it as part of my youngest sister's rebellion that she decamped to the Dense side. She would love that I work for a company called Knadel (no relation).

So when in 2012 an emergency arose and I was asked to organise the Wimbledon communal Seder on a week's notice, I channelled my mother. And since I knew for some people that the communal Seder might be their only real experience of Pesach that year, I could hear her voice loud and clear that I could not let them go home without a matzah ball.

Charlotte's Matzah Balls

This is for 16, but who needs just 16? Multiply as needed

¼ cup fat–Mama used schmaltz, rendered chicken fat, but I tend to go for olive oil

4 large eggs

1 cup medium matzah meal

1 teaspoon salt

¼ cup soup liquid (your choice – made up stock powder/cube works fine)

Mix fat and eggs together. In a separate bowl, combine matzah meal and salt, then add to the first mixture. Add soup liquid and mix well. Cover bowl and refrigerate for at least 2 hours.

Get a really large pot with a tight fitting lid. Fill ¾ full with boiling salted water. Reduce heat to slightly bubbling. Either lightly roll the balls of dough (for Dense), or simply drop in tablespoonfuls. Secret Number 1 for fluffy kneidlach: handle the dough lightly and as little as possible. This batter will make both fluffy and dense: just roll for dense, and use an ice cream scoop to drop fluffy ones straight into the pot.

Cover the pot and cook for 40 minutes, WITHOUT PEEKING (secret Number 2: do not uncover the pot). After 40 minutes, scoop balls gently out with a slotted spoon and place into simmering soup for 5 minutes before serving.

Do not simmer in the soup for much longer or they may disintegrate: if you don't want to eat them straight away, take them out of the cooking water and keep in a bowl. Or put them straight into serving bowls, so that they will be re-warmed when you ladle in boiling hot soup, which is what we did at the Wimbledon community Seder.

Other Matzah Ball Recipes

Matzah Balls

Diane Barnett

I make this with chicken soup. Usually I have roast chicken for one meal, then use the chicken carcass to make the soup. I skim the fat off the surface of the soup and use it for frying the onion for the matzah balls, which gives it a special flavour. Alternatively, olive oil can be used.

Makes about 7 medium matzah balls

1 medium onion

A little chicken fat (or olive oil)

4 matzahs

1 egg

About 2 tablespoons of ground almonds

A few slivered almonds (optional)

Salt and pepper

Matzah meal (for coating)

Finely chop and sweat a medium onion in chicken fat (or olive oil).

Meanwhile soak 4 matzahs in cold water. Drain into a sieve and press out the water. Put them in a bowl and add the onions, one egg, salt and pepper and stir. Add enough ground almonds to bind the mixture, and a few slivered almonds to add crunch if you wish.

Roll them into balls (I make them the size of a golf ball) and then roll in fine matzah meal. Drop into simmering chicken soup, for five or ten minutes. Or you can freeze them and just drop them into chicken soup next time you make it.

Kneidlach

Hilary Leek

This is Florence Greenberg's recipe for kneidlach which I use every year and also for Erev Rosh Hashanah. Florence was a friend of my mother from West London Synagogue, although a different generation.

1 breakfastcupful of medium matzah meal

1 breakfastcupful of boiling water

1 egg

1 teaspoon chopped parsley

2 tablespoonfuls of chicken fat (I use Tomor)

Salt and pepper

Nutmeg and ginger

Pour boiling water over the matzah meal and stir well until blended. Then add the egg, fat, parsley and seasoning. Mix thoroughly and put in fridge for at least 1 hour (I usually leave it for 4 hours minimum).

With hands dipped in cold water roll into tiny balls. Drop into boiling soup and simmer gently for 15 minutes with the saucepan uncovered.

As soon as they float to the top turn off the heat.

NB Because there are so many preparations for Seder I usually roll the balls well in advance and put them in the fridge until needed.

Marion's Matzah Balls

Marion Style

Makes about 12

2 large eggs

1 teaspoon salt

1 shallot

1 rounded tablespoon chicken schmaltz or light olive oil

25g (1oz) ground almonds

110g (4oz) medium matzah meal

Approximately 1 tablespoon finely chopped parsley

Finely chop the shallot and soften it in the fat for 5-10 minutes. Whisk the eggs until pale and fluffy. Gently mix together the shallot, salt, ground almonds and matzah meal and fold in the whisked eggs. They should be a consistency of damp sand. If necessary add a little more matzah meal.

With a very light touch roll them into walnut-sized balls with dampened hands. Place on a plate and cover with cling film.

Leave in the fridge for an hour.

Drop into boiling, salted water. Lower the heat and simmer for 30-40 minutes. Remove with slotted spoon.

Add to the soup for 10 minutes before you serve it.

Grandma's Pesach Biscuits

Yvonne Mason

This is a recipe that my mother Pearl Cooper passed down to me more years ago than I can remember. It is stuck into my favourite recipe book on a tatty piece of paper and the writing has faded. If you ask my children what they remember most about Pesach from their childhood I'm sure they will all say Grandma's Pesach biscuits. For us Pesach would not be Pesach without them. In her memory I have not converted the ounces into grams or the inch into centimetres – I will leave that to you.

Makes about 30 biscuits.

4oz potato flour

4oz cake meal

5oz soft butter

4oz caster sugar

2oz ground almonds

Juice and rind of half a lemon

1 egg

Dark chocolate – melted (optional)

Mix all ingredients together to form a large ball. Chill in fridge overnight.

Preheat oven to 190°C/375°F/Gas Mark 5. Sprinkle board with cake meal. Roll the biscuit dough until quarter of an inch thick. Cut the biscuits with a cutter and put onto lightly oiled tray. Bake for 15 minutes until pale golden. When the biscuits are cold you can half coat them in melted chocolate if you wish.

Chocolate Torte

Hilary Leek

A great cake any time of year.

200g (7oz) dark chocolate

4 medium eggs

170g (6oz) caster sugar

1 teaspoon vanilla extract

250g (9oz) ground almonds

200g (7oz) margarine or butter melted and cooled

Icing sugar for decoration

Preheat oven to 170°C/325°F/Gas Mark 3. Line a 24cm baking tin with non-stick baking parchment. Process the chocolate in a food processor until it is reduced to small pieces. Beat the eggs with the sugar and vanilla until thick and creamy for about 10 minutes. Fold in the chocolate, almonds and butter.

Spoon into the prepared tin, bake for 45–50 minutes until just firm to the touch. Leave to cool in the tin then turn out onto a plate. Dust with icing sugar and serve with crème fraiche or cream and berries.

Pesach Lemon Cake

Norma Golten

6 large eggs, separated

200g (7oz) caster sugar

200g (7oz) ground almonds

Zest of two unwaxed lemons and the juice from ½ lemon

Preheat the oven to 170°C/325°F/Gas Mark 3.

Whisk egg yolks and sugar together until pale and creamy. Fold in almonds with the zest and juice. Whisk egg whites until stiff and fold into yolk mixture.

Pour into a 23 cm (9½ inch) greased and lined tin. Bake on middle shelf for 30-40 minutes. Leave to cool in the tin. When cold make up lemon water and cover cake.

Mother and Daughter Passover Baking

Here are some of Lynne Sidkin and her mother Miriam's favourite Passover baking recipes.

Almond Macaroons

Miriam Goldman

225g (8oz) ground almonds

225g (8oz) caster sugar

2 large egg whites

Mix almonds and sugar. Beat egg whites lightly and mix together. Roll into small balls and put blanched almond on top. Bake in the oven at 170°C/325°F/Gas Mark 4 for 25 minutes.

Cinnamon Balls

Miriam Goldman

225g (8oz) ground almonds

225g (8oz) caster sugar

1 tablespoon cinnamon

3 egg whites

Mix together almonds, cinnamon and sugar. Beat egg whites stiffly and then add to dry mixture. Roll into small balls and bake 170°C/325°F/Gas Mark 4 for 20-25 minutes.

Almond Pudding

Lynne Sidkin

Delicious with fruit compote or fruit salad

110g (4oz) ground almonds

140g (5oz) caster sugar

4 eggs

Beat eggs and sugar until light and frothy. Add almonds and beat for 10 minutes. Pour mixture into a greased and lined 7-8 inch shallow square baking tin.

Bake in oven for approximately 50 minutes at 170°C/325°F/Gas Mark 4. Sprinkle with caster sugar when cool.

Chocolate Orange Brownies

Lynne Sidkin

Controversial brownies for Pesach – they contain "kosher for Passover" baking powder (really – google it). Undeniably delicious.

100g (4oz) unsalted butter

150g (5oz) dark chocolate

30g (1oz) cocoa powder, sifted

100g (4oz) ground almonds

1 teaspoons gluten-free baking powder

3 eggs

200g (7oz) dark brown sugar

1 teaspoon vanilla extract

Grated zest of 1 orange

Preheat the oven to 160°C/300°F/Gas Mark 2. Melt the butter and chocolate in a heat-proof bowl over a saucepan of gently simmering water. Leave to cool slightly.

In a bowl, combine cocoa, almonds and baking powder. Set aside. In another bowl, combine the eggs, sugar, vanilla extract and orange zest. Make a well in the centre of the dry ingredients. Pour in the egg mixture and melted chocolate, and stir from the centre until well combined. Pour into a lined baking tray 20 x 30 cm.

Bake for about 25 minutes or a little longer if you like them firmer. Leave to cool in the tray. Cut into squares and dust with icing sugar before serving.

Almond Macaroons

Almond Pudding

Recipes for those Pesach Egg Yolks

Crème au Chocolat
Sally-Ann Feldman

To use up 8 egg yolks at Pesach.

Serves 12

225g (8oz) kosher-le-pesach cooking chocolate

500ml (18 fl oz) milk

8 egg yolks

100g (4oz) granulated sugar

150ml (¼ pint) double cream

Preheat the oven to 180°C/ 350°F/Gas Mark 4.

Cut chocolate into very small pieces and melt in a saucepan, without water, over a very gentle heat.

When melted add milk and bring to boiling point, stirring the chocolate into the milk vigorously (or whisk) until incorporated.

In a large bowl beat together the egg yolks, sugar and cream with a birch or electric hand whisk. Continue beating for several minutes.

Now add the boiling milk very gradually, stirring constantly. Pour into either 12 small 8cm (3 inch) diameter ramekins or one large oven-proof dish.

Half-fill a large roasting tin with hot water and place the ramekins or dishes in it. Transfer to the oven and bake for 25 minutes for ramekins, up to an hour for one large dish or until the centre of the crème au chocolat is firm to the touch. Cool and chill lightly before serving.

Even more egg yolks? Have a look at the recipe for lemon curd earlier in this chapter.

Hollandaise
Miriam Edelman

3 egg yolks

1 tablespoon lemon juice

115g (4oz) butter, melted

Pinch cayenne pepper

Salt to taste

Put egg yolks in top of double boiler or bowl over hot, not simmering water. Beat with wire whisk until smooth. Add lemon juice and gradually whisk in melted butter, pouring in a thin stream. Slowly stir in 2 tablespoons of hot water, cayenne, and salt. Continue to mix for 1 minute. (Leave to sit if not thickened, whisk again.)

Mayonnaise
Miriam Edelman

1 egg yolk

½ teaspoon Dijon mustard or (for Pesach) dry mustard

½ teaspoon salt

Pinch cayenne pepper

1 tablespoon vinegar or lemon juice

¾ cup olive oil or salad oil (mild tasting)

Put yolk, mustard, salt, cayenne, and vinegar or lemon juice in a clean bowl, put the bowl on a towel to keep stationary, and whisk until blended. Beat in the oil, drop by drop (increasing flow as sauce thickens).

Tip: If hollandaise or mayonnaise curdles or 'breaks', try increasing the heat of your double boiler for the hollandaise, or put your mayo over a bowl of hot water. If that doesn't help, whisk in a teaspoon or more of boiling water, a drop at a time. Or, put another egg yolk in a new bowl and very slowly add in the sauce while whisking. With any of these methods, be patient and beat constantly with the whisk for as long as it takes.

The Meaning of Matzah and a Short History of Bread

Rabbi Sylvia Rothschild

The Bible tells us that people cannot live by bread alone (Deuteronomy 8:3), a statement so powerful it is repeated in the New Testament.

Bread is one of the oldest prepared foods. Evidence on rocks in Europe from 30,000 years ago shows starch residue left from the plants which had presumably been pounded to create flour in order to make early flat bread.

With the Neolithic age and the spread of agriculture, bread from grains became the mainstay of the human diet. Yeast spores are everywhere – in the air and even on the surface of cereal grains, so any dough left to rest in the open air will over time become naturally leavened. But people quickly learned to help the process along - Pliny the Elder reports that the Gauls and the Iberians used the foam skimmed from beer to produce "a lighter kind of bread than other peoples." Those who drank wine instead of beer in the ancient world used a paste composed of grape juice and flour that was allowed to begin fermenting, or else they used wheat bran steeped in wine, as a source for their yeast. But the most common source of leavening was to retain a piece of dough from the previous day to use as a starter for the new dough.

Probably that is why every year or so one had to start again, to not keep on endlessly adding a piece of dough from before to the new mix of flour and water, but to break what we would see as the cycle of infection and make a new start with this important food.

Bread means so many things to us – it was used to pay the workers' wages in ancient Egypt and the word is still used today to denote wealth – both "bread" and "dough" are slang expressions for money. The word "companion" denotes someone with bread (com + panis). The Roman poet Juvenal satirised superficial politicians and the public as caring only for "panem et circenses" (bread and circuses).

The cultural importance of "bread" goes beyond slang, to serve as a metaphor for basic necessities and living conditions in general. A "bread-winner" is a household's main economic contributor whose role is "putting bread on the table." A remarkable or revolutionary innovation is often referred to as "the greatest thing since sliced bread." Bread is the staple requirement in all human societies.

The word "bread" itself is curious – it has been claimed to be derived from the root of brew though it may be connected with the root of break, for its early uses are confined to broken pieces, or bits of bread. But in Hebrew the etymology is even more curious – "lechem", the Hebrew word for bread, is the same root as "lochem" – to do battle, and unlike the Teutonic languages, the third possible root "lacham" means not to separate, but to join together. Using all three meanings, Ludwig Kohler, the author of a dictionary of Biblical Hebrew, suggests that this third root – to be joined together, explains both battle and eating bread – in battle there is hand to hand combat and soldiers are bonded together in groups, in eating bread together people bond together in solidarity – breaking bread with someone is a powerful signifier of peace with them. Of course, the opposite may also be true – wars are fought over resources, and what is the most basic resource alongside water? Bread.

So what has this to do with the emblematic food of Pesach? Matzah is symbolic of two kinds of bread: both the bread of affliction and the bread of liberation. As we consider this festival and the foods we don't let ourselves eat – for Pesach should not be, as it increasingly seems to be becoming, a time when we can imaginatively create dishes that mimic chametz, with breakfast cereals and potato flour pasta made kosher for Pesach – we should be thinking of the staples of our lives, what they are based upon, how we are separated and how we are joined, how we add value to our lives rather than live them mechanistically.

By eating matzah we are helping ourselves consider what is freedom, what is poverty, and how fine the line between the two. We are reminding ourselves of what is basic and important in our lives and what is the froth of the leavening. Every so often we have to stop, to break the chain of habit, to start again from the beginning and Pesach is that time. Just as we break the cycle of infection of using a piece of dough from the previous day by making our bread with no additions except the elemental flour and water, so we take a week to live our lives in simplicity, to think about what we have been doing unthinkingly. Bread is freedom and bread is poverty.

Bread is broken and bread is joined. As we navigate the ambiguity and the possibilities of lechem in the form of matzah, we have the choice to think again. Are we in freedom? Do we oppress? Are we broken and separated from what matters? Are we joined to others in a strong bond?

The festival of Pesach is soon over, but I would hope that the thinking it demands of us goes into the weeks of the Omer as we build and count up towards Sinai and the accepting of Torah.

Unleavened Bread

It's rightly called "bread of affliction",
For matzah becomes an addiction
You'd better take care, though;
Like the Jews under Pharaoh,
It can't be released without friction!

Jerry Markison, The Jewish Limerick Book

SHAVUOT

Spinach Borrecas

Claudia Camhi

My great aunts and grandmother made these delicious filo pastry cheese and spinach triangles as a staple starter and for special festivals too. Their triangles were perfect bundles of crispness and taste.

Filling

200g (7oz) spinach

1 large potato

1 large whole egg

250g (9oz) pot of ricotta

150g (5oz) grated cheddar

2 teaspoons dry dill weed

Salt and pepper to taste

For the dough

1 cup sunflower oil

1 packet filo pastry cut into strips 8 cm (wide) 30 cm (long) and kept in a plastic wrapping to avoid the dough drying out.

To make the filling

Peel and cook the potato in boiling water until soft. Mash and allow it to cool.

Steam the spinach, squeeze any excess water and chop finely.

In a bowl mix the mashed potato, spinach, ricotta, cheddar, egg, dill, salt and pepper.

Preheat the oven to 180°C/350°F/Gas Mark 4.

To assemble the filo pastry triangles

Take two strips of filo pastry and place them side by side on a flat surface (vertical).

With your clean hands oil the surface of one strip. Sit the next strip on top of the first one so you get a double layered single one and oil again.

Lay a tablespoon of the filling near the top left corner of the strip.

A) Fold the top right corner of the filo pastry over the filling. This should form the long side of a triangle.

B) Then turn the left top corner down over itself. You will get the two shorter sides of the triangle.

C) Turn the top left corner over to the right side and you will have the filling wrapped up with filo pastry.

Repeat the process starting from A until the strip of dough is all used up.

Add oil to all the surfaces of the triangle with your hands and lay it on a baking sheet.

Begin again with another two strips of pastry repeating the process explained above until your pastry has been all used up. You should get about 18 borrekas.

Bake until the top is golden in middle rack of the oven for approximately 15 minutes.

Turn over and bake until golden, another 5 minutes.

Tips: The borrekas taste nicer straight out of the oven. They can be made a day in advance and reheated – make sure you cover them with aluminium foil. You can try to vary the filling leaving the spinach out. I have made them with different types of cheese or with chilli flakes. They can be eaten at room temperature as a picnic snack.

Rugelach

Miriam Edelman

Makes approximately 64

Dough

225g (8oz) salted butter, softened

225g (8oz) cream cheese, softened

5 tablespoons sour cream

1 teaspoon vanilla

250g (9oz) flour

Filling/Topping

300g (10½oz) dried fruit (raisins and sultanas mixed)

(Alternatives: can also use nuts, other dried fruits, chocolate, sour cherries, etc.)

50g (2oz) light brown sugar

2 tablespoons cinnamon

325g (11oz) jam

Milk to brush on top

Let the cream cheese and butter rest on the counter for 10 minutes — you want them to be slightly softened but still cool.

Cream together the butter and cream cheese in the bowl of an electric mixer. Blend in the vanilla and sour cream. Mix in the flour.

Divide the dough into 4 equal portions and wrap in cling film. Handle as little as possible. Chill the dough at least 4 hours, preferably overnight (or 1 hour in freezer).

To make the filling: Chop the raisins and sultanas. Mix together the fruit, brown sugar, and cinnamon.

Preheat the oven to 190°C/375°F/Gas Mark 5. Roll out each portion of dough on powdered (icing) sugar into a 25 to 30cm (10-12 inch) circle just under 0.25cm (¼ inch) thick on a lightly floured board or between two sheets of greaseproof paper.

Spread a light layer of jam (approximately 2 tablespoons) onto each dough circle. Sprinkle each circle with approximately 4 tablespoons of the chopped fruit mixture.

Cut each circle into 16 wedges using a sharp knife, pastry cutter or a pizza cutter. Roll each wedge from base to point.

Alternative: Roll into a rectangle instead of circle, spread and sprinkle as above, and slice into rounds.

Place point down (or, for alternative, solid edge up), 1 inch apart, on a lightly greased or baking parchment lined baking tray. Brush with milk if desired.

Bake for 15 to 17 minutes until golden. Remove to racks to cool.

Store in tightly covered container at room temperature up to 1 week, or in freezer up to 3 months.

Cheesecake

My Sultana Cheesecake

Diane Barnett

When I first got married, I tried all sorts of cheesecake recipes, till I came across this one. For the last forty years, I just use this one and don't vary the recipe – it is always popular. This should be made the day before you want to eat it to allow the flavour to mature.

180g (6oz) or 12 digestive biscuits, finely crushed

3 eggs

4 tablespoons caster sugar (plus a little extra for beating with the egg whites)

150ml (¼ pint) soured cream

450g (1lb) soft cream cheese

1 tablespoon sultanas

1 heaped tablespoon cornflour

Preheat the oven to 170°C fan or 190°C/375°F/Gas Mark 5.

Line a round 23cm (9 inch) tin with a white fluted paper lining (I buy mine from Lakeland) or line with baking parchment. Press the crushed biscuits into the base.

Separate the eggs. Beat the yolks with the sugar. Add the cream cheese and beat again till smooth. Add the sultanas, cornflour and sour cream and incorporate. Beat the egg whites with a little sugar till stiff and forming peaks. Fold the whites into the cheese mixture and then spoon on top of the biscuits.

Bake in the centre of the oven for about 25 minutes. Turn off the heat, open the oven door and leave for a further 15 minutes. Cool completely.

Connie's Cream Cheese Cake

Carra Kane

This recipe is from my grandmother Connie Simon and she is famous in the family for her desserts. Over the years I have enjoyed making it more and more. My kids asked if I could make it with a chocolate base so I used chocolate tea biscuits from the kosher section at Waitrose. Tasted good!

Filling

675g (24oz) Philadelphia cream cheese

1 cup sugar

1 teaspoon vanilla

4 eggs (I fold these in one at a time)

Crust

170g (6oz) Zweiback (in UK use digestives) or chocolate tea biscuits

1 teaspoon vanilla

2 teaspoons sugar

112g (4oz) stick melted butter

Topping

500g (1lb 1oz) sour cream

1 teaspoon vanilla

1 tablespoon sugar

I use a shallow glass 23 x 28cm (9 x 11 inch) tray or round spring pan.

Put the filling ingredients together in a mixer and beat for 5 minutes or until smooth.

Crush the biscuits into tiny pieces. I put them in a plastic bag and roll over thoroughly with a rolling pin. Mix the crushed biscuits with the other crust ingredients in a small bowl. Then press the crust into the pan to form the bottom and sides of the cake. Pour the cheese mixture on top of the crust.

Put in a cold oven and then set the temperature for 175°C/350°F/Gas Mark 4 for 45 minutes.

Small cracks form at the edges when done.

Prepare the topping by stirring the vanilla and sugar directly into the sour cream container, mixing well.

When the cake is done, remove from the oven and add topping at once.

Put back in the oven at 230°C/450°F/Gas Mark 8 for about 8 minutes.

No-Bake Chocolate Cheesecake
Lynne Sidkin

This is very easy to make and is a great dessert to have pre-prepared in the freezer. Just don't think about the calories!

200g (7oz) chocolate digestive biscuits
50g (2oz) butter or margarine, melted
100g (4oz) dark chocolate
150g (5oz) full fat cream cheese
150g (5oz) mascarpone cheese
50g (2oz) icing sugar, sifted
50g (2oz) amaretti biscuits, crushed

Line a 450g (1lb) loaf tin with greaseproof paper.

Crush the biscuits and tip them into a bowl. Add the melted butter or margarine and stir well until the crumbs are coated. Tip them into the loaf tin.

Gently push the crumbs to the edges of the tin until smooth and flat. Chill while you make the filling. Break the chocolate into small pieces and put in a glass bowl. Sit the bowl over a pan of simmering water, making sure the bowl does not touch the water. Melt the chocolate, stir and set aside.

In a separate bowl, use an electric whisk to whisk the cream cheese, mascarpone and icing sugar together until smooth. Stir in the melted chocolate until well combined.

Spoon the mixture onto the base and level. Chill for 2-3 hours.

Sprinkle the crushed amaretti on top before serving.

Mount Sinai Cake
Eleri Larkum

"Cake and Lego, what could be better. Amazing."
David

Family Favourites

SOUP

Carrot and Lentil Soup
Polly Conn

Serves 4-6

110g (4oz) red lentils

2 pints well-seasoned stock

3 tablespoons onions sliced

450g (1lb) carrots sliced

1 clove garlic crushed

Chopped parsley to garnish

Simmer lentils in stock for 15 minutes. Fry onions in oil until slightly golden. Add carrots and onions to lentils/stock. Simmer until carrots are soft. Add crushed garlic and liquidise.

Garnish with chopped parsley and serve.

Parsnip Soup
Polly Conn

Serves 4-6

3 tablespoons oil

450g (1lb) parsnips cubed

1 clove garlic crushed

1 onion chopped

25g (1oz) flour

1 teaspoon curry powder

2 pints well-seasoned stock

¼ pint single cream

Chopped chives to garnish

Gently fry the parsnip, garlic and onions in oil for 10 minutes. Stir in flour and curry powder and cook for 1 minute. Add the stock and simmer until parsnip is tender. Liquidise. Add cream and reheat gently.

Garnish with chopped chives and serve.

Pea Soup
Sally-Ann Feldman

This recipe has the (optional) addition of mushy peas to the ordinary ones. The only reason for this is that on the occasion that I made this for the Night Shelter for the Merton Homeless at the Synagogue, we had a lot of mushy peas left over from a panic visit we had to make to the fish and chip shop when our Synagogue oven broke down!

Serves 4

1 small onion, finely chopped

25g (1oz) butter

½ pint chicken or vegetable stock

400g (14oz) frozen peas

(for the mushy pea version I thawed the frozen peas and made up the quantity with the mushy ones – they are just peas, anyway)

Salt and pepper

½ pint white sauce (butter, flour and ½ pint milk)

2 tablespoons cream (optional)

Fry onion gently in the butter without colouring it, for approximately 5 minutes. Add stock, peas and seasoning, then cover and simmer for 8-10 minutes. When peas are soft liquidise them and add to sauce. Return soup to pan and re-heat. Stir in cream if used, adjust seasoning as necessary and serve garnished with parsley.

Leek and Watercress Soup

Ruth Magnus

This combination in a soup is a natural. It also happens to be delicious served chilled.

Serves 4

The whites of 3 large leeks (approximately 450g/ 1 lb) – washed and chopped

2 bunches of watercress, destalked and chopped (keep back some sprigs for garnishing)

2 medium potatoes (peeled and chopped)

50g (2oz) butter

850ml (1½ pints) light vegetable stock (or water)

150ml (¼ pint) double cream

Salt and freshly milled black pepper

Begin by melting the butter in a thick-based saucepan, then stir in the chopped leeks, potatoes and the watercress. Add some salt, then keeping the heat very low cover the pan and let the vegetables sweat gently for about 20 minutes (giving them a stir every now and then).

After that, add the stock or water and continue to simmer the soup with the lid on for a further 10-15 minutes or until the vegetables are absolutely tender.

When it has cooled, liquidise the soup in a blender or food processor, not too uniformly. Then stir in the cream.

Taste to check the seasoning. Then re-heat gently (without boiling) and, before serving, garnish with a sprig of watercress in each bowl.

Tip: this also works well without the cream.

Mushroom and Puy Lentil Soup

Hilary Leek

Serves 6

1 onion chopped

A few sprigs of fresh thyme

2 cloves of garlic chopped

150g (5oz) puy lentils

2 litres (3½ pints) vegetable or chicken stock

140g (5oz) mushroom selection

250g (9oz) closed chestnut mushrooms

Put onions, thyme, garlic and lentils in a large pan. Pour in all of the stock, cover and bring to the boil. Then simmer for about 20 minutes until the lentils are tender. Roughly chop the mushrooms and add to the simmering pan. Simmer for a further 5 minutes.

Remove the thyme sprigs and puree the soup until smooth-ish. Check the consistency. If you would like it a little runnier add a little boiling water to the mix.

Creamed Tomato and Pasta Soup

Camilla McGill

This is a really good light supper dish or for weekend lunches and goes down very well with children.

Makes 8-10 large bowls

55g (2oz) unsalted butter

3 tins of chopped or plum tomatoes (Valfrutto are the best make but any are fine)

2 small or one large onion

4 large carrots

4 sticks of celery

2 cloves of garlic

600ml (1 pint) chicken or vegetable stock (made with marigold powder is great)

1 bay leaf

4 teaspoons tomato puree

1 teaspoon molasses or dark brown sugar

Salt and pepper

150ml (5 fl oz) double cream (can leave out but it does make it delicious)

100g (4oz) tiny pasta - bows, or shells work best

Note: if you want to make this in a hurry then you could lightly steam the carrots and celery before adding them to the pan.

Slice the onion and chop the cloves of garlic. Melt the butter in a heavy based saucepan and add the onion first. Cook gently for 15 minutes if you have time as this makes the onion really sweet. Chop the carrots and celery into very small dice (½ cm square). Add to the pan with the garlic and stir gently for another 10-15 minutes. Pour in the 3 tins of tomatoes, stock, bay leaf, tomato puree and molasses or sugar.

Simmer until the carrots are nice and soft. Usually takes a good 30 minutes unless you have pre-cooked the carrots and celery.

Remove the bay leaf and puree really thoroughly in a blender. If you are adding the cream it works well to scald it first in a small pan and then add it to the hot soup.

Stir in the pasta cooked according to the pack - usually takes about 6 minutes to cook.

Grandma Dora's Borscht

Jo Freeman

This soup was made by my Grandma whose family came from somewhere in Poland. Great Grandpa Solomon liked to add smetana (sour cream and yoghurt) which we would buy in Hessel Street in the East End on a Sunday morning.

Makes 6 generous portions

1 medium onion

1 medium carrot

5 or 6 raw beetroots

1 litre (1¾ pints) stock made using Israeli parve bouillon

Juice of a large lemon

1 tablespoon sugar

Salt and black pepper to taste

Crème fraiche (optional)

Peel and chop all the vegetables. Put into a large pan and cover with the stock. Bring to the boil, cover and simmer for 45 minutes until the vegetables are tender.

Add the lemon juice and sugar and seasoning to taste. Then simmer for a further 5 minutes. Allow to cool and puree the mixture using a stick blender or put into a liquidiser. Return to the heat for a few moments serve piping hot.

Add crème fraiche before serving if required.

Tips

It tastes even better if you leave it overnight before serving. Freezes very well.

Soup, Beautiful Soup

Caroline Silver Lewis

In many a Jewish family, soup plays a major part of the eating ritual. I say ritual because that is what it is. Soup, like most food, belongs in the social category of Judaism. This may seem obvious but a meal in my family (and by family I mean generations of us) is not complete if there is no soup to start the meal.

I have moved on though from my grandmother's chicken soup to thinking about how soup either complements or becomes the repast in itself. On deciding what soup to make, I first have to consider several factors. What season is it? Is it for lunch or dinner? What is the main colour of the next course? Yes, colour! That is just as important for soup as the flavour and texture.

Let's start with the season. A winter lunch, for example, needs a good hearty soup including pulses accompanied by some good bread. But beware of it becoming sludgy, both in texture and colour. If you are using carrots and pulses, make sure you only use orange lentils so that the soup retains its glorious bright colour. If you blend it, adding greens will turn it to a dull brown. Not really appetising. Beware blending too when mixing different coloured vegetables.

For a soup to use as a starter at a heavy-ish dinner, such as Friday Night, or you want a light summer supper dish, then keep your soup thin. The colour itself should be tempting enough to dive in to. Consider beetroot, adding a handful of frozen peas and a few chopped carrots just before serving. Beautiful!

On making stock, for a thin soup don't go mad with stock cubes, but you can use one. Cook the vegetables (or meat) including an onion or two in large chunks big enough to strain off after. For a thick soup, follow the Indian method of thickening, that is, use plenty of onions. These, once blended with everything else add low fat thickness.

One other tip, except for cooking pulses or meat, vegetables lose colour and flavour if you boil them too long. Keep it really quick especially for anything green.

Before I finish, consider one more element. The flavours. The best way to do this is to close your eyes, consider the main ingredient to your soup and then imagine another flavour to go with it. Do not be afraid. Compare this to buying clothes or decorating your living room. Do you like the idea of the combination? Does it feel right? Taste it in your mind and if you like the idea then try it out. Returning to the carrots and red lentils above, for example, could you contemplate adding a sweet juicy orange blended with this? And some cardamon perhaps?

There is a soup for all tastes and moods, whether you are feeling hot or cold, thick or thin, rough or smooth. Be bold, use your imagination to let your creative juices flow into that saucepan.

Harira Soup

Merav Oppenheimer

I was born in the village of Demnat in the Middle Atlas in Morocco and this was the soup of my childhood. Our family left for Israel in the fifties when I was two years old. We arrived in Israel in a chilly January and one of my first memories is of my mother Zohara Waqunine serving us this warming soup during those first cold days in our new home.

My sisters Ohel and Rebecca and I still make this soup for our families and friends. Each of us cooks it a little differently, and some prefer it more or less thick. It is always delicious. Cheap, simple and nutritious it will warm you during a cold British winter. Like wine, it gets better with age so you can make a big pot of it and use it all week. You can add chicken or beef to the soup for a non-vegetarian version.

Serve with bread as a main course.

Serves 8

A mug of dried chickpeas, soaked overnight in a bowl of cold water

A mug of green lentils, soaked overnight in a bowl of cold water

1 tablespoon sunflower oil

1-2 medium onions, chopped

5 stalks of Mediterranean celery (available from Turkish shops, they have long, flavoursome stalks. If not available, use the inner stalks of English celery), cut into small pieces

Celery leaves from a bunch of Mediterranean celery (these are large leaves which you add whole to the soup)

A bunch of fresh coriander leaves, chopped

4 large Italian tomatoes, peeled (soak for 1 minute in just boiled water, then peel) and grated to make juice

1 tablespoon turmeric

Salt and black pepper

2- 2½ litres water flavoured with Telma chicken stock, adjust to taste

Optional Chicken thighs or other meat

1 tablespoon plain flour

Juice of half a lemon

Having soaked the lentils and chickpeas overnight, rinse well. Fry onion, celery and coriander leaves in a little sunflower oil till they are beginning to soften. Then add the chickpeas, lentils, water and stock, tomato juice, turmeric, black pepper, and a little salt to taste (depending on the saltiness of your stock).

[At this stage, for a meaty soup, you can add chicken thighs or other meat.]

Cover the saucepan loosely with a lid and simmer for about 40 minutes or until the chickpeas are tender (and the meat cooked).

Then remove about half a cup of the soup broth and mix well with the flour, making sure it is very smooth with no lumps. Then add the mixture back to the soup and stir well. This will thicken the soup. Then add the lemon juice, adjusting to taste. Simmer for a further 5 or 10 minutes. Remove the celery leaves before serving.

Tip You can use tinned chickpeas instead of dried which will reduce the cooking time.

Gooseberry Bushes and Gazpacho: Reminiscences and a Recipe

Diane Barnett

My first memory of food was as a very young child during the Second World War when rationing was in place. There wasn't much sense of "Jewish food" then. My mother (Milly Moss) pregnant with me, her first child, had moved down from Hull to live with her parents in Wembley whilst my father was away in the RAF.

I was of the generation where, because of the rationing, we didn't have the luxuries that we are used to now. To a certain extent, people cooked better then, with fewer fresh ingredients. Our neighbour owned chickens so we had a good supply of eggs and I would have a boiled egg for breakfast every morning. My grandfather grew raspberry and gooseberry bushes in the garden. I remember clearly the day during the Blitz that my grandparents' front door was blown in by a nearby bomb.

After the war, mothers spoilt their children when they could, although rationing continued for several years. I was the envy of all my friends when I had ice-cream for my fourth birthday party. My mother would also make indulgent puddings, like golden syrup tart and steamed chocolate pudding with chocolate sauce, which really felt extravagant when we had been used to chocolate as a very special treat to be had with the four ration points you needed to buy a bar of it.

In later years, my daughter Harriet loved her grandmother's Sunday lunches. There would be "best end of lamb" followed by my mother's idiosyncratic version of apple charlotte, which was actually apple with a topping of breadcrumbs and sugar.

For me, a love of cooking started when I married Neville over fifty years ago. My cousin gave me some sound advice: "there's no mystique to cooking. Just read the recipe carefully, and follow what it says exactly. If you like it, then you can make changes after that." This has always worked for me, and I have loved cooking since then.

I would try out traditional Jewish recipes, like chopped liver, chicken soup and fried fish. We still love a bowl of chicken soup with matzah balls – throughout the year – made from matzah and bound with ground almonds. But my cooking influences are wider than that and I wouldn't say I brought up my children Andrew and Harriet exclusively on traditional Jewish dishes.

Like many other Jewish brides of the 1960s, I was given a copy of Florrie Greenberg's *Jewish Cookery Book* for a wedding present. I still make her Passover almond pudding and like to have a look through my well-thumbed copy though now I also enjoy the recipes of Delia Smith, Jamie Oliver, Gary Rhodes and especially Claudia Roden.

I want to mention two particular family recipes. First there is my mother-in-law Bertha Barnett's signature dish: beef with pickled walnut. The walnuts can be bought in a jar. They are then mashed with some flour, stock and two tablespoons of vinegar. The meat is then braised in the mixture and has a lovely, rich flavour.

I also make fried fish like my mother and grandmother. The fish is coated in flour, then egg, and finally breadcrumbs before frying in oil. We usually eat it cold with salads. Cold fried fish prepared in this way originated amongst the Portuguese Jews in the Middle Ages and the method was brought to England by the Marranos (crypto-Jews) in the sixteenth century. As Claudia Roden explains in *The Book of Jewish Food*, Joseph Malin – an Eastern European immigrant – founded a fish business in 1860 in the East End of London, selling fried fish with chips. This winning combination of fish (eaten hot) and chips went on to become the British national dish.

An advert in my Florrie Greenberg Cookery Book. I was given a Sunbeam Mixmaster as a wedding present

Dona Maria's Gazpacho

Dona Maria gave me this authentic recipe for gazpacho when we were staying with her in Spain in the summer of 1963, the year Pope John XXIII passed away. My father-in-law's business was to import the sherry produced from her family's vineyards to England. Every morning, Dona Maria would go into the kitchen where the servants would be waiting for instructions on what to assemble and cook from the fresh ingredients they had gathered.

It is best to make this in a liquidiser, or a food processor.

450g (1lb) tomatoes (no need to skin or deseed)

1 whole red pepper (from a jar or tin of roasted peppers)

150g (5oz) bread, crusts cut off

½ wine glass of olive oil

¼ – ½ glass of (malt) vinegar

Liquidise the tomatoes and pepper. Soak the bread in water, then squeeze out the liquid. Whilst the processor is running, add the bread, a little at a time. With the liquidiser still running, add the oil and vinegar slowly. Then add as much water as you want, depending on whether you want a thicker or thinner consistency. Chill. When the weather is very hot, I like to make the soup thin and serve it as a drink.

To serve, spoon some of the following into the bottom of your bowl: diced green peppers, cucumber and tomato, chopped hardboiled egg, chopped avocado, croutons. Then pour the chilled soup over the top.

Chicken Soup and Kneidlach

Sally-Ann Feldman

Chicken Soup

1 whole chicken

1 chicken bouillon cube

Water

2 large whole onions

Carrots, peeled and cut into four, as many as you like

Leaves and top two inches of 6-8 stalks of celery

Large sprig of parsley

2 large squashy tomatoes

1-2 tablespoons salt, according to taste

Black pepper, to taste

Put the chicken in a large heavy saucepan and almost cover it with water. Add the salt and pepper and crumble in the chicken cube. Cover and bring to the boil. Uncover and remove any froth with a large, holed metal spoon. Add all the remaining ingredients. Bring back to the boil, then reduce the heat so that the liquid is barely bubbling. Cover and continue to simmer for a further 2 and a half to 3 hours or until the fowl feels very tender when the leg is prodded with a fork.

Strain the soup into one bowl and put the carrot into another. Discard the other vegetables. The bird should be put in a separate container. Refrigerate. Next day, remove any congealed fat, saving it for the kneidlach, and return the soup to the pan. Add the carrots and re-heat slowly before serving. The soup may be garnished with cooked vermicelli or kneidlach (matzah balls).

Chicken soup should always be made the day before it is served, as the flavour is incomparably better on the second day!

Kneidlach

One of the few cooking tips that my mother Winnie Lewis passed on to me was to add a pinch of cinnamon to a lot of savoury dishes including meatloaf, fried gefilte fish mixture and kneidlach. It just makes that little bit of difference.

You may not think that chicken fat is fashionable but I can only tell you that it makes such a difference to the flavour of the kneidlach. If you don't have enough, make up the quantity with soft margarine, preferably Tomor.

Makes eight kneidlach, enough for four people but I always make 3 or 4 times this amount – they all get eaten in no time!

1 slightly rounded tablespoon soft, rendered chicken fat (do not melt)

1 large egg

2 tablespoons chicken soup

½ level teaspoon salt

Pinches of pepper and cinnamon

2 level tablespoons ground almonds

50g (2oz) medium matzah meal (about 6 level tablespoons)

The secret of success is to use sufficient fat to make them tender yet firm. Providing the specified amount of fat is used, the amount of matzah meal may be increased if you prefer a firmer (though equally tender) texture. Ground almonds greatly enhance both the flavour and texture, but if you have none in the house, an equal quantity of medium matzah meal can be used instead. Beat the egg with a rotary whisk until fluffy, then stir in the tepid soup or water, the seasonings, matzah meal, chicken fat and ground almonds. It is a good idea to keep 1 level tablespoonful of meal in reserve and add it only if necessary, when the ingredients have been well mixed and you can see the texture. The mixture should then look moist and be stiff but still stirrable, yet not stiff enough to form into balls. Refrigerate or chill in a cold larder for at least one hour. (The mixture may be left overnight if convenient.)

Wet your hands under the cold water tap, take a walnut-sized piece of the now stiffened mixture, and roll it into a ball between your palms.

Have ready a large pan half full of boiling water. Add a teaspoonful of salt, then drop in the balls. When the water is barely bubbling, put on the lid, and simmer gently for forty minutes, without looking at the contents of the pan during that time. Uncover, lift out the kneidlach with a holed spoon, and lower them gently into simmering chicken soup. Simmer in the soup for 10 minutes more or so. Serve with the soup. Left-over balls can be allowed to remain in the soup overnight.

For other kneidlach recipes, see Passover chapter.

Beef, Vegetable and Noodle Soup
Ruth Magnus

Many years ago we were away on holiday and had the most wonderful Gulaschsuppe (goulash soup). This recipe comes a very close second to that soup and is actually a meal on its own.

Serves 8

450g (1 lb) shin beef

2.75 litres (5 pints) water

5 bouillon cubes

8 sticks of celery, thinly sliced

2 large (225g/8oz) carrots cut into 1cm (½ inch) cubes

1 rounded tablespoon tomato puree

1 medium (225g/8oz) onion, finely chopped

200g (½ lb) peeled potatoes, cut into 1cm (½ inch) cubes

50g (2oz) egg or Chinese noodles

½ teaspoon Italian herb seasoning

1 tablespoon chopped parsley

In a large pan combine the water and the piece of shin. Bring to the boil, skim the froth from the top with a metal spoon, then simmer for 1 hour. Add the celery, carrot, tomatoes, chopped onion, Italian herb seasoning and bouillon cubes and simmer for a further 30 minutes. Add the potato, peeled and cubed, and simmer for a further 30 minutes.

Lift out the meat with a slotted spoon, cut up small and then return to the soup. Drop the noodles into the soup and simmer for 5 minutes, then add the chopped parsley.

Taste and add salt and black pepper if required. Serve at once or, if possible, leave for 24 hours and reheat, as the flavour is then greatly improved.

Parsnip and Apple Soup
Ellen Sheridan

The recipe for this soup was passed on from the chef at the Petersham Hotel in Richmond. A weekday lunch, sitting at a table with a view over the Thames – highly recommended!

4 small to medium parsnips

1 green apple

1 carrot (peeled and roughly chopped)

1 onion or leek chopped

1 crushed garlic clove

Chilli sprinkles (optional)

1 organic vegetable stock cube

Kemp and salt to taste

2 tablespoons sunflower oil

1 litre (1¾ pints) water

Choose a pan with a lid that can hold all the ingredients with ease. Coat the bottom with oil and warm it up. Sauté the leeks and garlic until soft with the chilli, add the apples, carrots and parsnips and continue sautéing for a few minutes. Pour in the water and stock, and allow to simmer over a low heat for 30-40 minutes or until the vegetables are soft. Use a hand held blender to puree - a lovely warm treat for when the weather gets colder and the days somewhat greyer.

Sweet Potato and Lentil Soup

Ellen Sheridan

2 large sweet potatoes (peeled and roughly chopped)

1 carrot (peeled and roughly chopped)

1 leek, sliced

⅓ cup yellow split peas (rinsed, there is no need to soak)

½ cup red lentils (rinsed, there is no need to soak)

1 litre cold water

250g (9oz) watercress (rinsed)

1-2 tablespoons sunflower oil

Celery is optional

Salt and pepper, freshly ground chilli or chilli sprinkles, garlic, thyme etc. to taste depending on your preferences.

Choose a pan with a lid that can hold all the ingredients with ease. Coat the bottom with oil and warm it up. Sauté the leeks until soft. Add the sweet potatoes and carrots and sauté for a few more minutes. Pour in the water, the yellow split peas and red lentils and allow to simmer for 30 minutes covered with the lid. Just have it bubbling, not foaming, using a low to middle flame. Add the cress and allow to simmer for a further 15 minutes. The watercress should be soft and fall apart easily. Use a hand held blender to puree it. Nice and very comforting for the winter!

Winter Soup

Yvonne Mason

I love making soup in the winter. I keep it simple and always follow the same formula (call me boring if you like) then add whichever vegetables I fancy (or have in the house). I never measure anything. I just judge quantities by eye and adjust the liquid content accordingly - I guess this is the yin yang result of my rebellion against my scientific training.

When the kids were little it was a great way of getting veg into them without them noticing too much. The soup keeps in the fridge for a couple of days and the flavour improves after several hours of standing.

Onions, chopped

Stock

Milk

Vegetables, chopped

Seasoning

Suggested vegetable combinations

- Dried red lentils, carrots and celery (stir a squeeze of lemon in at the end and garnish with chopped parsley)
- Mushrooms
- Leek and potato
- Butternut squash (with or without mango). Great with lemongrass, ginger and coconut milk
- Peas (frozen is fine), spinach (frozen is fine) and mint

Fry a couple of onions until soft then add about a pint (570ml) of good quality stock (I use the parve chicken flavour Telma stock - it looks and tastes like chicken soup but is vegetarian - you can buy it in lots of big supermarkets now, even in South London). Bring to the boil, then add the chopped vegetables until cooked. The lentil combination will take about 40 minutes till the lentils are cooked.

Puree it all in the liquidizer. Add milk and seasoning and bring to the boil again. Be careful it doesn't boil over. You can add more milk, water or stock and seasoning or herbs to get the consistency and taste you like.

Tip

If you like a richer soup you can add cream.

Makes a great meal with some nice crusty bread.

Adam's Swiss Creamy Chestnut Soup

Adam Parker

The taste of Autumn/Winter Shabbat in Geneva.

Goes well with wine from the Lavaux region of Switzerland.

Knob of butter

3 onions, chopped

1 garlic clove, crushed

1.25 litres (4 fl oz) parve Chicken stock or vegetable stock

1 bay leaf

400g (14oz) vacuum-packed chestnuts – chopped into smaller pieces

1 tablespoon fresh rosemary

As much wine as you feel like. Or 2 tablespoons of sherry or vermouth

Salt and pepper to taste

Single cream to serve

In a saucepan, melt the butter and fry the onion, garlic and bay leaf till soft but not coloured (5-10 minutes). Add the chestnuts and continue to fry for a few minutes, but be careful that they don't stick to the pan and burn. Add the stock, rosemary and wine/sherry and bring to the boil.

Reduce temperature and simmer for 30 minutes. Remove the bay leaf and then blend the soup with a hand-blender.

Add water if needed to get the right consistency – a thin, silky, smooth soup. Add salt and pepper to taste.

Serve with a dash of cream if you feel like a little treat.

STARTERS, SIDES AND SALADS

Tal's Falafel

Tal Kalderon

This recipe was inspired by a fantastic falafel place I loved in Yehuda Halevi Street in Tel Aviv in the 1990s. The restaurant owner wanted to create falafel with a difference and came up with two kinds of falafel: green falafel, made with lots of coriander and orange falafel which contained sweet potato. The salads were fresh and healthy and were a welcome change from the usual side dishes of cabbage and chips you find at most falafel bars. Unfortunately, the restaurant has now closed down.

It wasn't until I came to the UK in 1999 to study at Aberdeen University that I made falafel for the first time. My uni friends loved it. You certainly couldn't buy falafel in Aberdeen.

Since my son Ilay and I have become involved in Wimbledon Synagogue, I've made some large batches of falafel for some Synagogue events, like the Hanukkah Fair and a Children's Fun Day. Even when I made this recipe with 3.5kg of chickpeas, the falafel sold out pretty quickly.

It is great served with sweet potato chips, Israeli/Arabic salad, tahina, humous and pitta breads.

For approximately 60 falafels

1 kg (2lb 3oz) chickpeas (If you don't have the time to soak the chickpeas overnight, you can boil them with bicarbonate of soda until softened or use tinned ones)

1 large head of garlic, peeled (optional)

2 onions, peeled and quartered

1 bunch coriander leaves

1 teaspoon bicarbonate of soda

1 tablespoon salt

1 tablespoon cumin

1 tablespoon sweet paprika

1 tablespoon cayenne pepper or white pepper, freshly ground

Vegetable oil for frying

The day before: soak the chickpeas in a large bowl in plenty of cold water and leave in the fridge overnight. Check occasionally to see there is enough water to cover all the chickpeas as they swell up.

On the day: drain the chickpeas, rinse well in cold water and pat dry.

Using a Magimix, or food processor, grind the chickpeas, garlic (if using) and onion. Add the bicarbonate of soda and the spices and mix well.

At this stage, you can refrigerate the mixture till you are ready to fry.

Just before you are ready to cook them, stir in the chopped coriander. If you find the mixture is too thin, you can add a little flour.

Using a spoon or by hand, form the falafel into balls.

Heat the oil in a large saucepan or wok. As falafel are deep fried, the oil should be at least double the depth of the falafel. You can check if the oil is hot enough by dipping a wooden spoon into the oil, bubbles should form around the spoon.

Place a few falafel into the hot oil. Fry until golden (approximately three minutes), turning them in the oil, then remove with a slotted spoon to a plate lined with some paper towel.

They are best eaten straight away but you could keep them warm in the oven for a little while.

Accompaniments
Sweet Potato Chips

Peel some sweet potatoes and cut them into wedges.

If you have lots of oil left from the falafel, simply fry them in the same pan. Alternatively, shallow fry, or place on a baking tray, coat in oil and bake in a hot oven for approximately 30 minutes or until soft.

Israeli/Arabic Salad

The main characteristic of this type of salad is that the vegetables are cut into very small chunks. You can vary what and how much you use but here are my suggestions.

2 large tomatoes (you cut them first and leave them at the bottom of a bowl, otherwise the juice will spoil the freshness of other vegetables)

1 cucumber with the skin on

1-2 yellow peppers

1 radish

2 or 3 spring onions

Mint leaves or flat parsley, as little or as much as you like

Juice from 1 lemon

At least 4 tablespoons of good extra virgin olive oil

Salt and pepper

Cut the vegetables into ½ cm chunks. Add the chopped herbs, lemon, olive oil and seasoning. Combine. Serve chilled or at room temperature within 1-2 hours of making it.

Egg and Onion

Josephine Urban

From Poland and Ukraine, no Yomtov or Shabbat meal is complete without this appetiser which sits on the table nestling between the chopped liver and herring.

Serves 6 as a starter

6 eggs

2 egg-size potatoes

4 spring onions

1 large onion

2 – 4 tablespoons light olive oil or sunflower oil

Salt and pepper to taste

Hard boil eggs and boil the potatoes. Chop large onion into very fine cubes, very small - and sauté in oil until golden and transparent.

Chop spring onions very finely and place in bowl. Add very finely chopped egg and potato and cooked onion. Mix carefully together adding salt, pepper and oil to taste (I use a two pronged carving fork for this).

Ingredients should be chopped finely, not grated. For reasons of authenticity substituting mayonnaise for oil is not advisable.

May be eaten next day if stored in fridge – but there will be no leftovers!

Nadine's Chopped Liver

Nadine Tuffin

My recipe for chopped liver is a mixture of various recipes that I have tried and collected from all around the world – from my South African mother, from Israel (where I grew up and experienced all my early Seders) and finally my many years in England where I make this traditional Jewish dish every year, and have made into my very own.

This can be enjoyed for Shabbat, Rosh Hashanah, Passover, before or after the fast for Yom Kippur or many other occasions.

Serves approximately 12 as an appetiser

350 - 450g (1lb) chicken livers (3 punnets of frozen chicken livers from the supermarket freezer)

1 tablespoon of olive or sunflower oil for frying

3 medium onions chopped

1 or 2 small hardboiled eggs

Freshly ground pepper to add while frying

Fresh coriander chopped and to add while frying

Fry the chicken livers with the onion and the coriander and add the freshly ground pepper. I tend to add quite a lot of both as the flavours of the fresh coriander and pepper really make this dish.

Make sure both the onion and the liver are well cooked and that the liver is not at all bloody.

I have quite often made this as an evening meal accompanied by mashed potatoes. My whole family love it. It is also at this point that I have to fight to keep everyone from dipping into the pan to taste…

Then add all the contents of the pan with one or possibly two small hardboiled eggs into a food processor and chop until blended and quite smooth.

Transfer to a bowl and garnish with some fresh parsley and enjoy with matzah and chrain.

Havurah Dinners

Havurah means a community of friends. Our havurah suppers for young families are held a few times a year on a Friday, after a short, family friendly Shabbat service.

Each family brings a dish to share and we often have a mix of home cooked and readymade food. To make sure everyone is happy, for the younger children, we usually have a staple of pizzas, baked potatoes with grated cheese or baked beans followed by ice cream, and the rest of us enjoy the other delicious food on offer. Here we share some of these dishes.

Greek Salad

Albert Ferro

I brought this along to a Friday Havurah family supper at the Synagogue.

Serves 4

50g (2oz) pitted black olives

3 large tomatoes, quartered lengthwise and then halved crosswise into eighths

1 large cucumber, cut into 2cm (¾ inch) strips and then halved

1 red pepper, de-seeded and diced

1 red onion, sliced very fine

1 packet of feta cheese, crumbled in

100ml (4 fl oz) good quality extra virgin olive oil

1 lemon

Mix it all up, and serve with wedges of lemon to squeeze over.

Sandy's Famous Mushroom Almond Pâté

Sandy Scher

Think of this as vegetarian chopped liver. I usually double the recipe so I have a batch left for myself.

Makes 8 ¼ cup servings

1 cup slivered almonds

¼ cup butter

1 small onion

1 clove garlic, minced or pressed

340g (12oz) mushrooms, sliced

¾ teaspoon salt

½ teaspoon thyme

¼ teaspoon white pepper (I often use black)

2 tablespoons salad oil (vegetable oil)

Spread almonds in a pan and toast in a 175°C/350°F/Gas Mark 4 oven for 8 minutes or until light brown. Melt butter in a wide frying pan over medium-high heat. Add onion, garlic, mushrooms, salt, thyme, and pepper. Cook, stirring occasionally, until onion is soft and most of the pan juices have evaporated. If you aren't sure, keep going. In a food processor or blender, whirl almonds to form a paste. With motor running, add oil and whirl until creamy. Add mushroom mixture and whirl until pâté is smooth.

Tabbouleh

Roland Appel

When my brother met his future wife, Jane, she would often make a tabbouleh, this being traditional of her family from Iraq. As a Sephardi welcomed into my family of Ashkenazi origin, Jane brought with her new foods and traditions. At their large family and friends' parties, there would always be a tabbouleh sitting on the table. I rather liked the dish as it was an exotic culinary addition to the other dishes we had known.

The tabbouleh I have re-created here is based on Jane's recipe. However, my memory for detail is not exact and I always take pleasure in re-creating with my own tweaks and changes. Please enjoy!

This will create sufficient for a large bowl, e.g. for a gathering of family or friends, or a family Shabbat in the Shul.

200g (7oz) bulgur wheat

400ml (¾ pint) boiling water

Large bunch parsley, washed and dried
Large bunch fresh mint leaves (remove tough stalks), washed and dried

4 small or 2 large red onions

200g (7oz) olives (green, pitted)

500g (1lb 1oz) sweet tomatoes (may be cherry or large – whatever type is available)

Juice of 2 lemons or 8 tablespoons bottled lemon juice

5 tablespoons olive oil

Salt (small amount to taste)

Place the bulgur wheat in a bowl, and cover with the boiling water. Stir then leave to cool.

Whilst waiting for the bulgur wheat to cool, chop and prepare the following items, and place in a separate large mixing bowl: the parsley, mint, onion and olives (finely chopped) and the tomatoes (cut into small pieces). Mix well, then add the bulgur wheat. Then add the lemon juice, olive oil and salt and mix again.

Tips: A very sharp knife is required, especially for the tomatoes. I found the chopping particularly easy with a hand food chopper or a food processor.

May be prepared the day before and kept in the fridge.

Marinated Cucumber Salad

Claudia Camhi

This recipe comes from Adela Ergas, my uncle's wife. Meeting at her place generally involves experiencing a lovely feast and a great time.

1 large cucumber

Small bunch of dill (preferably fresh)

Salt and pepper to taste

2 tablespoons of olive oil

Juice of two large lemons

Find a very sharp knife. Wash, pat dry and then finely slice the cucumber in rounds (keep the skin on for British cucumbers but any other cucumber should be peeled). The slices should be so thin that you see the light coming through and almost stick to the knife.

Place in a bowl and add all the rest of the ingredients.

Cover in cling film and refrigerate for an hour before serving.

Variation:

You can do the same with mushrooms but substitute the dill with some very finely cut chives and red peppers.

Very Very Easy Coleslaw

Vivienne Cato Koppel

Serves about 8

1 white cabbage

2 small red onions

About 4 large carrots

2 tablespoons mayonnaise

2 tablespoons white wine vinegar

Slice the cabbage and onions finely, grate the carrot (not too finely). It is easiest just to put them all through a coarse grater of a Magimix or such like, if you have one. Transfer to a large bowl, and add the mayonnaise and white wine vinegar. Mix it all through evenly: add more mayonnaise and/or vinegar according to your judgement – you want it to coat nicely but not be sloppy.

If any is left, it will keep (covered) in the fridge for a couple of days (it's not for freezing). It can be made a day in advance.

Janet's Jewel Salad

Janet Benjamin

This is my favourite feature salad at a dinner party. I created the recipe by borrowing from other salads I have tasted and it is influenced by all the delicious food always offered by Jewish South Africans. No matter who you visit there will be flavoursome and interesting salads and dishes on offer. Enjoy!

1 punnet of pomegranate seeds

250g (9oz) block of Greek Feta, crumbled

100g (4oz) walnuts, chopped

200g (7oz) delicate lettuce leaves mixed bag, favourite leaf is lamb's lettuce

200g (7oz) mixed baby tomatoes, yellow and red, halved

1 bunch organic spring onions, sliced finely

2 red romano/ sweet long peppers, cut finely

This is best served on a platter.

Start with your lettuce leaves, then tomatoes sprinkled on top, then red peppers, spring onions, feta and nuts. Just before serving sprinkle over the jewel-like pomegranates. Serve with a very good quality balsamic vinegar and olive oil.

Tip: you can add cucumber if you want to, as well as avocado to make it a richer salad.

Noodle Salad

Nicky Bannerman

250g (9oz) dried medium noodles

100g (4oz) unsalted cashews

½ red onion

1 fresh red chilli

Small bunch of coriander

1 or 2 tablespoons soy sauce

1 tablespoon extra-virgin olive oil

Juice of 1 lime

1 teaspoon sesame oil

1 teaspoon runny honey

Put the noodles in a large bowl, cover with boiling water and a plate, and leave to soak for a few minutes. Place the cashew nuts in a plastic bag or in a clean tea towel and bash to break up slightly with a rolling pin. Heat a frying pan and toast them, tossing a little.

Then add the honey, mixing well, and toast till golden. Peel the red onion and finely chop with the coriander stalks and the red chilli in a food processor. Add to a large serving bowl together with the soy sauce and extra virgin olive oil, the lime juice and the sesame oil. Mix well. Drain the noodles, refresh under cold water, then add to the bowl. Add the cashews and the coriander leaves and stir together.

Puy Lentil Salad

Claudia Camhi

I love pulses and in particular puy lentils as they do not need soaking the night before, keep their shape without turning into a puree and have a thin and soft outer layer. It is a good side dish for fish, potatoes or green salad.

150g (5oz) puy lentils

½ a red pepper

½ a green pepper

½ a purple/red onion

Salt and pepper to taste

2 tablespoons of olive oil

Juice of ½ a lemon

Rinse the puy lentils in cold water and place in a pan of 500ml (18 fl oz) of cold water. Wait until it boils, stir, cover and simmer on a medium heat until they are al dente (approximately 20 minutes).

Once cooked, drain and rinse the lentils in cold water and allow to cool down. Place in a serving bowl.

Cut the peppers and onion into very small cubes.

Add to the lentils and season with olive oil, lemon juice, salt and pepper.

Asparagus Salad with Sesame Seeds

Claudia Camhi

This salad was an invention of my sister Alejandra.

200g (7oz) asparagus

1 tablespoon of balsamic vinegar

2 tablespoons of olive oil

2 tablespoons of plain or toasted sesame seeds

2 teaspoons of salt for blanching the asparagus

Salt and pepper to taste for seasoning

Rinse and peel the asparagus stems if not tender enough. Bring a large saucepan of water to a boil and add 2 teaspoons of salt.

Place the asparagus in the saucepan and allow to cook for 2 minutes, remove and set in a bowl of cold water. Heat the sunflower oil in a large enough pan to fit the asparagus.

Pat dry the asparagus. Stir fry the asparagus until lightly golden on some of its surfaces. Be careful not to overcook.

Place on a serving dish and sprinkle over the sesame seeds. Drizzle with olive oil, balsamic vinegar and season with salt and pepper.

Warm Sweet Potato and Halloumi Salad

Andres Kupfer

Serves 4

4 medium sized sweet potatoes

A large salad bowl full of rocket, lamb lettuce and baby spinach leaves

250g halloumi cheese

2 lemons

A handful of pine nuts

A few leaves of fresh mint

3 tablespoons extra virgin olive oil

3 tablespoons pomegranate molasses

3 tablespoons water

Salt and pepper

Peel and cut the sweet potatoes into large chunks, toss them in two tablespoons of olive oil, the juice of two lemons and salt to taste. Roast them until crispy on the outside.

Slice and brush the halloumi with oil and cook on a griddle.

Toast pine nuts in a dry frying pan until light brown.

Make a dressing with the extra virgin olive oil, pomegranate molasses, water and salt and pepper to taste. Mix well.

Dress the salad leaves, then add the sweet potatoes, the halloumi and the pine nuts.

Finish by tearing the fresh mint leaves with your hands over the salad.

Serve warm with some chunky garlic bread.

Potato Bravas

Sally Lewis

This recipe is from Olga whose husband is a chef in a Spanish restaurant near King's Cross.

Serves 4-6

500g (1lb 1oz) waxy potatoes

300ml (10½ fl oz) olive oil

1 small onion, finely chopped

1 red chilli, finely chopped

400g (14oz) tin chopped tomatoes

½ teaspoon sugar

½ teaspoon salt

1 teaspoon smoked paprika

2 tablespoons sherry vinegar

1 egg

1 clove garlic, crushed

Chives, to serve

Preheat the oven to 200°C/400°F/Gas Mark 6. Peel the potatoes and cut into rough 2cm (¾ inch) chunks. Put a roasting tray with 2 tablespoons olive oil into the oven and leave to heat for 5 minutes, then take out, toss the potatoes in the hot oil, and bake for about 45 minutes until crisp and golden.

Meanwhile, make the sauces. Put 2 tablespoons of oil into a heavy-bottomed pan on a medium heat, and cook the onion for about seven minutes until golden and soft. Put in the chilli, and cook for another couple of minutes. Then add the tomatoes, sugar, salt and smoked paprika and stir well. Bring to the boil, and then turn down the heat and simmer for about 20 minutes until thick and dark. Take off the heat, add 1 tablespoon sherry vinegar, and adjust the seasoning if necessary.

To make the aioli, crack the egg into the small bowl of a food processor along with the garlic and 1 tablespoon sherry vinegar. Add 1 tablespoon olive oil and whizz until incorporated, then drizzle in the rest of the olive oil with the motor running, until you have creamy mayonnaise-style sauce. Season to taste. (You can also use a hand blender, but it's harder to drizzle and beat at the same time.)

Take the potatoes out of the oven and sprinkle with a little salt. Spread the tomato sauce on to the plates, put the potatoes on top, then add a dollop of aioli and a sprinkle of chives, and serve immediately.

Gratin de Courgettes Au Chèvre et Noisettes

Jessica Urvicz

6 courgettes, sliced in half lenghtways

60g (2½oz) hazelnuts, coarsely chopped

300ml (½ pint) single cream

Chopped fresh basil

Chopped fresh mint

Goat's cheese, cut in small cubes; alternatively half a feta cheese, approximately 100g (4oz)

50g (2oz) grated cheese

On a low heat, cook the sliced courgettes in the cream in a large pan until tender (20 to 30 minutes). Add basil and mint and stir for a couple of minutes. Then pour the courgettes into a baking dish, add the goat's cheese or feta, stir, then sprinkle in some of the hazelnuts and gently stir again. Sprinkle the remaining hazelnuts over the top, and then the grated cheese. Put your dish in the oven on 180°C/350°F/Gas Mark 4 until golden brown.

MAINS

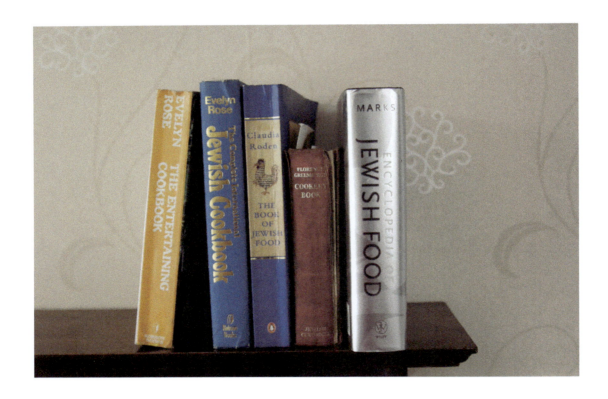

The Most Honest Recipe I Know
Rabbi Lionel Blue

Rabbi Lionel Blue, regular contributor to Radio 4's *Thought for the Day*, author of many books, including several cookery books, has kindly contributed two recipes to this collection.

Rabbi Blue with Rabbi Sheridan at Wimbledon

Arctic Chowder

Here is the most honest recipe I know. It is an arctic chowder from north east Canada.

I have used it on students, I made it for Lord Marks and above all it was wonderful for sailing, because you could spoon it out into mugs and it never made anybody seasick in force nine gales.

You need the following:

450g (1lb) white fish: cod or halibut fillets more or less (the fish can be smoked – a mixture is rather nice.)

1 litre (1¾ pints) skimmed milk

3 medium to large peeled potatoes cut in chunks

3 onions peeled and cut in chunks

A mug of frozen peas

A medium tin of sweetcorn well drained

Cooking is very simple. Skin the fillets and cut them into mouth-sized pieces. Heat the milk, throw in the onion and potato chunks, add salt and pepper but go easy.

When the potatoes and the onions are almost done, throw in the fish chunks, the drained peas and cook till the fish is done. Lastly add the corn and reheat.

Now, this sounds very ordinary but it is very, very, more-ish and if you are giving a dinner party it is a dish that is very comfortable for the cook. You can really enjoy your own party while doing the cooking. Do not try to make something elegant and smart out of it. Smart friends of mine who liked it, tried to improve it with sweet potato, sherry and other exotics. The results were awful! It is made from ingredients that marry each other, but the taste is delicious. The quantities don't matter – adjust them according to what you have got or haven't. It is a very good main course in wintery weather – and as I have said, honest cooking at its best.

Hummus Fit for Kings and Paupers

Rabbi Lionel Blue

How to make hummus not just out of a pot, but a dish fit for kings. It's very good at festival time.

Liquidize a tin or two of cooked chickpeas (I have never had time to do all the soaking and you can't taste the difference). Cream them carefully in a blender, with some of the liquid from the tin, which can help to make the hummus softer if it comes out too hard. In the blender, add half a cup of tahini and three cloves of garlic (I like garlic), the juice of two lemons, salt and pepper, paprika and chilli powder to taste.

Add 2 or 3 tablespoons of olive oil and mix in the blender (good quality olive oil). You get a rather unattractive brown paste, which may not seem festival-like, but honestly, it can become a regal dish. If your hummus appears to be too thick, then add some more of the liquid from the tin.

Spread the brown paste over a platter and make furrows in it with a fork. Pour good olive oil on top so it glistens in the furrows and dot the hummus with sliced black and green olives, thin slices of sweet onion or chopped spring onions, or sliced leek and red peppers in oil cut up into little bits. You can also add anchovies or indeed anything which makes your hummus look like jewels. Shower the edges of the platter with chopped parsley either flat or curly (that is more authentic).

This makes a truly wonderful dish as it is brought in.

By the way, it looks even nicer if you save some of the chickpeas and scatter them over. It brings an interesting change of texture.

Amazing Spinach Casserole
Carra Kane

This is a recipe you can make in advance, place in your refrigerator overnight and then cook the next day. My husband loves it cold, and eats it like a dip the day after. All the women in my family have their own version of this so I am not really sure where it originated. But I do know that every time I make this dish, everyone enjoys it. Have fun and feel free to change the amount. Sometimes I just use however much spinach I have in the freezer and stir in cream cheese and soup mix until it looks like the right combination.

300g (11oz) cream cheese

1 can cream of mushroom soup

1kg (2lb 3oz) frozen spinach

Worcestershire sauce

Seasonings of your choice - pepper, garlic granules, onion powder, etc.

Breadcrumbs

Butter

Defrost and drain your spinach. You will want to get as much water out as possible. Mix spinach, cream cheese, soup all together in a round Pyrex dish. Add a few dashes (4-6) of Worcestershire sauce and a bit of seasonings (I use garlic granules, onion powder, and pepper). Stir all together and taste, then decide if you would like to add more seasonings.

Use a spoon to flatten the top of the dish and clean the edges of the dish (makes it pretty when you serve later). Sprinkle breadcrumbs on the top so you can't see the spinach (I use seasoned breadcrumbs for added flavour). Place about 10-15 small knobs of butter (scattered evenly) over the top of the breadcrumbs. Bake in the oven, uncovered for 40-45 minutes on 180°C/350°F/Gas Mark 4 and serve hot.

Enjoy!

Chris' Puff Pastry Rolls
Victoria Druyan-Newman

This is very quick to prepare and popular with children.

Ready rolled puff pastry sheet

200g (7oz) plain cream cheese

200g (7oz) flavoured cream cheese (e.g. with chives, cracked pepper or chilli)

Grated cheese

Chives (optional)

Mix the different types of cream cheese together. Add some grated cheddar cheese into the mixture - enough to bind it.

Spread the mixture evenly on top of the puff pastry sheet. Cut chives (optional) on top of the mixture. Roll up the sheet, put in the fridge for an hour or so for it to soak and bind. Then cut into pieces of about 1.5-2 cm thick.

Lay the slices flat on a baking sheet and bake in a preheated oven at about 200°C/400°F/Gas Mark 6 until they puff up and become slightly brown, approximately 20 minutes.

Ratatouille Niçoise
Norma Golten

Serves 8

1 large onion

2 garlic cloves

1 red pepper

1 medium aubergine

3 medium courgettes

8 plum or vine tomatoes

5 tablespoons (or thereabouts) olive oil

1 bay leaf

3 sprigs thyme (I sometimes use dried)

Heat the oven to 200°C/400°F/Gas Mark 6.

Quarter the onion and thinly slice. Crush the garlic. Quarter the pepper and aubergine lengthways and finely slice across the pieces. Finely slice the courgettes. Peel, halve and deseed the tomatoes and slice each half into four pieces. Heat half the olive oil in a large frying pan and add the onions. Cook briskly, stirring often for 5 minutes then add the garlic and pepper. Cook, tossing occasionally, until wilted slightly. Scrape into a bowl. Add more oil to the pan and quickly fry the aubergine to colour. Tip into the bowl. In the last of the oil stir fry the courgettes to lightly colour and remove to the bowl. Give the tomatoes a quick fry so they collapse slightly and add to the bowl. Season, mix together and place in a baking dish. Put the bay leaf and thyme on top. Cover and bake for 45 minutes.

Courgette or Aubergine Gratin

Claudia Camhi

A staple vegetarian dish at my mother's place.

6 courgettes or aubergines washed and sliced in half lengthwise

Olive oil

Salt and pepper to taste

1 onion

250g (9oz) pot of ricotta

150g (5oz) grated cheddar cheese

2 eggs

100g (4oz) cheddar for the topping

1 teaspoon oregano

Preheat the oven to 180°C/350°F/Gas Mark 4.

Oil an ovenproof baking tray.

Carefully remove the flesh of the courgettes or aubergines with a tablespoon without damaging the skin. You should leave at least 0.5cm of flesh so the vegetable can be used as a container of the gratin (it should look like an edible canoe).

Chop and reserve the flesh for the filling of the gratin.

Line the tray with the hollowed side of the vegetables facing up, adding salt, pepper and oil. Roast for 20 minutes.

Meanwhile prepare the filling. Chop the onion into small cubes and stir fry until soft. Add the vegetable flesh, salt, pepper and 20ml of water and continue cooking until soft.

Add the ricotta and mix. Then allow to cool for a few minutes. Mix in the eggs and grated cheddar, keep some to sprinkle on top.

Fill the roasted vegetable canoes with the mix and top with cheddar. Return to the oven and bake until the top layer looks golden.

It can be served as a main with a side of rice.

Feel free to play with the filling by adding herbs and/or other vegetables to taste (mushrooms, peas, sweetcorn or even smoked salmon).

You can keep leftovers refrigerated and covered in cling film. Can be frozen.

Spinach Quiche

Claudia Camhi

This is a quick and versatile recipe and a tasty way to persuade my children to eat greens. It is a nice alternative for picnic and communal eating. I made it up by combining a recipe for aubergine pasties while trying to make a slightly lower fat version of a quiche (I am not sure if I really achieved the latter). My children love to play with the leftover dough.

Serves 8-10

Dough (for a 20 cm diameter/8 inch loose base tin)

250g (9oz) plain flour

80ml (3 fl oz) lukewarm water

40ml (2 fl oz) sunflower oil

½ teaspoon baking powder

½ teaspoon salt

Filling

2 large eggs

250g (9oz) pot ricotta

250g (9oz) pot of yoghurt (do not use fat free)

150g (5oz) grated cheddar plus some extra for the top

250g (9oz) steamed and finely chopped spinach

Dough

Preheat the oven to 180°C/350°F/Gas Mark 4.

Place the flour in a bowl and mix in the salt and baking powder. Add the oil and lukewarm water.

Briefly combine until you get a moist dough that does not stick to your hands. If too dry add lukewarm water. If too sticky add more flour. Don't overwork the dough. Pat it thinly on the tin and press down with a fork. There is no need to grease or oil containers.

Bake in middle rack of the oven until lightly golden, about 15-20 minutes, but do not allow the edges to get too dark.

Remove from oven.

Filling

While the base is baking, make the filling. In a bowl mix eggs, ricotta, yoghurt, cheddar and finely chopped steamed spinach. Make sure you have removed all excess water from the spinach by placing in a sieve and squeezing.

Pour filling on the baked base and even out its surface. Sprinkle the top with grated cheddar.

Bake for approximately 45 minutes at 180°C/350°F/Gas Mark 4 until the top is golden.

For picnics, you can double the recipe and bake on a 30cmx38cm (12 x 15 inch) baking tray.

Tips

- You can also combine different types of flour. I have done this recipe with potato flour or with 200g (7oz) of white flour and 50g (2oz) of wholemeal. The texture changes but it still works well.

- Make sure to use lukewarm water. If the water is too hot the dough becomes hard to manage.

- Do not work the dough - just combine it into a manageable mix.

- Do not forget to prebake to avoid sogginess. There is no need to use parchment or weigh it down with beans.

- I do not add salt to the filling because the cheese is savoury enough.

- It can last up to a week if covered with cling film and refrigerated.

Variations

- Onion and basil (finely chop 1 leek, 1 red onion, 1 white onion and stir fry in sunflower oil until soft but not golden. Add a small handful of finely chopped basil to soften at the last minute. Then mix with the ricotta, yoghurt and cheddar and proceed as above)

- Smoked salmon and fennel

- Sun dried tomatoes and basil

- Leek finely chopped and stir fried until softened

- Different types of cheese with some marjoram

- Spice it up with chilli flakes.

Curried Nut Roast
Hilary Leek

Serves 4

225g hazelnuts, brazil nuts or walnuts, finely chopped

2 medium onions

1 medium pepper (preferably green), de-seeded and finely chopped

Cooking oil

75g (3oz) whole-wheat breadcrumbs

1 clove garlic, crushed

1 teaspoon dried or 2 teaspoons chopped fresh mixed herbs e.g. thyme, sage, parsley

1 tablespoon mild curry powder or 1 teaspoon Madras curry powder

225g (8oz) peeled and chopped tomatoes (I use a tin of chopped tomatoes)

1 egg, beaten

Salt and freshly milled black pepper

Preheat the oven to 220°C/425°F/Gas Mark 7. Use an 18cm (7 inch) square cake tin, greased.

Fry the onions and chopped pepper in a little oil until soft – about 10 minutes.

Meanwhile, mix the nuts and breadcrumbs together in a large bowl, add the garlic, herbs and curry powder. Stir in the onions, pepper and tomatoes, mix very thoroughly and season. Now add the beaten egg to bind the mixture together. Finally, pack the mixture into the prepared tin and bake for 30-40 minutes.

You can serve this with a fresh tomato sauce.

Easy Pizza
Gila Godsi

Makes two thin crust pizzas or one thick crust.

Dough
1 small tub (170g) Greek yoghurt (Total)

250g (9oz) self-raising flour

Pinch of salt

Sauce
Tomato puree/passata

2 teaspoons olive oil

Pinch of oregano

Cheese

10 cherry tomatoes cut in half

10 basil leaves

1 red pepper cut into strips

½ yellow pepper, cut into strips

Courgette sliced into thin strips (with vegetable peeler)

2 cloves garlic, finely sliced

1 red onion cut into thin rings

Preheat the oven (200°C/400°F/Gas Mark 6).

Add the yoghurt to the flour and salt and mix until you get a firm but malleable dough. Let the dough rest for about 15 minutes. Lightly grease a large tray with the oil. Roll out the dough and place on the tray.

Spread the tomato paste and sprinkle with oregano and salt. Place the slices of cheese and then add the vegetables on top. Bake for about 20 minutes.

You can change the toppings and add or take away according to preference. For example, I also added a bit of olive oil to the tomato topping for flavour and left out the garlic.

Quick Carrot and Courgette Pancakes

Claudia Camhi

My friend Mei taught me this easy and versatile recipe. It is a quick snack that goes down well with children as the carrots and courgettes are nicely disguised in a pancake. It is important that the vegetables are finely grated to get the right texture.

Makes 6

1 finely grated carrot

1 finely grated courgette

4 eggs

4 level tablespoons plain flour

1 level teaspoon baking powder

1 level teaspoon Chinese 5 Spice (sold in most supermarkets)

Salt to taste

1 tablespoon sunflower oil for frying the pancakes

In a bowl whisk the whole eggs, Chinese spice, salt, flour and baking powder. Add the courgette and carrot to this mix.

Lightly oil a 13-15cm (5-6 inch) non-stick frying pan and heat.

Add a ladle of this mix and fry on both sides as you would a plain pancake. It just takes about 2 minutes on one side and a minute or less on the other side.

Serve straight away. They can be reheated in the microwave.

Serve as a snack cut into wedges or grate cheese over and roll up before serving.

Courgette Bake

Claudia Camhi

My mother Patricia whisked up this recipe on a recent visit to London and it was truly amazing. A good way to get children to eat greens.

5 courgettes

1 onion

2 eggs

250g (9oz) pot of ricotta

250g (9oz) pot of mascarpone

50g (2oz) grated cheddar

Salt and pepper to taste

2 tablespoons sunflower oil

Preheat the oven to 200°C/400°F/Gas Mark 6.

Wash, dry and grate the courgettes. Place them in a bowl and microwave them for 4 minutes. Place the courgettes in a sieve and squeeze out the excess fluid.

Chop the onion into small cubes and stir fry in sunflower oil until lightly golden. In a separate bowl mix the ricotta, mascarpone, eggs, salt and pepper. Then add the onion and courgettes.

Oil a baking dish and place the mix in it. Top with the grated cheddar.

Bake for 40 minutes or until the top layer looks golden.

This will keep refrigerated, covered in cling film and can be reheated.

Grandma Freda's Braised Chestnut and Mushroom Pie

Stella Mason

This is a family favourite that my mother Freda made. Many of you may remember her when she moved to the area in her last years. Her grandchildren loved to visit her in Eastbourne and it was her great pleasure to cook for them. This pie was enjoyed not only by my sons but their friends who thought it a great treat to be invited to visit Grandma Freda by the seaside. They asked her for the recipe and I received a handwritten script which has remained in my folder for at least 20 years - I never seem to have time to make it! I pass it to you in the hope that you have sufficient time to treat your family.

900g (2lbs) mushrooms

225g (8oz) dried chestnuts

350g (12oz) stoned prunes

4 cloves garlic

2 sweet red onions

2 strong English onions

1 bunch fresh sage

½ bottle red wine

1 egg, beaten

450g (1lb) plain flour

225g (8oz) margarine

190ml (⅓) pint water

Salt and pepper

A pinch of sugar

20cm (8 inch) loose bottom cake tin lined

Soak the prunes and chestnuts overnight in separate containers.

The next day, drain the chestnuts and place in a covered casserole with a little water and half the wine. Add a pinch of sugar, a little salt and black pepper. Cover and cook in a slow oven until fairly soft. Then chop coarsely.

Stew prunes until plump, then drain and chop. Wipe and thickly slice the mushrooms. Chop two cloves of garlic. Melt 25g (1oz) margarine in a heavy bottomed saucepan over a low heat. Add the garlic and cook for a couple of minutes. Add the mushrooms, cover and cook slowly for 15 minutes.

Peel the onions and cut each onion in two long lengthwise slices and sweat with remaining garlic in 25g (1oz) of margarine. When softened, add the sage and remaining wine and simmer for 10 minutes.

Melt 175g (6oz) margarine with the water. Sift the flour with 1 teaspoon of salt. Make a well in the middle, pour the hot water and melted margarine in and work together, kneading lightly. Line the tin with the pastry, reserving some for the top of the pie.

Place a layer of mushrooms over the base of the lined tin. Then add a layer of chestnuts, a layer of onions and a layer of prunes. Repeat the layers and fill the pie shell up ending with a layer of mushrooms. Roll out the remaining dough and cover the pie, sealing the edges with egg beaten with a tablespoon of water. Use trimming to decorate. Brush the top with egg. Cut an inch across the pastry in the centre and fold back the cut.

Bake at 200°C/400°F/Gas Mark 6 for 1 hour. Brush with egg again and cook for a further 15 minutes.

Seven Veg Tagine

Alethea Cooper

Serves 8

This tagine was very well received by the adults at a recent Friday night Young Family Shabbat meal. See if you can adapt the veggies to include those the children like - no reason why they shouldn't enjoy it too.

1 tablespoon olive oil

2 onions, cut into thin wedges

3 garlic cloves, thinly sliced

½ teaspoon paprika

1 teaspoon ground cumin

½ teaspoon ground ginger

1 large cinnamon stick

Grated rind and juice of 1 orange

1 teaspoon Harissa paste

4 carrots, cut into chunky matchsticks

450g (1lb) small, tender okra (can use green beans instead)

1 small butternut squash (about 450g/1lb) peeled and cut into chunks

450g (1lb) turnips (trimmed and cut into wedges)

800ml (1½ pints) hot veg stock

2 x 400g (14oz) tinned plum tomatoes

3 tablespoons tomato puree

4 tablespoons clear honey

2 x 400g (14oz) cans chickpeas, drained

250g (9oz) pack ready to eat prunes

15g (½oz) fresh coriander, chopped

Seasoning

Heat oil in the base of a large heavy based pan (large enough to take all the ingredients) and fry onions over low heat for 5-6 minutes. Add garlic, paprika, cumin, ginger and cinnamon stick and cook, stirring for 2 minutes. Stir in orange rind and juice, Harissa paste, carrots, okra, squash, turnips, stock, tomatoes and tomato puree. Bring to the boil and simmer, uncovered for 25 minutes.

Then stir in the honey, chickpeas and prunes. Bring back to the boil and simmer for 15 minutes. Discard cinnamon stick. Stir in coriander and season to taste.

Best served with couscous to soak up the juices.

Tzimmes

Miriam Edelman

As far as I can tell, anything that is a baked mixture of at least two vegetables qualifies as tzimmes. This is the traditional tzimmes in my Russian/Romanian Ashkenazi family, and one of my favourite foods.

5 sweet potatoes

500g (1lb) carrots - about 4 large

2 tablespoons butter

1 tablespoon flour (optional, runnier without)

1 teaspoon lemon juice

1-4 tablespoons liquid (orange juice, water from boiling carrots, other)

100g (½ cup) brown sugar

Fruits: 750g raisins, sultanas, prunes, figs, apricots; fresh or tinned plums; apples

Boil the sweet potatoes in their jackets until just al dente, not soft. Cool, peel, cut into chunks.

Peel carrots, cut into chunks, and boil until al dente. Set aside to cool.

In a large baking dish, make a paste of the butter and brown sugar, and flour if using. Add lemon juice and liquid to make a runny, slightly thick gravy. Add the fruit and stir to coat. Add sweet potatoes and carrots; mix.

Bake at 180C/350F/Gas Mark 4 for 30 minutes. Serve warm or cold.

Easy Roasted Vegetables

Wendy Levy

This is one of my favourite recipes and is loved by all the family. It is so easy to throw together and once in the oven you can, almost, forget about it while you get on with something else.

Serves 2-4

1 red pepper

1 yellow pepper

2 red onions

Half a butternut squash

2 or 3 large potatoes

2 tablespoons pine nuts (optional)

4 tablespoons olive oil

3 tablespoons soya sauce (optional)

Crushed clove of garlic

Rosemary/garlic/salt mix from Waitrose

(or 1 teaspoon garlic powder or granules, 2 stems fresh rosemary or 1 teaspoon dried rosemary and ½ teaspoon salt)

Salt and pepper

Preheat the oven to 200°C/400°F/Gas Mark 6.

Chop the peppers, onion, butternut squash and unpeeled potatoes into chunky pieces and place in a large baking dish. Drizzle with the olive oil and mix in the garlic, herbs, salt and pine nuts. Mix together and bake for 60 minutes. Remember to stir/turn every 20 minutes. Only add soya sauce half way through. Leaving uncovered in oven while baking will allow the vegetables to crisp (my preference), otherwise cover with foil if you want a 'softer' bake. Drizzle evenly and mix through.

Plaice Fillets with Smoked Salmon

Lynne Sidkin

When I married and left home - nearly 30 years ago - I started a recipe book with favourites that my mother would cook and also cuttings of very simple recipes I thought I would like to try. The book is now full and so well-used that it is held together by a rubber band! It contains this very straightforward recipe that has become a firm favourite at supper parties.

Serves 4

4 skinned plaice fillets

170g (6oz) smoked salmon

40g (1½oz) butter/margarine

40g (1½oz) plain flour

150ml (¼ pint) dry white wine

300ml (½ pint) milk

3 tablespoons single cream

1 tablespoon lemon juice

Salt and pepper

Sprinkle the fillets with salt and pepper. Place a layer of smoked salmon on what would have been the 'skin side' of each fillet. Roll up loosely towards the tail end and place in a lightly greased shallow dish.

Melt the butter or margarine and stir in the flour. Cook for one minute. Gradually add the wine, followed by the milk and keep stirring until sauce thickens. Remove the pan from the heat and stir in the cream and lemon juice. Pour over the fish, cover the dish with foil and cook at 160°C fan oven/300°F/Gas Mark 3 for 50 minutes.

This can be prepared during the day up till the baking stage, refrigerated and cooked in the evening. I serve it with baby new potatoes and a 'medley' of different coloured vegetables.

Lorna's Fish Pie
Lorna Cohen

A sociable standby that can be prepared fresh or frozen for a last minute get together: this is a much loved creation that has evolved over the years in the Cohen family household.

Accompany with a deliciously dressed salad of nuts, avocado, crisp red pepper and salad leaves.

I have served this to all the North and South Londoners who came to my son's Aufruf in January 2011 on a wonderful snowy Shabbat. It is not a specifically Jewish recipe but Jewish in a way that helps the hosts feel relaxed and able to look after their guests and not have to jump up and down with serving vegetables etc. It's warm, never the same twice and nourishing.

Serves approximately 6

Approximately 1 kg good fresh fish e.g. salmon, cod, haddock or maybe a slice of smoked haddock (not the artificially dyed).

Knob of butter

1 teaspoon milk or substitute

400g (14oz) grated cheese e.g. cheddar, Lancashire, Cheshire

½ a celeriac

2 medium sized potatoes

1 parsnip

1 turnip or swede if preferred

Optional: You can add a few mushrooms or a few leaves of spinach to the fish but make sure you drain off all liquid before adding the puree of root vegetables

Cook root vegetables and blend together with salt, pepper and a little butter or milk so it's a smooth lumpless consistency.

Cook fish in a 30 x 20 x 6 cm (12 x 8 x 2.2 inch) dish for 5 minutes in heated oven (140°C/275°F/Gas Mark 1) with butter and milk so that it is undercooked. Take out and sprinkle on half the grated cheese.

Put the puree on top of the fish and the rest of the grated cheese and cook for approximately 15 minutes at a much higher temperature (approximately 180°C/350°F/Gas Mark 4) and, if desired, grill for last 3 minutes to brown the top.

Take out and serve, piping hot, with a green vegetable or salad.

Yoghurt Coriander Fish
Claudia Camhi

Yoghurt is one of the ingredients that Sephardic Jews took from their stay in Turkey. My mother Patricia makes this recipe as a quick, original and easy way to infuse the summer flavours into a fish dish. Our summer lunches are usually relaxed, outdoors and informal and this plate is a favourite one of her staple buffet of salads, sides and fish. It allows plenty of hands-free time to enjoy the company of the grandchildren without having to pay too much attention to preparation.

Serves 8-10

2 large salmon fillets or other mild tasting white fish

1 generous bunch of chopped fresh coriander leaves

2 tablespoons of Dijon mustard

500g (1lb 1oz) pot plain yoghurt (not fat free)

Salt and pepper to taste

1 tablespoon sunflower oil

Preheat the oven to 200°C/400°F/Gas Mark 6.

Oil a ceramic baking container and lay the salmon fillets in it. Season with salt and pepper. Cover with aluminium foil and cook in the oven until 5 minutes before it is ready (approximately 20 minutes).

Prepare a yoghurt mix by blending the Dijon mustard, yoghurt and coriander with an electric blender (the hand held one used to puree baby food works very well).

Remove the foil and cover with the yoghurt mix. Bake for 5 more minutes. Once bathed in the yoghurt sauce and placed back in the oven the sauce will take on a flan-like consistency.

Serve hot.

It goes well served with rice or potatoes. Do not overcook to avoid the fish and the sauce getting too dry.

Gefilte Fish (Fish Cakes)
Estelle Lerner

Makes 14 – 15 cakes

675g (1lb 8oz) fish

    450g (1lb) skinned cod or haddock

    225g (8oz) herring or mackerel filleted but not skinned

    (or other fish e.g. salmon)

2 eggs

2 onions

2 tablespoons matzah meal

Generous bunch parsley

½ cup water

Salt and pepper

Cut up onion and mince (or chop) in a food processor. Add fish, cut into cubes, chopped parsley and mince together. Add other ingredients. Be careful not to over-mince fish. It should not be mushy.

Allow to stand at least 20 minutes. Mixture should be soft enough to form into cakes or patties. You may need to add more water or matzah meal.

Put 1 or 2 tablespoons of matzah meal on greaseproof paper and turn each cake in it.

Put enough oil in a frying pan to cover a third the depth of a fishcake. When hot add fishcakes and cook 16 – 18 minutes in gently bubbling oil until golden brown.

To freeze, place uncooked fishcakes on cling film on tray or plate. When frozen put in plastic bag. When needed place on cling film and thaw, preferably overnight in fridge, before proceeding.

Rosie's Fried Fish
Adele Lazarus

Adele came across the Wimshul Cooks blog because her son who works in the food industry read Rabbi Sybil's blog article on Heston Blumenthal and thought it would amuse her. She was inspired to send us her prized family recipe for fried fish which we are very pleased to include here.

Everyone's mother, let alone buba, makes the best fried fish. I must, however, make a special plea for my late mother's fish. Mum was a self-taught, adventurous cook and every important Yomtov was marked, not only by her delicious baking, but by her superlative fish. I was her faithful tweeny who was permitted to assist over many years. Now my sister and I try very hard to replicate and almost succeed in achieving the impossible, Rosie's fried fish.

About 1kg (2-3lbs) hake (whole fish)

About 700g (1 ½ lbs) haddock fillets

6 medium eggs (3 eggs plus 3 egg yolks to every 3lb or 1 kg 350g of fish)

1 medium to large onion

3 tablespoons medium and fine matzah meal, mixed

1 tablespoon ground almonds

Just under 1 teaspoon salt

1 teaspoon sugar to each pound (450g) of fish

2 pinches white pepper

Keep some old but not burnt oil from previous frying of fish. Any jar does. This forms the basis of oil you fry the fish in.

Mince the fillets and flesh from the hake together. I use a plastic washing up bowl, kept for the purpose. Weigh the fish.

Chop the onion in a Magimix. Spread in a thin layer over the top of the fish. Add seasoning and sugar. Mix in with a large spoon or by hand. Mix the fine and medium matzah meal together. Mix into fish mixture. Add 1 egg and 1 yolk to every pound (450g) of fish. Add the ground almonds. Mix everything together by hand, very thoroughly. This takes a few minutes.

If making for Pesach you can't use a cube of bread to test the oil's heat. Instead take a small frying pan, put in 2 tablespoons of the old oil heat and fry a very small ball of fish. Remove when brown. You are testing for seasoning and flavour. You might need more salt, sugar, or more matzah meal if too soft. Mixture should be firmish. Add more to the bowl of fish you have taken the small ball from. Mix again.

Now make the balls by rolling some fish about the size of walnuts between your wetted hands. Or more fish if you want bigger balls. You must keep wetting your hands. Dry hands make it impossible to roll the sticky fish mixture. Put all the balls on a large tray at the side of your hob.

To fry the fish: you need two decent frying pans with 5cm (2 inch) high sides, two spatulas, two knives, a roll of kitchen paper, a large tray with a double layer of kitchen paper across all of it and a large bottle of either sunflower oil or corn oil.

Pour some old oil in each pan. Add 4cms of oil to each pan. Heat on medium heat 3 to 4 minutes until it starts to make a noise! Try out by putting in a small fishball in each pan. Don't overcrowd the pan. Put a few fishballs in each pan. Cook until rich brown on one side and using a knife / spatula carefully turn over. Cook again till a rich brown then carefully remove with slotted spoon/spatula. Place on the tray with kitchen paper. Keep replacing with raw fishballs until all have been fried. You will need to replace the kitchen paper if it gets too oily. Leave the oil to cool before disposing of it.

Tips

- 5lb (2kg 300g) of fish would be enough for 2 average families.
- 6lb (2kg 700g) of fish = approximately 80 medium fish balls.
- Close doors, open windows
- Scarf over hair (optional) - Mum never did but always wore a 'pinny'!
- Don't prepare in advance, it makes for wet fish.
- Freezes very well. Freeze in portions.
- It takes almost all morning!

Fish Cakes

Josie Knox

For the girl who doesn't like fish, except for these...

I usually use half ordinary white fish (pollack or coley are fine) and half salmon (for oily fish benefits) but you can use whatever mixture you like.

Makes around 12 and serves 2 to 3 per person

500g (1lb 1oz) fish filleted, skinned and cut into small chunks (keep white and salmon separate)

1 medium or large egg

Juice of 1 lemon

Parsley, large handful

Medium matzah meal

Salt and pepper

Sunflower or other bland oil for frying

Put the white fish (or half if you are using all the same fish) in a food processor with the egg, lemon juice and parsley and blitz until it is a paste and the parsley is chopped very finely. The mixture will be quite wet. Add the salmon or other half of the fish and pulse so that the chunks are broken up but can still be seen clearly in the mixture. Add salt and pepper if wanted.

Tip into a large bowl and add matzah meal to bind together and reduce the wetness. I usually do this by eye but try approximately 5 to 6 tablespoons. You want enough to bind the mixture but not so much that it makes the cakes hard or dry. Allow to stand for a few minutes to allow the matzah meal to absorb some of the moisture. You can always add a bit more matzah meal at this stage if it's still very wet.

Divide the mixture into 12 and form into patties. Coat them with matzah meal and shallow fry in the oil on a medium heat for 4 to 5 minutes each side until golden brown. Then drain on kitchen paper.

(You could deep fry but I find these cook just fine in shallow oil. There may be a paler ring around the sides of the patties but they will still be cooked through.) Serve hot, warm or at room temperature.

These are at their lightest and best when eaten on the day of cooking, however they will keep in the fridge for a couple of days or can be frozen and reheated.

Mixed Ecuadorian Ceviche (Fish Marinated in Lemon and Lime Juice)

Francisco Conesa

Francisco, who has been working at the synagogue for over seven years, is also a professional chef trained in the UK and has several years of experience working in restaurants. His training focused on French cuisine but he is sharing with us a typical Ecuadorian dish of his homeland, perfect for summer.

Serves 4

200g (7oz) sea-bass fillet, skinned and cut into 1.5 cm by 1.5 cm pieces

250g (9oz) salmon fillet, skinned and cut into 1.5 cm by 1.5 cm pieces

Juice from two lemons and two limes

½ a finely sliced red onion, salted for a few minutes and rinsed in running cold water

A handful chopped coriander

1 skinned and finely diced tomato

1 tomato liquefied and passed through the sieve

100g (4oz) sliced, fried and salted plantain (sold in health stores)

2 finely sliced red chillies

A dash of olive oil

Salt and pepper to taste

Place the diced fish in a serving bowl. Add the lemon and lime juice. Cover with cling film and refrigerate for 1½ hours. Just before serving remove from the refrigerator and add all the rest of the ingredients except for the plantain that should be sprinkled on top at the last minute.

Spanish Chicken Casserole
Camilla McGill

Adapted from Evelyn Rose

Serves 6-8 people

2 large onions

1 fat clove garlic

2 red peppers

2 large carrots

6-8 skinless chicken thighs but chicken breasts fine too

1 heaped tablespoon flour seasoned with 2 teaspoons paprika and 15 grinds black pepper

5 tablespoons olive oil

1 carton (500g) passata (sieved tomatoes)

1 tablespoon sun dried tomatoes or tomato puree

100-150ml (3 ½ - 5 fl oz) chicken stock (from a cube or fresh)

150ml (5 fl oz) fruity red wine

2 teaspoons dark brown sugar

1 teaspoon salt

15 grinds black pepper

125g (4½oz) green or black pitted olives

225g (8oz) or 1 cup frozen petit pois

Preheat the oven to 180°C/350°F/Gas Mark 4.

Prepare the vegetables: Finely chop the onion and garlic. Cut peppers into 1.25cm (½ inch) squares (roughly). Peel and cut carrots in long strips lengthways and then across to make very small dice.

Dip the chicken thighs in the seasoned flour which you put on a plate. Heat 3 tablespoons of olive oil in a large frying pan to a medium-high heat. Brown the chicken pieces on both sides for about 2-3 minutes each side. Lift out of the pan and arrange in a roasting tin that leaves some room around the edge for the sauce.

Add some more olive oil to the frying pan (approximately 2 tablespoons). Cook the onion slowly on a fairly low heat for about 20 minutes so it is soft and sweet. Add the garlic and cook 3-4 minutes more. Then turn up the heat to medium and add 300ml (½ pint) passata – you can always add more later if you think you need it, add tomato puree or sundried tomato paste, red peppers, carrots, stock, sugar, red wine, pepper grinds and salt. Simmer uncovered on a low heat for about 20 minutes till the carrots are quite soft and the mixture is thick and juicy. Then pour into the roasting tin so that the sauce half-covers the chicken thighs. It might need a little more stock to make sure they are covered enough.

Cover the roasting tin tightly with foil and bake for about 30 minutes – half way through you can open up the foil and pour some of the sauce from the edge on top of the thighs. In the meantime, cook the frozen petit pois for a short time till almost cooked. Uncover the chicken after 30 minutes and add the olives and the petit pois and cook for a further 10-15 minutes.

Nice served with tagliatelle or rice and a green salad. Enjoy.

Wok Fried Honey Soy Chicken
Jacky Schmid

This is a very quick, tasty and easy recipe that I use when I have been out with the kids and they are hungry so need something that takes under 10 minutes to prepare. Always popular with them.

Chicken Breasts

Soy sauce

Sesame seeds (generous amount)

Runny honey

Carrots

Oil for frying

Rice for however many you are serving

Roughly cut chicken into small cubes and place in a bowl. Add soy sauce, sesame seeds and good dollop of honey so all soaking nicely. Cut carrots into very small cubes. Put rice on (I use the small bags – 3 for 4 kids). Heat oil in the wok. Add chicken mixture and carrots and stir fry in the wok. Make sure the chicken is cooked through.

Put rice on plates and add the chicken mixture on top.

You can prepare the chicken mix and cover and leave in fridge whilst out. If oil is hot enough the honey will start caramelizing, which my kids like!

Be careful - the sesame seeds can spit out of the wok whilst cooking.

Yummy Sesame Chicken Schnitzel

Jacky Schmid

This recipe is from my friend Emily Schwartz who I grew up with and is the sister of Jeremy Cohen, a Wimshul member. A delicious alternative to chicken nuggets.

Chicken Breasts
Matzah meal
Sesame Seeds
Seasoning
Beaten Egg
Oil to fry
Humous

Roughly cut chicken breasts into 3-4 pieces. Lay on cling film on chopping board with space in between and cover with cling film. With a rolling pin or something similar bash out the chicken until it is evenly thinned.

Mix the dry ingredients and place on a plate. Dip chicken into egg and then in the dry ingredients until coated.

Fry in oil about 3 minutes on each side but check it is cooked through. Dry excess oil off on kitchen roll.

Serve with humous, delicious to dip in.

The thinner the chicken the nicer it is. Make sure the oil is hot when you place the chicken in it so it seals and crisps the coating.

Chicken in Vegetable Sauce

Ellen Sheridan

6 chicken thighs and breast

1 leek

2 peppers (any colours)

150g (5 fl oz) double concentrated tomato puree (about half a tube)

1 tablespoon olive oil

1 teaspoon brown sugar

1-3 teaspoons Worcester sauce

1 tablespoon lemon juice

½ teaspoon English mustard (optional)

Optional spices – chilli, garlic, thyme, sage

Preheat the oven to 180°C (with fan)/400°F/Gas Mark 6.

Mix finely chopped leek and finely chopped peppers in a pan and sauté lightly for a few minutes with a small amount of olive oil. Add about half a litre of water with the tomato puree. Add brown sugar, Worcester sauce (makes it spicy, to taste), lemon juice and English mustard (optional). Add optional spices. Simmer for 5-10 minutes (avoid heavy boiling, the longer it simmers the nicer).

Place skinned chicken thighs and breasts in a baking dish. Spoon over the vegetable mix. Cover the dish and cook for an hour to an hour and a half. Take off the cover towards the end (last 15 minutes).

Chicken Paprika

Nick Parish

This is a staple Friday night dish in our house.

1 chicken in eight pieces

100g (3½oz) Tomor

1 onion, chopped

1½ - 2 tablespoons paprika

1 tablespoon flour

400ml (¾ pint) chicken stock

1 tablespoon tomato purée

150ml (5 fl oz) non-dairy cream

Lemon juice to taste (approximately ⅓ lemon)

Season chicken. Melt Tomor in large frying pan/casserole and fry onion until translucent. Add paprika and then chicken, and cook slowly until chicken is golden. Sprinkle chicken with flour, add stock and tomato purée and stir well. Cover, bring to boil and simmer for 20 minutes. Add cream and lemon juice, stir well and cook for five minutes more without boiling.

Sweet and Sour Meatballs

Sally Lewis

This is based on a recipe by Claudia Roden from her classic, *The Book of Jewish Food*.

These are good served hot with steamed rice or potato kugel and can also be eaten cold. I haven't met a soul yet who hasn't liked them.

1 large onion sliced

4 tablespoons sunflower oil

3 garlic cloves, crushed

800g (1lb 12oz) chopped tomato (Cirio are the best)

Juice of 1 lemon

3 tablespoons brown sugar

4 ginger biscuits

1kg (2lb 3oz) minced beef

1 medium onion grated

Fry the sliced onion in the oil until golden, then add the garlic and stir until only very slightly coloured otherwise the sauce tastes bitter. Add the tomatoes, salt, pepper, lemon juice and sugar. It is best to add the sugar first and then gradually add the lemon juice until you get the correct sweet and sour balance. Break the ginger biscuits into the sauce. Simmer for about 15-20 minutes until the sauce is very thick.

Mix the meat with the grated onion and salt and pepper and work to a paste with your hands. If you have a Magimix you can chop the onion as finely as possible, then sit the mince on top in two batches and pulse until mixed, being careful not to over process. This is much quicker.

Roll into 2.5cm (1 inch) balls and drop into the sauce. They will produce a lot of liquid so if your sauce is very thick to start with you will have a richer and tastier sauce at the end.

Cook on a very low heat for at least 1½ hours. I do mine in the oven (180°C/350°F/Gas Mark 4) with the lid half on and turn the meatballs half way through the cooking time. Depending on the thickness of your sauce you can cook them uncovered for the last half hour. If necessary you can always add a little more water. Cook until they are slightly browned.

They are especially good and tender if you add about 25% cooked beef from a leftover roast which you mince in the magmix and then add to the uncooked mince prior to forming into balls.

For a variation I often add a couple of tablespoons of chopped coriander to the meat mix.

Bell Peppers Stuffed with Beef and Rice

Victoria Druyan-Newman

This is one of my favourite Russian dishes from my childhood (at least one that doesn't take four hours to cook).

7-8 medium bell peppers of any colour, preferably with flat bottoms

500g (1 lb 1oz) lean ground beef

⅔ cup rice

1 onion

1 carrot

1 tablespoon vegetable oil

1 teaspoon salt

½ teaspoon ground black pepper (optional, to taste)

About 600-700ml (21-24 fl oz) of liquid tomato passata (can add a bit of sun dried tomato paste for a stronger taste)

1 tablespoon paprika

2 bay leaves

Pour hot water over the rice and let it soak for 2 hours.

Core and seed bell peppers. If they cannot stand on their own, cut small slivers off the bottom part of the pepper taking care not to make a hole in the bottom.

Dice the onion. Peel and grate the carrot using a coarse grater. Add enough oil to a frying pan to cover the bottom, add onions and carrots and sauté on medium-high stirring often, until onions are soft and golden. Drain on a paper towel.

In a large bowl, mix beef, rice, carrot and onion mixture, salt, and pepper. Stuff peppers with the mixture. Stand stuffed peppers upright in a large pot making sure they don't fall on their sides.

In a saucepan, mix tomato passata, paprika, and two cups of boiling hot water.

Pour enough sauce over stuffed peppers to just cover their tops. If there is not enough sauce, add more hot water to the pot to make sure that peppers are covered. Add bay leaves.

Place pot on the stove and heat it up on high quickly until the sauce is almost boiling, then turn the heat down to medium low. Cover pot with lid and simmer for 45 minutes.

Michael's Rice Recipe

Judith Ish-Horowicz

My sister Ruth's long term partner, Michael Goldberg came from Israel to see my mother recently, visiting her every day, spending many hours with her and staying with me. Already having a houseful, I was really appreciative when he offered to prepare his 'renowned rice' with its magic ingredient, a drop of wine. It was delicious and, having persuaded him to cook it again for our 18 Shabbat dinner guests, he has now given us the recipe, but I'm not sure he'll want to stay with us on his next trip!

1 cup rice

1 onion chopped

1 teaspoon salt

½ teaspoon turmeric

2 cups water, including small amount of wine (white or red)

Oil

Rinse the rice well in a strainer and allow to dry. Heat oil in a saucepan, add onion, fry until it starts to brown. Add rice, stir fry for about 5 minutes. Add salt and turmeric, stirring well. Add water and wine, stir well, cover pan and bring to boil.

Turn the heat low and simmer for 20 minutes. Do not open pot and do not stir.

Check that rice is cooked, remove from stove and allow to stand for 5-10 minutes.

My Dinner with Heston Blumenthal
Rabbi Sybil A. Sheridan

It all started when I was invited to the New Israel Fund dinner. Amos Oz was speaking. Excitedly I told my husband about it, confident that we would both be going.

"Sorry," he said, "I have invited Heston Blumenthal for dinner."

"Are you mad?"

"No. He is giving a talk at Maidenhead Synagogue and we always entertain the speaker beforehand and he is the one person I simply can't take to a restaurant. You will have to cook." (Feminists please note: no suggestion that he might wield a saucepan for the occasion.)

I was not happy. Firstly it meant missing the NIF dinner, secondly… What on earth was I to cook? I enjoy spending time in the kitchen, but my repertoire is limited to the things that four growing boys consume. Potatoes mostly. I complained volubly to all my friends. "Keep it simple," they all advised. "Don't try and impress." "Cook something Jewish. I bet he doesn't get that often."

That was a good idea.

I looked at my ancient copy of Evelyn Rose. Given to me by my mother-in-law Gabrielle Romain on our engagement, with the inscription "To my future daughter-in-law whose husband will never say, 'It's not as good as my mother made it.'"

I began to get quite excited, but I wasn't going to let my husband off that easily. Whenever he mentioned the dinner, I would groan and mutter. I had Heder and the Synagogue AGM that day. We had invited my niece and nephew aged 8 and 12 to stay for the Friday and Saturday before. When exactly did he think I would find the time to cook?

But in my head the menu was beginning to take shape. I would use the last of the vegetables in our new organic vegetable patch. We had marrow and onions, parsnips and a few runner beans – I could make quite a tasty soup with that. Then, I thought, slices of prime bola the way my grandmother-in-law Cecily Harding made it, with lemon peel, braised in the slow cooker all day. I would cook tsimmes and maybe the kids would have fun making dumplings.

I pondered over a dessert. Here, Wimshul Cooks came to the rescue with wonderful recipes. I was offered homemade biscotti to have with the coffee, and a very special honey cake. I realised that had I played it differently I could probably have had the whole meal cooked for me!

Then, one morning over breakfast, my husband looked at me cheerfully.

"I have good news," he said, "Heston is not coming for dinner."

"What?"

"He is filming that afternoon and is not sure what time he could get to us so I told him not to worry about dinner, just turn up for the talk."

"WHAT?"

"I knew you would be relieved. That's a whole load of stress off your mind."

"But I enjoyed the stress. I enjoyed the challenge."

"I'm confused. I thought you would be pleased."

"Pleased? Don't you realise what a great anecdote this has made? Now you've gone and spoiled it!"

How could he do this to me? Men! I just don't understand them!

Oma's Braised Beef

My grandmother-in-law, like many of her generation, did not believe in measurements, hence the vagueness of the recipe but it is so easy and it does work.

Slices of prime bola – one per person
Flour and seasoning
A little oil
An onion
Beef stock
Bay leaf
Juice and zest of a lemon

Peel and slice the onion then fry it in the oil until soft and golden. Transfer to a casserole dish. Cover the slices of prime bola in seasoned flour and fry quickly on both sides. Transfer to the dish and cover with the beef stock, add the bay leaf and lemon and cook for a long time in a low oven.

Mushroom Spelt Risotto
Heston Blumenthal

Chef Heston Blumenthal has kindly contributed this recipe to our cookbook. His website describes his route to the top as "an unconventional one, involving rule-breaking, unusual experiments and an exploding oven".

Herbs and acidulated butter contribute their flavours to this risotto, which can also be used as a side dish. One of the key ingredients here is dried shiitake mushrooms, which are especially rich in the umami taste. It's worth having some in your store cupboard, so that you can add them to any dish where you want to enhance a mushroom flavour.

Serves 4

For the risotto

50g dried shiitake mushrooms

750g vegetable stock

15g groundnut or grapeseed oil

100g peeled and finely chopped shallot (approx. 2 large banana shallots)

4 cloves of garlic, peeled and finely chopped

200g pearled spelt

15g unsalted butter

200g button mushrooms, finely sliced

30g whipping cream

50g mascarpone

To finish and serve

60g acidulated butter

40g parmesan cheese, grated

5g parsley leaves

5g tarragon leaves

Salt and black pepper

Put the dried shiitake mushrooms into a saucepan with the vegetable stock and place over a high heat. Bring to the boil and allow to boil for 5 minutes. Remove the pan from the heat and allow to infuse for 30 minutes before straining into a clean pan. Set the mushrooms aside and gently warm the stock for using in the risotto.

Heat half the oil in a clean wide-bottomed saucepan over a medium heat and sweat the shallot and garlic (approximately 7–10 minutes). Remove when soft but not coloured and set aside.

Heat the remaining oil in the same saucepan, then add the spelt and toast over a medium-high heat for 3–4 minutes.

Pour in half of the warmed stock, stir and allow to cook for 10 minutes. Continue adding stock one ladle at a time until the spelt is tender and all the liquid has been absorbed.

In the meantime, melt the unsalted butter in a small frying pan over a medium-high heat. When foaming, add the button mushrooms and cook until caramelized in colour (approximately 10 minutes).

Add the caramelized mushrooms, shallots, garlic, cream and mascarpone to the spelt and cook for a further 4–5 minutes, stirring regularly.

Stir in the acidulated butter and, once melted, add the Parmesan and remove from the heat. Allow to rest for 3 minutes.

Roughly chop the herbs. Season the risotto with salt and freshly ground pepper and add the chopped parsley and tarragon just before serving.

Acidulated Butter

100g peeled and sliced onion

185g dry white wine

300g white wine vinegar

250g unsalted butter, cubed

Boil the onion, wine and vinegar over high heat until reduced by three quarters. Whisk the butter through the liquid, leave to infuse for twenty minutes, then strain. Roll into a log and wrap in baking paper. Keeps for a week in the fridge or a month in the freezer.

Chicken with Garlic Potatoes and Rosemary
Andrew Earis

I first began playing the organ at Wimbledon Synagogue for Shabbat services around 15 years ago, whilst I was a student at Imperial College and the Royal College of Music. This was just after the move from Worple Road to Queensmere Road, when the Synagogue was still a building site! A few years after that I became Director of Music and took over the running of the Synagogue Choir, on the retirement of Raph Gonley. In 2009 I became Director of Music at St Martin-in-the-Fields in Trafalgar Square where I run all of the church music and concerts programme – over 1000 events each year! I still come back to Shul once or twice a month to play the organ, and to see all of the great friends I have made over the years.

8 chicken thighs

800g (1lb 12oz) baby new potatoes, halved

2 cloves garlic, thinly sliced

2 tablespoons fresh rosemary leaves

2 tablespoons olive oil

Preheat oven to 240°C/220°C fan/475°F/Gas Mark 9. Cut two deep slashes through skin and flesh of chicken to the bone. Place chicken and potato in large, heavy-based flameproof baking dish. Brush with olive oil, roast, uncovered, 30 minutes. Add garlic and rosemary to dish, roast, uncovered, for a further 10 minutes or until browned.

Serve with a mixed salad.

Flory Solomon's Indian Selection
Nina Portugal

I am really delighted to be able to contribute these family recipes passed down by my mum Flory Solomon. Flory was from Bombay and these recipes are just some of the traditional dishes that would be made for Shabbat, festivals and family dinners. For Flory, preparing food was a symbol of love and affection. She took pride in making new dishes for family and friends and enjoyed holding 'Indian cookery' classes in the Shul as well as several Kiddushim. I hope you enjoy these recipes as much as we do.

Tomato Bhaji

Serves 4

4 medium onions

7 medium tomatoes

½ level teaspoon red chilli powder

1 level teaspoon turmeric (haldi) powder

1½ level teaspoons sweet paprika

1 level teaspoon coriander powder

1 level teaspoon garlic powder

Salt to taste

Oil for frying

Fresh chopped coriander leaves

Slice onions. Chop tomatoes. Heat oil in wok or frying pan, add sliced onions. Fry till brown. Add the masalas - chilli, turmeric, sweet paprika, coriander and garlic powder. Fry for a minute, then add salt and chopped tomatoes and fry till tomatoes are soft and the juice of the tomatoes has evaporated. Add chopped green coriander leaves, fry for two seconds till it is all mixed in. Serve hot with chappatis, naan or as a side-dish to the main meal.

Potato Bhaji

2 big or 3 medium potatoes

1 big or 2 medium onions

½ level teaspoon red chilli powder

½ level teaspoon turmeric powder

1 level teaspoon garlic powder

1 level teaspoon red sweet paprika

1 level teaspoon coriander powder

2 or 3 medium size tomatoes (optional)

Salt to taste

Oil for frying

A few sprigs of fresh green coriander (optional)

Peel potatoes, cut into small pieces and leave in water till you are ready to use them. Slice onions. Heat the oil in a frying pan and fry onions till light golden brown. Add chopped tomatoes (optional). Add all the masalas (spices), fry for a minute, add salt and the potatoes. Fry again till the potatoes are nicely coated with the masalas. Cover the frying pan. Lower the heat and cook potatoes on a low fire, stirring frequently till potatoes are cooked. Add chopped fresh green coriander (optional). Serve hot with chappatis, rice or as an accompaniment.

Spicy Tuna Fish Cakes

Makes approximately 18. Serve as a starter.

1 can of tuna steaks or chunks in water

2 small potatoes (boiled)

1 small onion (finely chopped)

½ level teaspoon red chilli powder

½ level teaspoon turmeric powder

1 level teaspoon coriander powder

1 level teaspoon red paprika

½ level teaspoon garlic powder

¾ level teaspoon cumin powder

A few sprigs of fresh green coriander (chopped)

¾ level teaspoon mint (optional)

Salt to taste

Oil for shallow frying

1 or 2 eggs (beaten) as required

A little rice flour or make a batter to coat fish cakes

In a bowl put the finely chopped onion with the salt. Crush onion and salt. Add tuna, boiled potatoes and all the above masalas (spices), mash the tuna and potatoes and mix thoroughly, adding the chopped fresh green coriander and mint.

Make flat rectangular small fish cakes, dip in the rice flour and keep aside till you are ready to fry them. Dip fish cakes in the beaten egg and shallow fry till brown.

Spinach Bhaji

Serves 2 to 3

1 packet (250/300g – 9-10oz) fresh spinach

2 large or 3 medium onions

1 small green chilli (chopped)

3 tablespoons desiccated coconut

Salt to taste

Oil

Put the spinach in a bowl, wash, drain and chop.

Heat oil in a saucepan. Slice onion. Add onion and chopped green chilli together with salt. Cover and let the onions cook for 3 minutes till soft. Add chopped spinach and cook for about 8 minutes till all the juice has evaporated. Then add the desiccated coconut, stir for a minute till it is thoroughly blended in with the cooked spinach. Serve with chappatis or pitta bread.

Tuna Fish Curry

Serves 2

1 can tuna steaks or chunks

2 tablespoons tomato puree

A few curry leaves

1 clove fresh garlic (crushed/chopped)

1 teaspoon Kashmiri/Vindaloo paste **or**

½ teaspoon red chilli powder

½ teaspoon turmeric powder

½ teaspoon cumin powder

1 level teaspoon coriander powder

A few sprigs of green coriander (chopped)

2 tablespoons tomato ketchup

Salt to taste

Oil

Heat oil in a saucepan. Add curry leaves and crushed garlic. Cover for a few seconds till garlic is brown (not burnt). Add tomato puree, stir for a minute or so, and then add all the above masalas (spices) except the chopped coriander and tomato ketchup. Add tuna. Stir well till thoroughly coated. Cook for about 4 minutes on a medium heat, then add tomato ketchup and chopped green coriander. Simmer for a few seconds. Serve with rice (khichdi) or any other rice.

Rice with Red Lentils (Khichdi)

Serves 3-4

1 cup basmati or any other rice

¼ cup red lentils

1 medium onion (sliced)

½ teaspoon turmeric powder

½ teaspoon garam masala powder

Oil

Salt to taste

Wash rice and lentils together and leave aside.

Heat oil in a saucepan and fry sliced onions till brown. Add turmeric and garam masala powders, together with salt and stir. Then add washed rice and lentils, stir well till blended with the ingredients. Add 1¾ cups of boiling water. Let it boil, cover with lid, then reduce heat to very low. Let it cook for 20 minutes.

Curried Corn

Serves 2-3

1 can of corn (or frozen corn)

1 medium onion (sliced)

½ teaspoon turmeric powder

1 teaspoon coriander powder

1 level teaspoon garam masala powder

1 heaped teaspoon Green Masala (recipe given in next column)

Coconut cream (cut into 2 small pieces)

Oil

Salt to taste

Few sprigs of fresh green coriander, chopped (optional)

Heat oil in a saucepan. Fry sliced onions till lightly brown. Add the green masala, turmeric and coriander powders and salt. Stir well for about two minutes reducing heat slightly. Then add the corn with a ¼ cup of water, stir well and let it cook for about 8 to 10 minutes on low heat. Add the garam masala powder and coconut cream, mix well till coconut cream has dissolved, then add the fresh coriander (optional). Can be eaten as a side-dish to a main meal or with chappatis, pittas or rice.

Fresh Green Masala

This green masala paste can be used when cooking pulses, mince or green fish curry.

1 bunch fresh green coriander

6 cloves of garlic

2 pieces of ginger

4 green chillies

Chop the above ingredients. Put in liquidiser (adding a little water) or in a mincer till it is like a paste. Use as required. The rest should be kept in the refrigerator or also can be frozen.

Tandoori Chicken

Chicken Pieces (6 to 8)

1 teaspoon garlic powder

3 to 4 teaspoons tandoori masala powder

Salt to taste

For the sauce

2 or 3 tablespoons mayonnaise

2 or 3 tablespoons tomato ketchup

Marinate chicken pieces with garlic powder, salt and tandoori masala powder and cook till tender on slow fire. Cool the cooked chicken, add the mayonnaise and tomato ketchup mix till all the pieces are coated well. It should be dry. Put in the oven to brown, turn chicken pieces so the other side browns. Serve hot.

Curried Chicken

Few pieces of chicken

1 large onion

Tomato (or tin of tomatoes/tomato puree)

¼ teaspoon chilli powder

1 teaspoon coriander powder

½ teaspoon turmeric powder

½ teaspoon garlic powder

Oil

2 teaspoons tomato ketchup

Water

Slice the onion and fry in oil till brown. Chop the tomato and add (or add the tomato puree or tin of chopped tomatoes), then the spices. Add chicken pieces and stir well for a minute, add water and let it cook on a low heat. When cooked add tomato ketchup, stir and serve with rice.

Mince Koftas (Meatballs)

225g (½ lb) minced chicken or beef

1 large onion

½ a tomato

Green Masala

Tamarind pulp

Garlic powder

Coriander powder

Coconut cream

Fresh coriander leaves (kotmir)

Oil

Cut onion finely. Reserve a little, brown the rest in oil. Cut half a tomato and add to the browning onion. Add all the masalas and coconut cream, pour in a little water and let it boil. In the meantime mix the reserved onions with the minced chicken or beef. Break an egg into the mixture. Add green masala, salt, coriander powder. fresh chopped coriander and combine. Form balls and fry them in oil till golden brown. Then add them to the mixture, cover with a lid and let it cook for some time. When cooked and all water is evaporated add the tamarind pulp with a little bit of sugar. Sprinkle some more fresh coriander over the koftas.

Coriander

PUDDINGS, CAKES AND BISCUITS

Blinis

Ludmilla Silverov

This is my mother's recipe and one of her favourite dishes which she would make when I was growing up in the western part of Ukraine. My mother would go to the market in the morning and buy fresh curd cheese (tvorog) homemade by the women of the village (she had her favourite whose curd cheese tasted the best) and of course that made them even tastier.

When I make them they are delicious though not quite as good as my mother's.

Batter

500ml (17 fl oz) milk

4 eggs

2 cups plain flour

2 tablespoons caster sugar

Pinch of salt

A few drops vanilla extract

Knob of butter or sunflower oil for frying

Beat the eggs, sugar and salt in a mixer for a few minutes. Gradually add the milk with the mixer running. Then add the flour gradually mixing with a spoon first and then beating with the mixer attachment until it is smooth. Add the vanilla extract. Leave it to stand for 15-20 minutes.

Before frying the blinis, mix it with a spoon and if you feel that the mixture is a bit thick, add a little bit of water. Then make the pancakes, frying on both sides in a little butter or sunflower oil if you prefer. Place the cooked pancakes on a plate. Then prepare the filling.

Filling

500g (1lb 1oz) tvorog (or other curd cheese), available from Polish shops

2 tablespoons of caster sugar (you can add more or less, to taste)

1 egg yolk

A few drops vanilla extract

Raisins (optional)

Coating

100g (4oz) butter

Combine the filling ingredients well.

Preheat the oven to 160-180°C/350°F/Gas Mark 4. Grease the ovenproof dish (has to be with a lid) with a little butter.

Once all the blinis are fried, fill them by spreading about one tablespoon of the filling on each one, then rolling them up into a cigar shape. I leave them open at the ends.

For the coating, melt the butter. Then brush each filled pancake with melted butter and transfer to a dish, laying them side by side. Then complete another layer perpendicularly.

Once all the blinis are in the dish, cover with a lid and put in the oven for 30 minutes.

Tip

These can be prepared ahead of time. You can then just put the dish with the rolled blinis in the oven half an hour before you want to eat them. You can also bake the dish ahead, cool and refrigerate, then either fry them in the frying pan for a few minutes with a little butter or microwave them. Fried is tastier.

If you can't find curd cheese, you could use cream cheese. In this case, omit the egg yolk.

Betty's Lockshen Pudding

Betty H. Burge

You can't beat Betty's lockshen pudding recipe, with its easy method, and delicious served hot or cold. Betty's pudding has been by far the most popular post of the Wimshul Cooks blog. In fact, at one point, we had TV researchers, who had found Betty's recipe online, knocking on our door wanting to interview Betty about it. Betty knows how to welcome people to the Shabbat service, having handed out prayer books for many years, as well as providing practical support at the Kiddushim afterwards.

It was my mother Ada Samuel's recipe and I am now the only one in the family making lockshen pudding. Need I say more! When I go to the family in Nottingham, two puddings accompany me; when I go to cousins in St Albans, one pudding. I even made one in exchange for some magnet links put on four pieces of my jewellery!

225g (8oz) cooked broad lockshen (I use tagliatelle)

115g (4oz) margarine (shmultz!)

3 beaten eggs

115g (4oz) sugar

115g (4oz) raisins

2 teaspoons cinnamon

Combine all the ingredients and tip into a well-greased 20 x 20 x 5cm (8 x 8 x 2 inches) tin.

Put into 180°C/350°F/Gas Mark 4 oven and cook for 45 minutes. Leave longer if necessary.

Tips

Serve hot or cold as a dessert, or nosh when feeling like it.

This freezes very well.

Chocolate Mousse

Dani Freeman

1½ bars (270g) Bournville chocolate

6 eggs

½ a pat (125g) butter

Break up the chocolate and butter and melt it in the microwave in a microwavable bowl for 2 to 3 minutes or until it is melted.

Separate the eggs to white and yolk. Mix the yolks with the melted chocolate and butter. Whisk the whites until soft peaks form. Mix the whites with the chocolate mixture, cover and put in the fridge.

Two hours later it will be ready.

Chocolate Mousse

Io Epstein

125g (4½oz) bar of chocolate (mixture of whatever you like – I use just dark chocolate if we are eating meat or mix half and half dark and milk if not)

4 eggs

3 teaspoons of caster sugar

A dash of milk (or soy milk if eating after meat)

Break up the chocolate and melt in the microwave. Separate the eggs. Add the yolks to the melted chocolate and beat in. Beat the egg whites till stiff then beat in the sugar. Fold the beaten egg whites into the chocolate mixture and put in the fridge until set (though I often make it at the last minute and stick it in the freezer for a short blast which seems to do just as well). Very easy!

Can keep in the fridge for 3 days.

Chani Smith's Avocado Dessert

Diane Barnett

Chani Smith is the wife of our former Rabbi, Danny Smith. Among her many accomplishments, Chani produced many delicious recipes. Until she gave me this recipe I had not thought of avocados being used in a dessert. The recipe works with medium to large avocados and with or without the liqueur.

2 avocados

⅓ cup caster sugar

1 tablespoon lemon juice and 1 tablespoon liqueur – Cointreau is ideal or 2 tablespoons lemon juice

275ml (¼ pint) double cream (if you want a very creamy result use ½ pint)

Process the avocado, sugar, lemon juice and liqueur, if used, until smooth and lump free. Beat cream until it forms soft peaks and fold into avocado mixture. Cover tightly with cling film and refrigerate.

It is important to cover the dessert tightly with cling film or the dessert will lose its vibrant green colour.

Put into a lined 20cm (8 inch) tin. Sprinkle with the flaked almonds.

Honeycomb Ice Cream

Cynthia Hipps

This ice cream is delicious and easy.

5 tablespoons granulated sugar

2 tablespoons golden syrup

1 teaspoon bicarbonate of soda

500g (1lb 1oz) whipped cream

400g (14oz) tin of condensed milk

First make the honeycomb. Melt sugar and syrup in a pan. Boil the mixture to medium brown colour, stirring all the time. Remove from the heat, sieve bicarbonate of soda over it and stir. Pour onto the oiled baking sheet and cool. When the honeycomb is solid, break into small pieces with a rolling pin. Whip cream until sloppy. Beat in the condensed milk, and whip until thick. Fold in the honeycomb and freeze.

Plum and Ginger Ice Cream with Crumble Topping

Victoria Prever,

Jewish Chronicle Food Editor

My ice cream churning machine is a favourite kitchen gadget. Smooth, soft ice cream can be mine in under an hour, so I regularly use it. If you do not have an ice cream maker you can still make delicious ice cream – it just takes a bit longer.

Plums and ginger are a perfect combination, and the crunchy, cinnamon crumble makes a great topping. If the ice cream is enough of a challenge, try serving it in a sandwich. Simply freeze the ice cream in a shallow tray about 2 inches deep, and cut rounds of it out with a biscuit cutter. Serve the ice cream patty between two thin, ginger snap biscuits.

450g (1lb) dark plums, about 8 large plums quartered and pitted

120g (4½oz) soft light brown sugar

3 tablespoons syrup from a jar of stem ginger

90ml (3 fl oz) water

250ml (9 fl oz) double cream

1 – 2 balls stem ginger very finely chopped

For the crumble topping

80g (2¾oz) plain white flour

60g (2½oz) butter

60g (2½oz) soft light brown sugar

½ level teaspoon ground cinnamon

For the ice cream: put the plums, sugar, ginger syrup and water in a pan and simmer until soft – 10 to 15 minutes – until tender. Puree in a blender.

Stir in the chopped ginger and double cream. Refrigerate until cold, then churn in an ice cream maker in accordance with the manufacturer's instructions.

If you do not have an ice cream maker, pour into a container with a lid and freeze for about 1½ to 2 hours until the outer edges of the mixture are solid and the centre still liquid. Beat well until it is all slushy then return it to the freezer. Repeat after 1½ - 2 hours. After another 1½ - 2 hours it should be frozen, so give it a final blitz in a food processor until smooth. Return to the freezer to firm up.

To make the crumble topping: preheat your oven to 190°C/375°F/Gas Mark 5. Combine the ingredients in a bowl and rub the butter into the flour until it comes together to form little crumbly lumps of dough the size of peas.

Line a baking sheet with silicone and sprinkle with the crumble mixture. Bake for about 10 minutes and leave to cool.

Serve the ice cream sprinkled with the crumble topping.

Roasted Nectarine Ice Cream

Victoria Prever,

Jewish Chronicle Food Editor

This delicate ice cream is a taste of pure summer. To turn it into a dinner party dessert, roast a few extra nectarines per guest and serve with a scoop of ice cream and whole Amaretto biscuits on the side. Garnish with fresh mint sprigs.

Serves 4 – 6

4 large ripe nectarines, halved and stoned

1 tablespoon caster sugar

250g (9oz) mascarpone cheese

170g (6oz) caster sugar

200ml (7 fl oz) whole milk

1 tablespoon Amaretto liqueur (optional)

3 or 4 small Amaretto biscuits, crumbled (optional)

Preheat your oven to 200°C/180°C Fan/Gas Mark 6. Put the halved nectarines in a roasting tin, cut side up. Sprinkle them with the tablespoon of caster sugar.

Roast them for about 20 minutes until they feel soft when pierced with a knife and the skin peels off easily.

When cool enough to handle, peel off the skins and blitz them in a blender or food processor with the mascarpone, milk and sugar and blitz to a smooth puree.

Stir in the Amaretto – if using – and churn in an ice cream machine.

If you don't have a machine, pour the mixture into a shallow freezer-proof container with a lid. Freeze for a couple of hours until almost solid then whisk until smooth. Return to the freezer and repeat twice more to break down the ice crystals.

Serve with the crumbled biscuit sprinkled over the top if wished.

Pavlova Made with Love and Dedication

Mindi Ison

When I married 55 years ago I could not cook. I had a Law Degree but no practical abilities for married life save that I had attended a term on a baking course where I learnt to bake a pavlova. I have been baking pavlovas ever since for all sorts of joyous occasions.

I make various versions but my favourite is a lemon pavlova that I like to make in a 28cm (11 inch) quiche dish which I wipe lightly with sunflower oil.

For the basic pavlova

4 (large) egg whites

225g (8oz) caster sugar

2 teaspoons cornflour

1 teaspoon vinegar

1 teaspoon vanilla

Lemon filling

4 egg yolks

112g (4oz) caster sugar

3 generous tablespoons lemon juice, freshly squeezed

1 teaspoon lemon rind

150ml (5 fl oz) soured cream

200ml (7 fl oz) whipping cream to decorate

Place the egg whites in a bowl, a Kenwood or whatever other electric mixer you use with a whisk attachment and turn the speed to full, then add a pinch of salt. Whilst the whites are beating mix the cornflour in to the caster sugar and sieve into a bowl. When the whites are stiff add a dessertspoon of the sieved sugar mixture and whisk until stiff. Repeat until all the sugar mixture is finished.

NB This procedure takes a little time but do not be tempted to add more than a spoon at a time and do not add the next spoonful until the egg whites are stiff again. I do a few exercises between the spoonfuls. It is very good for one's figure to make up for eating the pavlova.

Finally beat in the vinegar and vanilla.

Spoon the stiff mixture into the quiche dish building up the circumference so that it looks like a low wall. But as the pavlova will expand during baking leave the wall a few centimetres from the side of the dish.

Place in a cool oven 140°C/275°F/Gas Mark 1.

After 1 hour turn the oven off and leave pavlova in the oven until it feels firm to the touch. I usually leave it overnight as I only seem to find time to bake in the evening.

Lemon mixture

Place egg yolks and sugar in a thick bottomed pan and beat with a wooden spoon until pale and creamy. Add the lemon rind and lemon juice and then place pan on a very low heat and stir continuously until the texture of mayonnaise. Turn off the heat and the lemon will thicken up further as it cools.

When it is completely cold stir in the sour cream and spoon into the base of the cooked meringue. Place in the freezer. Meanwhile whip up a small carton of whipping cream or double cream with 2 teaspoons of caster sugar and spread on the frozen lemon. Put back in the freezer and leave until about an hour before you need the cake and then decorate with fresh fruit such as raspberries and kiwi. Keep in the fridge till needed.

Enjoy. The contrast of the sharp lemon and sweet meringue is delicious even after 55 years of tasting.

Tiramisu

Claudia Camhi

This dessert is a favourite for all at home and a must on a lazy weekend late summer lunch when the whole family gets together. Our children join in the drizzling and mixing. There is rarely any left.

250g (9oz) pot of ricotta

250g (9oz) pot of mascarpone cheese

2 eggs

1 teaspoon vanilla extract

1 cup granulated sugar

Enough sponge fingers to line your container

⅓ cup coffee liqueur (Kahlua)

½ a cup filter coffee

1 tablespoon cocoa powder for dusting

Line a dish with the sponge fingers. Mix the coffee with coffee liqueur. Drizzle the coffee liqueur and coffee mix on top of the biscuits and allow it to soak in. In a separate bowl mix the ricotta, mascarpone, vanilla and two egg yolks until creamy.

Make a syrup by mixing the sugar and ½ a cup of cold water in a pan. Bring it to a rolling boil. It takes more or less 20 minutes at full fire to obtain the right consistency. In a separate bowl and 5 minutes before the syrup is ready, begin beating egg whites with an electric mixer until stiff peaks are formed. When ready slowly pour in the syrup whilst you continue beating the egg whites. Fold this meringue into the cheese mixture (ricotta and mascarpone). Lay this mix on top of the sponge fingers. Dust with cocoa powder and refrigerate for a couple of hours.

Keep refrigerated. You can make a non-alcoholic version. It tastes better the next day!

Rice Pudding

Sara Levy

This is my mother-in-law Joan Levy's gluten-free rice pudding (my husband's favourite). Whenever Scott goes away on a business trip I like to surprise him with a huge pot of rice pudding upon his return. He is not a great one for sweet treats, but he will eat a bowl of the rice pudding for breakfast, lunch and dinner.

4 cups cooked rice (I use brown basmati but you can use any white or brown rice, better even if it is a day old out of the fridge)

4 eggs, beaten

4 cups of semi skimmed milk

¼ cup sugar

1 cup raisins

1 tablespoon ground cinnamon

Butter

Put the cold, cooked rice in an oven dish and pour on the milk. Pour in the beaten eggs and raisins (add more if you like). Add the sugar. Sprinkle in the cinnamon. Gently stir it all together so it is mixed evenly. Dot some small pieces of butter on top.

Cook in the oven at 180°C/350°F/Gas Mark 4 for about an hour. When the rice pudding doesn't jiggle and looks set in the middle you can take it out of the oven, or just turn the heat off and let it cool down in the oven. Great served warm or straight out of the fridge! The consistency of the pudding is different every time I make it and it takes anywhere from 50 - 70 minutes depending on your oven. Enjoy!

Sam's Fruity Crumble
Sam Dayan

This warm comforting dish is perfect for the autumnal months, which conveniently coincides with Rosh Hashanah. I get up early in the morning to prepare both the fruit mixture and crumble topping and then simply pour one over the other when we return from Synagogue. If your family lunches are anything as over-supplied and lively as ours, the crumble will have ample time to cook during the meal.

2 bananas

3 conference pears

1 cooking apple

2 ripe nectarines

150g (5oz) blackberries

Juice of 1 orange

2 teaspoons cinnamon

80g (3oz) demerara sugar

50g (2oz) light soft brown sugar

For the topping

125g (4½oz) plain flour

125g (4½oz) porridge oats

125g (4½oz) demerara sugar

150g (5oz) unsalted butter

Peel and core the cooking apple, then cut up all the fruit into bite-sized pieces and put them into a bowl.

Add the sugars and cinnamon and mix until all the fruit is well integrated. NB the quantities given for the sugars can only ever be a suggestion, as it really depends on how ripe the fruit is. As ever, the best way to adapt to your ingredients is constant tasting!

Squeeze the orange and then pour the juice over the mixture. Not only does this enhance the flavour but also ensures that the fruit keeps in good condition for longer, which is important if preparing the pudding significantly in advance of cooking.

Mix the flour, oats and sugar together in a separate bowl.

Dice the butter and then proceed to rub it into the flour mixture so that it forms large crumbs. This process only works if the butter is cold; once it has reached room temperature, it is nigh impossible to make the topping. If you are struggling, try dicing the butter beforehand, keeping it in the fridge and then only rubbing it in bit by bit i.e. take a quarter of the butter and rub it in while keeping the rest cold in the fridge and then move on to the next quarter and so on.

Pour the fruit mixture into the cooking dish and just before cooking cover with the topping.

Cook in the oven for 35 minutes at 190°C/375°F/Gas Mark 5. The topping should be golden brown. Ice cream, crème fraiche and Greek yoghurt are all delicious accompaniments. Enjoy!

Pears in Honey, White Wine and Cardamom

Claudia Camhi

This is my own recipe, a little twist on "apples and honey" and a dairy-free pudding as well if you choose to leave out the crème fraiche.

4 tablespoons runny honey

Lemon peel

Juice of ½ a lemon

2 cups of white wine

2 cups of water

4 crushed cardamom pods

4 tablespoons caster sugar

8 firm and preferably small pears

Crème fraiche (half-fat)

Place the wine, water, honey, sugar and cardamom in a pot that has a lid. Place the pot on low flame with the lid on and allow to come to a boil.

Peel the pears, leaving the stems and place to simmer in the pot, covered with the lid, until soft. This may take 15 to 20 minutes depending on the size of the pears and their firmness.

Add the lemon juice. Once the pears are soft, place in a container, allow to cool and refrigerate.

Serve with a dollop of crème fraiche.

A variation is to simmer the pears in red wine with three cloves, no honey, a small cinnamon stick, orange peel and 6 tablespoons of caster sugar. I do not use crème fraiche with this option.

Rhubarb Compote

Anne Clark

Serves 6

A quick, delicious and unusual way of preparing rhubarb without the addition of refined sugar.

500g (1lb 1oz) rhubarb (approximately)

1 orange

Sultanas or raisins (generous handful)

Ground almonds, ground cinnamon, ground mixed spice (to taste)

A little water

Sweetening: a little honey, or date syrup or concentrated apple juice or maple syrup or agave nectar or a combination of some of these things!

Put washed, chopped rhubarb in saucepan. Add peeled, chopped orange, sultanas or raisins, ground almonds, cinnamon and a little ground mixed spice. Simmer gently with a little water until soft, stirring from time to time. Sweeten to taste. (Use sugar, if you must).

Store in fridge. Eat chilled or at room temperature.

Gefiltefest

Gefiltefest is the UK's annual Jewish food festival, held north of the river (Thames). The Gefiltefest co-ordinators got in touch with Wimshul Cooks to ask if we would like to volunteer at the festival.

The challenge? To assist the chefs and food writers who were giving cookery demonstrations during the course of the day. A keen team of five jumped at the chance. We all had a great day, watching and assisting really impressive chefs, such as Silvia Nacamulli and Kim Kushner, handing out tasters of what had been cooked to the appreciative audience, and picking up a few tips along the way. Michael Leventhal, the founder of Gefiltefest, Silvia Nacamulli and Kim Kushner have kindly contributed their recipes to this book.

Perfect Chocolate Brownies

Michael Leventhal

For the following brownie recipe I've taken the ingredients of Tarryn Klotnick – a wonderful Gefiltefest volunteer – and used a few techniques from the French cook David Lebowitz, mixed in with my own ideas.

200g (7oz) dark chocolate. The better the chocolate, the better the brownies.*

175g (6oz) unsalted butter

175g (6oz) caster sugar

50g soft dark brown sugar

130g (4½oz) plain flour

3 eggs

Vanilla essence

150g (5oz) pecan nuts

*If you are using less than 75% cocoa, reduce the amount of sugar (because the chocolate is less bitter).

Preheat the oven to 170°C/325°F/Gas Mark

3. Line a tray with two sheets of silver foil perpendicular to each other and grease the top sheet. In a medium saucepan melt the butter, then add the chocolate and stir gently on a low heat until everything is smooth and melted.

Remove from the heat, stir in the sugar and a drop of vanilla essence. Beat in the eggs, one by one.

Add the flour and stir very energetically for about 75 seconds until the batter becomes smooth and glossy. Don't skip this crucial step!

Stir in the chopped pecan nuts – they should be toasted first for just 5 minutes on 170°C/325°F/Gas Mark 3.

Bake for 30 minutes – underbake rather than overbake – then leave to cool completely before taking out and cutting. If you put a knife into a jug of hot water it will slice through the brownies more easily.

If you freeze them in the tin before cutting you'll get perfect lines and they won't crumble so much – but there are less crumbs for you to hoover up yourself!

Pizza Romana
Traditional Roman Jewish Candied Fruitcake

Silvia Nacamulli   www.cookingforthesoul.com

The Pizza Romana, also called Pizza di Piazza, is a traditional fruitcake that Roman Jews eat for happy family occasions such as weddings, bar/batmitzvah and brits. It is a unique delicacy from the Roman Ghetto. It is still a mystery why it is called pizza as it is sweet and it has nothing to do with the pizza we all know and eat worldwide!

These delicious fruitcakes are usually given in a little sachet, together with cinnamon and almond biscuits, at the Mishmara. The Mishmara is a traditional Roman Jewish evening of prayers and singing (and food of course!) on the Thursday evening before the main event.

Most people buy the Pizza Romana already made from Boccione, a wonderful little bakery in the main square (Piazza) of the ghetto in Rome. However in my family we enjoy baking our own. This is my version of it.

Makes 18-20 large or 26-28 stick size fruitcakes

100g (3½oz) raisins

100g (3½oz) unskinned almonds

100g (3½oz) pine nuts

200g (7oz) glace cherries or mixed candied fruit

100ml (3½ fl oz) Marsala or sweet wine

230ml (8fl oz) sunflower, corn or vegetable oil

1 teaspoon of vanilla extract

170g (6oz) white caster sugar

500g (1lb 1oz) white flour (ideally '00' grade, otherwise all-purpose plain white flour)

A pinch of salt

Preheat the oven 220°C/425°F/Gas Mark 7.

Place in a bowl the raisins, almonds, pine nuts and the chunks of glace cherries/candied fruit together with the Marsala or sweet wine and the vanilla extract.

For a fuller taste, leave the fruit and nuts to soak for a few hours or overnight.

In a separate bowl mix the flour, the sugar, the oil and a pinch of salt. Mix thoroughly, either by hand or with an electric mixer. Now add the soaked nuts, candied fruit and wine. Mix and work the dough until you get a homogeneous consistency. It is normal if it appears a little crumbly.

Spread a little flour on a clean surface, cut the dough into 3-4 parts and create with each piece long, chunky rectangular blocks. Now divide each long block into 5-6 pieces of 5-6cm (2 inches) in length, 4-5cm in width (1½ inches) and 2cm (¾ inch) in height. Otherwise cut it into smaller sticks to have finger size fruitcakes.

Lay an oven tray with parchment paper and place the fruit cakes on the tray. Bake for 20 minutes until golden and slightly burned. If you are making small size cakes then bake them for 16-18 minutes. Remove from the oven, leave to cool down before removing from the tray.

Eat warm or at room temperature. These cakes last for several days in a jar. Enjoy!

La Pasta - Orange Sponge Cake

Kim Kushner, author of 'The Modern Menu'

Cake in Spanish is pastel. Many Spanish-speaking Jews who came from Morocco would make this simple, light cake to serve on the Sabbath and referred to it as pasta, a twist on pastel. The syrup and candied orange slices can be made one day in advance, covered separately, and refrigerated. Return the orange slices to room temperature and re-warm the syrup slightly before serving.

Serves 9-10

Cake

6 large eggs

1¾ cups sugar

½ cup rice bran oil or vegetable oil

½ cup orange juice

1 teaspoon vanilla

2 cups plain flour, sifted

2 teaspoons baking powder

Candied orange slices and syrup

1 cup sugar

¾ cup orange blossom honey

3 tablespoons green cardamom pods, crushed

1 teaspoon vanilla

1 small orange, peel on, thinly sliced

Preheat the oven to 160°C/325°F/Gas Mark 3. Grease a 23cm (9 inch) bundt pan with oil.

Using a standing or handheld mixer fitted with the whisk attachment, beat the eggs and sugar on medium-high speed until pale yellow and smooth, about 4 minutes. Add the oil, orange juice, and vanilla and beat until thoroughly combined. Add the flour, 1 cup at a time, and baking powder, until thoroughly incorporated. Pour the batter into the prepared pan and bake for about 1 hour, until the cake springs back when tapped or a cake tester inserted into the cake comes out clean. Let cool.

Meanwhile, prepare the candied orange slices: line a baking sheet with parchment paper. Bring the sugar, honey, cardamom, and 3 cups of water to a boil in a medium-heavy saucepan, stirring until the sugar dissolves. Stir in the vanilla and add the orange slices. Reduce the heat to medium-low and simmer, turning the orange slices occasionally, until they are tender and the syrup is reduced to 3¼ cups, about 40 minutes. Arrange the orange slices in a single layer on the baking sheet. Strain the syrup and reserve.

Remove the cooled cake from the pan and place on a cake platter. Drizzle the syrup over the top of the cake and arrange the orange slices on top. The cake may be covered tightly in plastic wrap 2 days in advance of serving.

Light Chocolate Cake

Camilla McGill

Adapted from Heavenly Chocolate Heartache by Harry Eastman

Delicious and healthy. Enjoy!

Serves 12

You will need either one deep or two normal 20cm (8 inch) round cake tins. Loose bottomed ones are the easiest.

3 medium eggs

160g (5oz) caster sugar

200g (7oz) peeled and grated butternut squash or sweet potato. This is the weight once it is peeled. Don't grate it until you are about to use it. Use a very fine grater.

3 tablespoons dark cocoa powder

120g (4½oz) flour (works well with plain or spelt flour)

80g (3oz) ground almonds

1 teaspoon baking powder

1 teaspoon bicarbonate soda

¼ teaspoon salt

125ml (4½ fl oz) buttermilk or milk mixed with a teaspoon of lemon juice to make buttermilk

For the icing

65g (2¼oz) unsalted butter softened

220g (8oz) icing sugar sieved

65g (2¼oz) mascarpone or cream cheese

4 teaspoons cocoa powder

A pinch of salt

Grease the tins with some butter or margarine and line with circles of greaseproof paper.

Preheat the oven to 180°C/350°F/Gas Mark 4. If you have a fan oven put it at 160°C.

Whisk the eggs and sugar in a large mixing bowl for a minimum of four minutes until they are pale and fluffy and have at least doubled in size. Beat in the butternut squash or sweet potato that you have just finely grated.

Add the sifted flour, cocoa powder, baking powder, bicarbonate of soda, salt and ground almonds. Mix well. Add the buttermilk and beat again to make sure all the ingredients are mixed in.

Pour evenly into the two tins or the one deep tin if you don't have two.

Place in the middle of the oven and bake for 30 minutes until they are risen, springy and look cooked and have mostly stopped hissing when you put your ear to them.

Cool the cakes on a wire rack. When they are cool, turn them out and remove the paper from the bottom and leave to cool completely. If you made the cake in one pan, slice the cake carefully horizontally so you can fill with icing later.

To make the icing, beat the butter with half of the icing sugar in a mixing bowl with a wooden spoon. Mix them together till they form a nice thick paste. Then beat fast for 10 seconds to loosen the butter even more. Add the mascarpone or cream cheese, cocoa powder (sifted) and salt as well as the remaining sifted icing sugar. Beat together till combined.

Refrigerate the icing for 15 minutes before using. Then give it a good mix again. Spread icing over the middle layer and top of the cake.

Apple Cake

Ella Raz-Rhodes

This is an Israeli recipe.

1kg (2lb 3oz) cooking apples

2 cups of self-raising flour

1¼ cups of sugar

5 eggs

½ cup chopped nuts or almonds

½ cup of sultanas (optional)

Cinnamon

Preheat the oven 160-180°C/350°F/Gas Mark 4. In a food processor, mix together the flour, sugar and eggs.

Peel apples and core and slice them.

In a lightly greased dish arrange the apple slices and sprinkle with the nuts, cinnamon and sultanas and mix up. Pour the flour mixture on top of the apples and bake until the top is pale brown for about 25 minutes.

Check with a sharp knife that the apples are soft before turning off the heat.

Fruit Cake

Paulina Bystritsky

I vary this cake a lot and it always comes out a bit differently so I will give rough quantities and you can play around with the recipe as well! It usually takes less than 10 minutes to get the preparation done and about 40 minutes in the oven.

Basics

4 eggs and 2 egg whites

¼ cup of light brown sugar (Or a few teaspoons of sugar, and the rest of the ¼ cup replaced with honey)

1 banana, mashed with a fork (and mixed with up to 1 tablespoon of sunflower oil – optional, makes the taste more moist but more oily)

1 cup of ground almonds

1 cup of self-raising flour

The extras

Juice of half a lemon

2-3 teaspoons vanilla extract or vanilla powder

¼ teaspoon ground cinnamon

A drizzle of honey

Cranberry juice concentrate works well here, but optional

½ cup of dried chopped fruit

½ cup of walnut pieces

Beat the egg whites separately with the sugar, until not runny, then add pre-whisked yellows. If feeling a bit lazy, just mix all the eggs with the sugar with a whisk for a short time.

Add the banana (and oil) purée. Add the ground almonds and then the self-raising flour. Your mix should be quite runny.

Now add the lemon juice, vanilla, cinnamon and a drizzle of honey.

Once you feel the mix is right in consistency, runny enough but not too runny, you can finally add the chopped dry fruit, and the walnut pieces. You should still be able to stir the mix, make sure it is not overpowered by the dried fruit and walnuts, but that there are fruit and nuts throughout.

Oil a 30 cm (12 inch) cake tin and preheat the oven (160°C with fan/350°F/Gas Mark 4). Pour in the mix, which probably comes up half way to the top of the tin – don't worry, it will rise.

Bake in the middle to lower part of the oven for at least 30 minutes. Check with a toothpick for readiness, when the toothpick comes out moist but not covered with cake mix it is done.

You can 'glaze' the cake with a variety of ingredients such as lemon juice or cranberry juice concentrate. Cover with tin foil to cool slowly.

Almond Cake

Susan Zisman

As well as being a Shul member, Susan has worked in Apples and Honey Nursery for many years, retiring in 2013. She was well loved by the nursery children, more of an extra grandma than a teacher.

225g (8oz) softened butter

225g (8oz) caster sugar

150g (5oz) self-raising flour

4 eggs

½ teaspoon almond extract

75g (3oz) ground almonds

Flaked almonds for decorating

(Optional tin of black cherries)

Preheat oven to 180°C/350°F/Gas Mark 4.

Cream softened butter with the sugar and almond extract. Add 1 egg with 2 dessertspoons of flour. Repeat until all eggs and flour are used. Then add the ground almonds and incorporate.

(If adding cherries, cut into quarters and coat in ground almonds then gently fold into the mixture with a spoon).

Put in to a lined 20cm (8 inch) tin. Sprinkle with flaked almonds and bake for 50 minutes until golden brown,

"Magic Red" Cake

Eleri Larkum

The name for this beetroot seed cake is inspired by my younger son who helped me make it. The colour is truly stunning, and has to be seen to be believed. As does the next part, when, during the cooking process, the colour disappears. Once cooked, you're left with an ordinary cake-coloured cake, only flecked with red. A mini miracle.

225g (8oz) self-raising flour

½ teaspoon bicarbonate of soda

1 teaspoon baking powder

½ teaspoon ground cinnamon

180ml (6 fl oz) sunflower oil

225g (8oz) light brown sugar

3 eggs separated

150g (5oz) raw beetroot

Juice of ½ a lemon

75g (3oz) raisins

75g (3oz) mixed seeds (sunflower, pumpkin, linseed, pine kernels, poppy seeds, or any seeds or nuts you have)

For the icing

8 tablespoons icing sugar

Lemon juice

Poppy seeds

Preheat the oven to 180°C/350°F/Gas Mark 4. Grease and line a rectangular 20 x 9cm (8 x 4 inch) loaf tin.

Beat oil and sugar together, add egg yolks one by one. Grate beetroot coarsely and fold into mixture, then add lemon juice, seeds and fruit. Sift the flour and raising agents together and stir slowly into the mixture. Beat the egg whites till soft peaks, and fold into the mix.

Pour into the lined tin, and take a moment to admire the colour. It takes 50-55 minutes to cook but cover with foil after 30 minutes to prevent the top from burning. Test it with a skewer to see if it's done – it should be moist, but not sticky. Leave in the tin to cool for at least 20 minutes. Make a thin icing to drizzle over the top, and sprinkle over some poppy seeds.

Like any moist cake made with oil, this keeps beautifully, and possibly even improves with age.

Yoghurt Cake

Claudia Camhi

I got this recipe from Graciela Ergas in Chile, an inspiring woman that would welcome everyone to her home and gather people around the table to engage and share in lively and parallel conversations. An experienced cook/baker like her would just know what is right in terms of times and amounts and would rarely measure or weigh ingredients. I make this recipe using a 250ml or 8 fl oz cup. People always ask me for the recipe. It works very well as an easy and quick recipe for Shavuot.

2 large eggs

1 cup of sugar

¾ cup of sunflower oil

1 cup of plain yoghurt (do not use fat free)

2 cups of plain flour

1 teaspoon of vanilla extract

2 teaspoon of baking powder

Preheat the oven to 180°C/350°F/Gas Mark 4.

Prepare the tin according to manufacturer's instructions.

Use a whisk to mix eggs, sugar, oil, yoghurt and vanilla extract in a bowl. Whisk flour and baking powder in until the mixture looks creamy. Do not over mix. Put batter in baking tin making sure not to fill more than ⅔ of your container.

Bake in middle rack for 45-55 minutes (the timing will vary depending on oven and tins).

It is ready when you insert a cocktail stick at the centre of the cake and it comes out dry.

The plain batter allows for plenty of experimenting in shapes and flavours:

- You can use a loaf tin, cupcake tin or a doughnut shaped mould. Double the recipe for larger tins.
- Add 2 tablespoons of poppy seeds and the zest of a lemon.
- Add a handful of sultanas, currants or any other dry fruits and or nuts you like. Make sure you dust the fruits in flour so they don't sink to the bottom.
- For a marbled outcome: Place ⅔ of the plain batter in the tin. Then take ⅓ of the batter and mix in 3 tablespoons of cocoa powder. Place it on top of the plain batter and let the oven do the rest.
- Bake the plain batter in a round tin. Once baked and cooled cut it in half and fill it with strawberries and cream. Dust the top with icing sugar.

The cake should last for a week at room temperature as long as it is covered in cling film.

Alec Cake

Helen Bramsted

Every summer, when our children Leah and Alan were growing up, we would join our friend Alec on his boat for a day, travelling along the Thames towards Henley. One time he produced a wonderful cake with boudoir biscuits around the edge and topped with chocolate mousse and cream – we were so impressed that he could make this on board, and even more so, when he told us that the secret was that half the ingredients were shop bought. From then on it became our preferred family birthday cake. It's best not to count the calories though!

1 sponge base (I get mine from Waitrose)

1 packet of boudoir biscuits

6 eggs

175g (6oz) chocolate (I use half cooking chocolate and half Bournville)

1 small pot of double cream

Chocolate flake for decoration

Put the sponge base in a springform cake tin. Slice the boudoir biscuits in half lengthways and arrange them around the inside edge of the tin, with the sugary side facing outwards.

Next make the chocolate mousse. Separate the eggs. Melt the chocolate in a bowl over a pan of hot water. Add the egg yolks to the melted chocolate and combine. Whip the egg whites till stiff and, when the chocolate mixture has cooled a little, fold in the whites. Then whip the cream.

Spread the mousse evenly on the top of the sponge, then spread the whipped cream on top of that. Crumble the flake over the top. Refrigerate and serve cold.

Banana Ginger Cake

Sharon Tyler

The recipe is based on a recipe from the Australian Women's Weekly magazine and has been tasted at many Shul events.

90g (3½oz) butter (room temperature)

2 tablespoons golden syrup

¼ cup caster sugar

¼ cup brown sugar

1 egg

⅔ cup mashed banana (2 bananas)

1½ cups self-raising flour

½ teaspoon bicarbonate of soda

2 teaspoons ground ginger

1 tablespoon milk

Frosting

1½ cups icing sugar

30g butter

2 tablespoons lemon juice

¼ cup chopped glace root ginger

Preheat oven to 180°C/350°F/Gas Mark 4.

Grease a 20cm (8 inch) ring pan and line the base with baking parchment. Cream the butter, golden syrup and sugars in a small bowl with electric mixer until light and fluffy. Add egg, beat until combined and then beat in banana. Transfer mixture to a large bowl and stir in the sifted dry ingredients and the milk.

Pour the mixture into the prepared pan. Bake in a moderate oven for about 30 to 45 minutes. Stand 5 minutes before turning on to a wire rack to cool. Spread cold cake with frosting and sprinkle with ginger.

To make frosting, combine sifted icing sugar with soft butter and enough lemon juice to mix to a spreadable consistency.

I often add more than 1 tablespoon of milk to the cake batter to make it a 'dropping' consistency. Check if a skewer comes out clean to know it is cooked.

Tea Bread

Cynthia Hipps

This tea bread is extremely easy and can be eaten with or without butter.

2 cups mixed dried fruit, soaked in enough cold tea to cover for at least half an hour and preferably overnight

2 cups self-raising flour

1½ cups soft brown sugar

2 eggs

Preheat the oven to 180°C/350°F/Gas Mark 4 After soaking the dried fruit, drain the tea liquid off, reserving the liquid. Add the self-raising flour, sugar and eggs to the dried fruit. Add some of the cold tea if the mixture seems a little stiff. Put in lined and greased 900g (2lb) loaf tin and bake for 40 to 60 minutes.

Gateau Lawrence (Chocolate Cake)

Helen Barnett

For the Cake

180g (6¼oz) dark chocolate

175g (6oz) butter/margarine

125g (4½oz) sugar

200g (7oz) ground almonds

4 eggs separated

For the Icing

100g (4oz) dark chocolate

50g (2oz) butter/margarine

Preheat the oven to 150°C/300°F/Gas Mark 2.

Break chocolate into small pieces and melt. Cream together butter and sugar until soft and creamy. Add ground almonds, egg yolks and melted chocolate. Beat until well blended. Whisk whites until stiff, add to mixture, and fold in with a metal spoon. Pour into a round loose-bottomed 23cm (9 inch) tin, bake for 45 minutes (light crust will form on the top). Cool before removing.

Icing

Melt chocolate and butter, drizzle over cake, leave to set.

Chocolate Torte

Lynne Sidkin

200g (7oz) plain chocolate

3 tablespoons water

110g (4oz) margarine

3 eggs, separated

140g (5oz) caster sugar

90g (3¼oz) ground hazelnuts or almonds

60g (2½oz) self-raising flour

Glaze

150g (5oz) plain chocolate

90g (3¼oz) margarine

Preheat the oven to 170°C/325°F/Gas Mark 3. Line a 23cm (9 inch) tin.

To make the torte, melt the chocolate with the water (I do this in the microwave). Beat in the margarine, a little at a time.

Whisk the egg yolks with the sugar and then stir into the chocolate mixture. Fold in the nuts and flour.

Whisk the egg whites until stiff, then fold into the mixture. Pour mixture into tin, bang on surface to remove any air bubbles, and bake for 45-50 minutes. Allow to cool.

To make the glaze, melt the chocolate and then beat in the margarine. Spread over the cake and down the sides.

"Emma's" Brownies

Helen Barnett

3 eggs

200g (7oz) white chocolate drops

250g (9oz) plain chocolate (at least 75% cocoa)

75g (3oz) butter

175g (6oz) caster sugar

175g (6oz) self-raising flour

Pinch of salt

1 teaspoon vanilla

Line a 30 x 23 cm (12 x 9 inch) tin with baking paper.

Melt plain chocolate and butter (can microwave). Beat sugar, eggs and vanilla. Add melted chocolate. Stir in flour and salt. Add white chocolate buttons.

Bake in oven at 170°C/325°F/Gas Mark 3 for 16/17 minutes (depends on oven). They should be a bit squishy – don't over bake.

Healthy Carrot Cake
Cynthia Hipps

This is a recipe given to me by an old university friend who now lives in the US. Every time I make it, someone asks for the recipe.

1 tablespoon lemon juice

150ml (¼ pint) milk

110g (4oz) butter

235ml (8 fl oz) honey

225g (8oz) carrots, grated

110g (4oz) raisins

110g (4oz) stoned dates, chopped

1 egg beaten

110g (4oz) wholemeal flour

110g (4oz) strong white flour

2 teaspoons bicarbonate of soda

1 teaspoon baking powder

1 teaspoon ground cinnamon

½ teaspoon grated nutmeg

50g (2oz) chopped walnuts (optional)

Preheat the oven to 180°C/350°F/Gas Mark 4. Grease the bottom of a 20cm (8 inch) tin and line with greased greaseproof paper. Combine the lemon juice and the milk and put on one side.

Melt the butter and honey in a medium saucepan. Remove from the heat and add carrots, raisins, dates, egg and reserved sour milk.

Sift the flours with the bicarbonate of soda, baking powder, cinnamon and nutmeg. Add the chopped walnuts if using. Mix everything together and pour into the baking tin and bake in the centre of the oven for 1- 1¼ hours. Leave in the tin to cool partially before turning onto the rack.

Date and Walnut Cake
Hilary Leek

Makes 10 generous helpings

175g (6oz) chopped dates

1 cup boiling water

½ teaspoon bicarbonate of soda

225g (8oz) caster sugar

50g (2oz) butter, softened

1 egg, beaten

1 teaspoon vanilla essence

225g (8oz) plain flour

½ teaspoon baking powder

Pinch salt

110g (4oz) chopped walnuts

Preheat the oven to 190°C/375°F/Gas Mark 3. Grease a tin approximately 25 x 15 x 5cm (10 x 6 x 2 inches) or two smaller ones and line with baking paper.

Pour boiling water over dates and quickly add bicarbonate of soda. Set aside.

Cream together the butter and sugar and gradually beat in the egg, vanilla essence, flour, baking powder and salt. Finally, add walnuts and combine with date mixture. Turn into the tin, smooth level and for decoration you could sprinkle on 25g (1oz) of demerara sugar, or even caster sugar.

Bake for 35 minutes until firm to the touch.

Passion Cake
Hilary Leek

Serves 10 (at least)

275g (10oz) plain flour

50g (2oz) chopped walnuts

1 level teaspoon bicarbonate of soda

3 eggs

2 level teaspoon baking powder

2 ripe bananas

1 level teaspoon salt

175g (6oz) grated carrots

175g (6oz) soft light brown sugar

175ml (6fl oz) oil

Frosting

75g (3oz) butter

½ teaspoon vanilla essence

75g (3oz) cream cheese

Finely chopped walnuts for sprinkling

150g (6oz) icing sugar (can add more)

Heat the oven to 180°C/350°F/Gas Mark 4. Grease and line a 22.5cm (9 inch) round cake tin. Sift the flour, bicarbonate of soda, baking powder and salt into a medium-sized mixing bowl. Add the brown sugar, chopped walnuts and eggs. Peel and mash the bananas and add to the bowl, then add the grated carrots and oil. Mix ingredients together and then beat well for 1 minute to make a soft cake batter.

Pour the mixture into the prepared cake tin and spread level. Place in the centre of the preheated oven and bake for 1 hour. Allow to cool in the tin for 5 minutes, then turn out on to a wire rack and leave until completely cool.

Put the butter and cream cheese into a mixing bowl sift in the icing sugar, add the vanilla and beat until soft and creamy. Slice cake horizontally and sandwich layers with a little of the frosting. Spread remainder over top and sides. Sprinkle with the finely chopped walnuts.

Blue Poppy Seed Cake
Carol Plummer

100g (3½oz) blue poppy seeds

225ml (8 fl oz) milk

225g (8oz) butter or margarine

225g (8oz) light raw cane sugar

3 eggs, separated

225g (8oz) plain wheatmeal flour

1¼ teaspoons baking powder

Preheat the oven to 180°C/350°F/Gas Mark 4.

Line and grease a 20cm (8 inch) cake tin. Bring the poppy seeds to the boil in the milk, then turn off the heat and let them soak for 25 minutes in a covered pan.

Meanwhile cream the butter and sugar together until light and fluffy. Add the egg yolks, one at a time, and beat them in thoroughly.

Mix the flour and baking powder together and fold this into the creamed mixture. Then stir in the soaked poppy seeds and milk.

Next, whisk the egg whites until they are stiff and fold them in carefully. Spoon the mixture into the prepared tin and bake the cake for 1 hour or until the centre feels firm and a skewer when inserted into the cake comes out clean.

Let the cake stand in the tin for 10 minutes, then turn it on to a cooling rack.

The Cake for All Seasons
Marcelle Jay

This recipe is known in France as "Four Quarters." The reasons for this evocative name are that there are four seasons to the year, and there are four ingredients in the cake (that need to be of the best quality possible).

I did not create this recipe - it is the great standby of most middle class French households, and I have translated the recipe from the book *Je Sais Cuisiner* which has sold 3 million copies, and has been popular for four generations.

3 eggs (medium sized)

Their weight in

a) plain flour

b) sugar (preferably FairTrade caster sugar)

c) butter (best quality, slightly salted)

Grated lemon rind (from about ½ a lemon)

Preheat the oven to 180°C/350°F/Gas Mark 4 and prepare the cake tin. Modern silicone loaf or other shape tins are ideal.

Beat the egg yolks with the sugar until the mixture is runny and light in colour. Slowly add alternately some of the sifted flour, and some of the softened butter until these are used up. The grated lemon rind is added at this stage. Then carefully fold in the stiffened egg whites and finally pour the mixture into the cake tin ensuring that it is only two thirds full.

The cooking time should be between 40 and 50 minutes.

Let the cake cool. A light dusting of icing sugar is a suggestion if you feel it requires it.

The advantages of this cake for what I call "batch-baking" are obvious, as most of us can adapt the proportions using larger eggs, or multiply the quantities.

I love "marrons glaces", sweet chestnuts and, as a luxury, one can cut up the real thing, and artistically decorate the cake for a special occasion, or else try out the cream of marrons glaces that you can dot around, much as one would use tomato paste on ravioli. It is there to be enjoyed.

One Bowl Brownies
Amy Shocker

110g (4oz) unsweetened chocolate

170g (3/4 cup) butter or margarine

2 cups white granulated sugar

3 medium eggs

1 teaspoon vanilla extract

1 cup flour

Nuts or flavoured chocolate chips, eg. white chocolate or mint are optional

Heat oven to 170°C/325°F/Gas Mark 3. Line a rectangular cake pan (9 x 13 inch or 23 x 33cm) with foil, extended over the edge to form handles. Grease foil.

In a large microwavable bowl, microwave chocolate and butter on high for 2 minutes or until butter is melted. Stir mid-way, and continue to stir afterwards until chocolate is all melted. Stir sugar into chocolate mixture until well blended. Mix in eggs and vanilla until blended. Stir in flour.

Spread in prepared pan and bake 25-30 minutes, until toothpick comes out with fudgy crumbs. It is best to check it at 25 minutes to be sure it is still slightly 'undercooked' or they will be too cake-like.

Cool in pan, lift out of pan onto cutting board and cut.

Tip: I like to wrap them in foil and freeze them once slightly cooled down, and then cut from frozen when I need them. They thaw quickly.

Red Velvet Cupcakes

Emma Samuels-Lee

70g (2½oz) butter

1 egg

150g (5oz) plain flour (I use gluten free and also add a teaspoon of xanthan gum)

25g (1oz) cocoa

40ml (1½ fl oz) red food colouring

Splash vanilla extract

120ml (4 fl oz) buttermilk

½ teaspoon bicarbonate soda

1 teaspoon white vinegar

300g (10½oz) icing sugar, sifted

50g (2oz) cool butter

125g (4½oz) cream cheese, cold

Preheat the oven to 170°C/325°F/Gas Mark 3.

Beat the butter and the sugar until light and fluffy and then slowly add the egg and beat in.

In a separate bowl, make a paste by mixing together the cocoa powder, red food colouring and vanilla extract. Add to the butter until evenly combined then slowly pour in half the buttermilk.

Add half the flour and beat until everything is well incorporated. Repeat this process until all the buttermilk and flour have been added. If using an electric mixer turn on high until smooth and even. Turn the mixer down to low speed and add the bicarbonate of soda and vinegar. Beat until well mixed, then turn up the speed again and beat for two more minutes.

In a separate bowl, mix the icing sugar and butter. Add the cream cheese in one go and beat until the frosting is light and fluffy. Spoon the cake mixture into the paper cases until two-thirds full and bake in the preheated oven for 20 to 25 minutes, or until the sponge bounces back when touched.

When the cupcakes are cold, spoon the cream cheese frosting on top.

Gluten-Free Carrot and Cinnamon Cupcakes

Emma Samuels-Lee

Makes 36

450g (1lb) sugar

4 eggs

350g (12oz) vegetable oil

450g (1lb) gluten free plain flour

2 teaspoons bicarbonate of soda

2 teaspoons gluten free baking powder

2 teaspoons cinnamon

1 teaspoon salt

2 teaspoons vanilla extract

225g (8oz) chopped nuts and/or sultanas

680g (1lb 8oz) freshly grated carrots

Frosting

4 tablespoons unsalted butter

75g (3oz) cream cheese

1 teaspoon vanilla extract

Icing sugar

Preheat the oven to 180°C/350°F/Gas Mark 4.

Beat together the sugar and eggs in a large mixing bowl then add the oil and vanilla and beat just until smooth.

In a separate bowl combine gluten-free flour mix, bicarbonate of soda, baking powder, cinnamon and salt. Add the dry ingredients to the wet ingredients and beat. Stir in grated carrots, raisins and nuts. Pour the batter into prepared pans.

Bake for 30-35 minutes or until they pass the toothpick test. Cool on a wire rack.

While muffins are cooling beat together the butter, cream cheese and vanilla in a large mixing bowl. Add icing sugar and beat until smooth and creamy. Pipe from a piping bag on top of the cupcakes.

Continental Plum Tart

Liz Ison

My grandmother Else Nathan, who was born in Mannheim, Germany, moved to London in 1936 with her husband, parents and two young children.

This recipe evokes memories of her and her close circle of cousins and friends who used to visit each other's houses for coffee, cake and conversation.

110g (4oz) butter, cubed

110g (4oz) caster sugar (plus more for sprinkling on top of the plums)

1 egg

225g (8oz) plain flour

Pinch of salt

6-8 plums, halved and stoned

Grease and line a 20cm (8 inch) tart tin with a removable bottom. Preheat the oven to 170°C/325°F/Gas Mark 3.

Measure everything except the plums into a bowl and mix with the tips of your fingers till it looks like crumble. Put half the crumble mixture into the tin, pressing down gently. Arrange the plums, cut-side up, sprinkle with some sugar, then cover with the remainder of the crumble mixture. Bake for 30-45 minutes. Serve warm or cold.

Crazy Cake

Miriam Edelman

This is a Depression-era recipe, when eggs in particular were hard to come by. I promise you cannot taste the vinegar! It is traditionally dairy-free, and if you use a healthy oil it can be low cholesterol. Or, you can substitute yoghurt (especially non-fat) for all or part of the oil to make it lower in fat. But most importantly it's easy, incredibly fast, and very yummy.

200g (7oz) sugar (1 cup)

210g (7½oz) flour (1½ cups)

4 tablespoons cocoa

1 teaspoon baking powder

½ teaspoon salt

250ml (8½ fl oz) warm water (1 cup)

125ml (4 fl oz) vegetable oil (½ cup) (sometimes I use a bit less, or yoghurt instead or in combination)

1 teaspoon vanilla

1 tablespoon vinegar

Sift the dry ingredients. Then pour over the remaining ingredients. Stir thoroughly. Pour into greased and floured 20cm (8 inch) square pan. Bake at 180°C/350°F/Gas Mark 4 until a toothpick inserted in centre comes out clean/dry.

Middle Eastern Specialities

Gila Godsi

I have a long association with Wimbledon, having worked at Apples and Honey Nursery for many years. My family are of Iraqi descent but had lived for generations in Sudan and consider themselves Sudanese Jews. The Kak (salty biscuits) and the baklava are basic staples of Middle Eastern baking and there are variations of them throughout the region. Every woman has her own version. My mother Sara learnt the art from her mother-in-law. Her own mother didn't like to cook but was a whizz with the sewing machine. Now my daughter Daisy and I carry on the baking traditions.

Pantespanya (Pain d'Espagne)

This is our family 'go-to' cake. Having called it Pantespanya all my life, it wasn't until I was an adult that I asked my father what it meant. It is the Arabic pronunciation of Pain d'Espagne (Spanish bread) – say it in an Arabic accent and you'll see!

My father Mayer Godsi's favourite, this was baked at all celebrations and festivals (apart from Pesach) despite its plainness. My mother Sara recalls how she had to bake eight of these for my brother's Brit shortly after coming out of hospital. Then her sister-in-law decorated them and she got all the praise and the compliments and my mother's efforts went unrecognised. She still gets outraged to this day – and my brother was born in 1958!

This makes quite a big cake. We still use my mother's deep, battered and dented 28cm (11 inch) cake tin.

225g (8oz) sugar
225g (8oz) self-raising flour
8 large eggs
1 teaspoon baking powder
2 tablespoons sunflower oil
1 teaspoon vanilla
Juice of two tangerines

Preheat the oven to 170°C/325°F/Gas Mark 3.

Separate eggs. Put yolks in smaller bowl and whites in larger bowl. Whisk egg whites and ¾ of the sugar until stiff. Mix yolks with tangerine juice, oil, vanilla and rest of sugar until light and fluffy. Add 2 tablespoons of flour and baking powder. Fold this mix in with egg whites and then gradually fold in the rest of flour.

Pour into the cake tin and place in oven.

After 10 minutes, reduce heat to 160°C/320°F/Gas Mark 2½ and leave for 40 – 50 minutes until golden brown. Test with skewer.

Do not open the oven door to check until it is nearly cooked.

Leave to cool for a bit in oven before removing.

Covered it keeps well for a few days but when it gets a bit dry, my father loved it sliced and toasted with jam on top!

My mother's story of the decorated cakes is interesting because in all my years of eating and baking this cake, I've never known it to be decorated with anything. It is eaten plain in our family.

Kak B'milch (Salty Biscuits)
Gila Godsi

Another family tradition. My mother made these all year round and my grandfather loved them with his tea. They are hand-sized savoury biscuits and he would squeeze them in his hand to break them into his tea. Then he would eat them with a spoon like a cereal. Needless to say both my children now eat them this way!

Mahlab is the crushed dried kernel of a cherry stone and can be bought from middle-eastern shops. It gives the Kak their flavour but can also be left out.

This recipe makes a couple of big Quality Street tin-fuls.

1kg (2lb 3oz) strong white bread flour

2 sachets (14g) instant yeast

400g (14oz) margarine

1 cup of lukewarm water

1 teaspoon crushed mahlab

Handful of nigella seeds

½ cup sesame seeds, lightly roasted

Salt

For glaze, 1 egg beaten

Tip yeast and salt on flour taking care the yeast and salt don't touch each other. Add nigella seeds, sesame seeds and mahlab. Add margarine and mix until cookie crumbs texture. Add water a little at a time until dough binds. Make a hole in the dough, cover and leave to rise for a couple of hours.

Preheat oven to 180°C/350°F/Gas Mark 4.

Cut a slice of the dough and squish gently into a long sausage. Cover the rest so it doesn't dry. Slice the sausage into pieces and make into small rings about 4cm (1½ inches) in diameter.

Glaze with egg.

Bake in the oven for about 20 minutes until golden brown.

Covered, they keep for weeks.

Balawa

Daisy Abboudi (Gila's daughter)

My grandmother Sara Godsi taught me how to make balawa (the Arabic pronunciation of baklava). This is her recipe.

Filling

300g (10½oz) raw almonds, peeled

2-3 heaped serving spoons caster sugar

2½ serving spoons of blossom water

A sprinkling of cinnamon (enough to lightly cover the contents of the bowl)

If the almonds are bought with skins on, soak the nuts in water boiled from the kettle for as long as it takes for the skins to get soft and wrinkly then peel them off.

Blend the almonds, cinnamon and sugar together in a food processor until a coarse mixture has formed. Add the blossom water and briefly mix again to blend into a loose and crumbly paste.

Syrup

1kg (2lb 3oz) caster sugar

Tap water

1 tablespoon blossom water

½ lime

Put the sugar in a pan on the hob on a high heat. Pour in enough water to cover the sugar by 2cm. Bring to the boil and stir gently but constantly with a metal spoon until all the water is dissolved. Lower the heat and simmer.

How to know the syrup is ready:

- Lift the spoon out of the pan and wait for the constant dribble of syrup to end
- When the mix turns into droplets then start counting. It's ready when 7 droplets fall off the spoon.

Add the lime and carefully bring the syrup back up to the boil - it should remain clear. Stir in the blossom water, take the mixture off the heat and leave to cool.

Pastry/ Assembly

800g (28oz) filo pastry (If you can buy this from a Greek or Lebanese store it will come out better. Their pastry is thinner than the standard supermarket type).

250g (9oz) unsalted butter, melted

Preheat the oven to 170°C fan/375°F/Gas Mark 5.

Grease a shallow rectangular tray (about 4-5cm/1½ - 1¾ deep). Place 2 sheets of filo pastry vertically on the horizontal tray. Brush with butter. Fold the overhang in. Turn the tray around 180° and repeat, brushing each layer with butter until you have used up half of the pastry.

Spread the almond mixture over the pastry making sure to get an even layer on the whole tray. Layer the remainder of the pastry as before. Don't press the pastry down if possible - this keeps the balawa light and fluffy. Fold the final sheet of pastry so that it fits the tray as exactly as possible and lay it over the top. Cut the balawa with a sharp knife across, down and diagonally to create triangles.

Bake for about 30 minutes (until the pastry is a light golden brown). Pour the cold syrup over the hot balawa as soon as it comes out of the oven.

Oatmeal Chocolate Chip Cookies

Miriam Kramer

This is my favourite fast, easy-to-make and tasty recipe for cookies.

Makes about 60 cookies.

250g (9oz) unsalted butter

185g (6½oz) soft brown sugar

185g (6½oz) caster sugar

2 eggs

1 teaspoon vanilla essence

235g (8¼oz) plain flour

1 teaspoon bicarbonate of soda

¼ teaspoon salt

185g (6½oz) old-fashioned (not microwave) porridge oats

375g (13oz) chocolate chips (I think white are best but others are fine)

125g (4½oz) toasted and chopped walnuts (optional)

Preheat the oven to 180°C/350°F/Gas Mark 4. Line two rimless baking sheets with parchment baking paper.

In a large bowl, using an electric mixer on medium speed, beat the butter and both sugars until creamy. Add the eggs and vanilla and beat again until smooth. In another bowl stir together the flour, bicarbonate of soda and salt, and then add the dry ingredients to the wet ones and beat on low speed until smooth. Stir in the oatmeal porridge, chocolate chips and nuts if using.

Drop rounded tablespoonfuls (I use a small ice cream scoop) of the dough onto the prepared sheets, spacing them about 4cm (1½ inches) apart. Bake for 10-12 minutes until the cookies are golden brown. Transfer the cookies to a wire rack to cool completely.

When cool they should be stored in an airtight jar.

Jason's Almond Citrus Macaroons

Jason Burns

This is an old Burns household favourite.

Makes 18 macaroons

112g (4oz) raw almonds

450g (1lb) shredded unsweetened coconut

1 teaspoon vanilla extract

2 tablespoons marmalade

3-4 tablespoons honey

4 egg whites

Preheat the oven to 175°C/347°F/Gas Mark 4.

Blitz almonds until ground. Add coconut, vanilla, honey and marmalade and pulse until a thick paste is formed in a bowl. Whisk egg whites until stiff. Gently combine coconut mixture and egg whites in a bowl.

Drop small amounts of macaroon mixture onto a greaseproof paper lined baking sheet. Place in the oven for 15-20 minutes or until golden brown on outside.

Cool before eating (if you can resist them!) Store in an airtight container.

Cottage Cookies
Berlin Leiman

This recipe makes the best cookies ever. It originates from Estonia and is made by our nanny Marina.

Makes about 25 cookies.

250g (9oz) cottage cheese (tvorog) from a Polish shop (full fat, or medium but not low fat)

200g (7oz) unsalted butter (at room temperature)

320g (11oz) plain flour

Granulated sugar to dip the cookies in before baking

Preheat the oven to 190°C/375°F/Gas Mark 5.

Combine the butter and cottage cheese together. Add the flour gradually till it reaches playdough texture.

Roll the dough 0.5cm (¼ inch) thick and cut into circles using a glass.

Spread some sugar onto a plate. Press each circle into the sugar, generously coating on both sides (the sugar caramelises during baking, keeping the inside of the cookie moist). Then fold each cookie in half, and then in half again so it looks like a quarter of a circle.

Bake for 20 minutes till a golden colour.

Chocolate Fridge Cake
Nicki Zisman

I always double or even quadruple this recipe for an event or just to feed all of my boys!

110g (4oz) butter

2 tablespoons golden syrup (maple flavour if possible)

1½ tablespoons drinking chocolate

225g (8oz) crushed digestives

175g (6oz) Cadbury's dairy milk chocolate for topping

(Optional - any combination of nuts, dried fruit, coconut you like)

Melt the butter, syrup and drinking chocolate in a pan. Add the crushed biscuits and any of the optional ingredients.

Press into 18cm (7 inch) square tray.

Melt chocolate in the microwave or in a heat-proof bowl over simmering water and then spread over the top.

Marion's Recipes
Camilla McGill

My mother Marion has been married to David for over 60 years and has four children (I am the youngest) and 10 beautiful grandchildren on whom she dotes. She regularly cooks delicious meals for the family and thinks nothing of making Shabbat dinner or Sunday lunch for at least 15. She is an amazing cook and presents her dishes with such a delicate touch.

Marion was born in 1930 in Brighton and moved to London in 1940 during the war - in time for the Blitz! Her father (Charles Bild) was from a family of 11 children with 7 girls. Marion's aunts were all great cooks and it was probably from them that she got her inspiration as her mother (Anne) wasn't particularly interested. Anne was what was known as a good plain cook. Having moved to London Marion's father died very suddenly aged 42 in 1942. Her mother was left with three young children to look after. Anne was an exceptionally feisty woman who had to fend for her children and did so by running fish and chip shops and coffee bars and even a launderette over the years. She worked till she was 79 and went on to live to 102.

Marion's Ginger Biscuits
Marion Style

Makes 30-35 biscuits

175g (6oz) unsalted butter

175g (6oz) light muscovado sugar

3 tablespoons agave syrup (or golden syrup)

350g (12oz) white spelt flour

2 teaspoons bicarbonate of soda

2 teaspoons ground ginger

1 teaspoon ground cinnamon

Slices of crystallised ginger to decorate

Heat the oven to 160°C (140°C fan)/325°F/Gas Mark 3.

Line two baking sheets with baking parchment.

Melt the butter, sugar and syrup together over a gentle heat. Sift the flour, bicarbonate of soda and spices together in a mixing bowl and beat in melted butter, sugar and syrup to form a soft dough.

Take teaspoons of dough and gently roll into balls with wet hands. Place onto the lined baking sheets spacing well apart. Press a small piece of crystallised ginger into the centre of each one.

Bake until golden, about 10-12 minutes.

When you take them out of the oven, bang trays sharply on worktop to give them a crazed surface.

Leave on tray to cool for 1-2 minutes then transfer to a wire rack.

Chocolate Chestnut Cake
Marion Style

Serves at least 12

415g (14oz) tin of chestnut puree unsweetened

5 eggs separated

225g (8oz) caster sugar

110g (4oz) softened butter

Grated rind of an orange

150g (5oz) dark chocolate (70%)

3 tablespoons Cointreau, brandy or orange juice

Grease and line a 25cm (10 inch) springform cake tin.

Loosen chestnut puree in the tin with a fork (or put it into a bowl and do this).

Either with an electric whisk, in a kitchen aid or in a Magimix-style machine, beat egg yolks and sugar until pale and fluffy. Add the chestnut puree and soft butter.

Add the ground almonds, orange rind, grated chocolate and brandy or orange juice. Mix together gently but thoroughly.

Beat egg white until stiff. Fold egg white into chocolate mixture.

Bake 40-50 minutes until it just stops wobbling. It will firm up out of the oven as well.

Cool in the tin.

Turn out onto a serving plate and either dust with icing sugar and serve or top with whipped cream and fresh berries. Strawberries, raspberries or blueberries all work well. Serve with crème fraiche.

Kamish Broit
Sophie and Aaron Vallance

This recipe has been passed down from Aaron's great-grandma Beck, to Grandma Marilyn, to mum Sherry and now Sophie has taken up the Kamish Broit baking baton.

Kamish Broit are traditional Ashkenazi biscuits, also known as Mandelbrodt. They are like Italian cantucci, also 'twice-baked', but with more give and heartiness. However, it's their deliciousness that makes them so popular in our home – one is never enough! The question is whether you are a dipper or not; options include in tea, coffee or hot milk.

Biscuits

3 eggs

1 cup sugar

1 cup vegetable oil

1 teaspoon baking powder

1 teaspoon vanilla extract

1 cup ground almonds

3 cups plain flour

Topping

½ cup sugar

1 tablespoon cinnamon

Beat eggs. Add sugar, oil, and vanilla and beat well. In a separate bowl, mix flour, ground almonds, and baking powder. Fold into the mixture. It should be a bit sticky. Shape into two fat logs (easiest with wet hands).

Bake at 165°C/325°F/Gas Mark 3 for 25 minutes and let cool for 20 minutes.

Slice (by the inch) before it is cold. Dip the slices into the topping. Put slices back into the oven and dry out at 100°C/212°F/Gas Mark ¼ for two hours.

Sandwich Cookies

Eleri Larkum

Cookies

1½ cups plain flour

¾ cup cocoa powder

½ cup granulated sugar

½ teaspoon salt

¼ teaspoon baking powder

185g (7oz) unsalted butter, softened

3 tablespoons milk

1 teaspoon vanilla extract

Filling

110g (4oz) unsalted butter, softened

1½ cups icing sugar

¼ teaspoon salt

1 tablespoon vanilla extract

Put the flour, cocoa, sugar, salt and baking powder in a food processor and pulse till combined. Add the butter and combine. With the processor running, add the milk and vanilla extract. Cut out some greaseproof paper or lay out some clingfilm. Press the batter into a log about 5cm (2 inches) in diameter and wrap in the paper, twisting the ends of the paper like a sweet or wrap tightly in the clingfilm. Refrigerate for an hour or until needed.

Preheat the oven to 180°C/350°F/Gas Mark 4. Line baking sheets. Cut the log into thin slices about 3-5mm (⅛–¼ inch thick) and lay on the sheets leaving space between each one. Bake for 12-15 minutes. Cool before filling.

To make the filling, combine all the ingredients in a food processor. When you are ready to serve, spread 1cm (½ inch) on a cookie and top with another cookie to form a sandwich. Keep the remaining filling in the fridge and store the cookies in an airtight container, making up more sandwiches when you want them.

COOKIE GALLERY

Cookies made and iced by Eleri Larkum

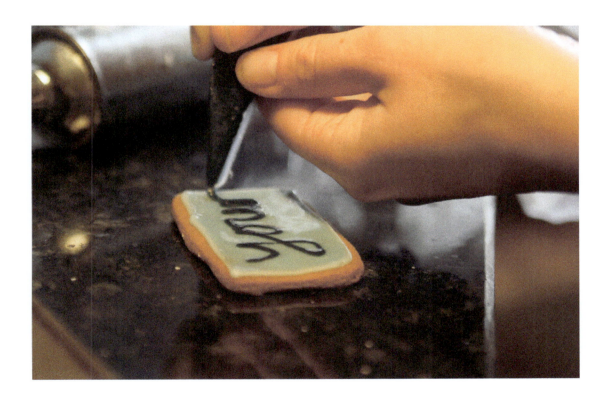

Thank you very much to those who purchased a personalised cookie for enabling this cookbook to happen!

The Ish-Horowicz and Bower Family

Lisa, Maurice, Owen and Jenny Woolf

Jennifer Ison and Daniel Dayan

Benjamins x

Hilary and James Leek

Gila Godsi

Sara Godsi

The Isons

Alison, David, Liat and Beth Kelin

The McGill Family

Rabbi Sybil Sheridan

Judy, Bob, Emma and Alice
Weleminsky-Smith

Sherrards is pleased to have supported many a Wimbledon Synagogue Kiddush!

We serve delicious platters of biscuits, cakes, sandwiches and savouries suitable for all occasions.

18 The Market Place, Falloden Way,
Hampstead Garden Suburb, London, NW11 6JJ
Tel: 020 8455 2111

www.sherrardsbakery.co.uk

Index of Contributors and their Recipes and Articles

A		
Daisy Abboudi	Balawa	312
Mel and Barry Angel	Eingemachts (Beetroot Jam)	209
Roland Appel	Tabbouleh	251
B		
Nicky Bannerman	Noodle Salad	252
Diane Barnett	My Sultana Cheesecake	226
	Gooseberry bushes and Gazpacho: Reminiscences and a Recipe	237
	Matzah Balls	214
	Dona Maria's Gazpacho	239
	Chani Smith's Avocado Dessert	287
Helen Barnett	Lekach (Honey Cake)	121
	"Emma's" Brownies	305
	Gateau Lawrence	305
Janet Benjamin	Janet's Jewel Salad	252
Heather Bieber	Memories of an East Ham Pesach	207
	Passover Lochen	207
Rabbi Lionel Blue	The Most Honest Recipe I Know: Arctic Chowder	257
	Hummus Fit for Kings and Paupers	258
Heston Blumenthal	Mushroom Spelt Risotto	278
Helen Bramsted	Alec Cake	302
Betty H. Burge	Betty's Lockshen Pudding	286
Jason Burns	Jason's Almond Citrus Macaroons	314
Paulina Bystritsky	Fruit Cake	300
C		
Claudia Camhi	Cooking and Learning at Apples and Honey Nursery	72
	Almond, Honey and Whisky Lemon Cake	122
	Aromatic Stuffed Pepper	132
	Persian Latkes	144
	Barley Soup	165
	Persian Aubergines	165
	Iced Pomegranate Grains	169
	Recollections of Chilean Pesaj (Pesach)	202
	Pesaj Spinach Minna Drizzled with Grape Syrup	203
	Spinach Borrecas	224
	Marinated Cucumber Salad	251
	Puy Lentil Salad	253
	Asparagus Salad with Sesame Seeds	253

	Courgette or Aubergine Gratin	260
	Spinach Quiche	260
	Quick Carrot and Courgette Pancakes	263
	Courgette Bake	263
	Yoghurt Coriander Fish	267
	Tiramisu	290
	Pears in Honey, White Wine and Cardamom	292
	Yoghurt Cake	302
Vivienne Cato	Very Very Easy Coleslaw	252
Anne Clark	Gluten-free Latkes	145
	Anne's Amazing Apple Sauce	145
	Rhubarb Compote	292
Malcolm Cark	Fairtrade at the Synagogue	95
Lorna Cohen	Lorna's Fish Pie	267
Josette Cohen	Shabbat Lunch with a French Twist	47
	Saumon Poche with Creamy Sauce	47
Francisco Conesa	Mixed Ecuadorian Ceviche (Fish Marinated in Lemon and Lime Juice)	270
Polly Conn	Carrot and Lentil Soup	231
	Parsnip Soup	231
Alethea Cooper	Seven Veg Tagine	265
D		
Sam Dayan	Fruity Crumble	291
Victoria Druyan-Newman	Chris' Puff Pastry Rolls	259
	Bell Peppers Stuffed with Beef and Rice	274
E		
Andrew Earis	Chicken with Garlic Potatoes and Rosemary	279
Miriam Edelman	Baked Potato Latkes	144
	Date Butter	162
	Seven Biblical Species Cookies	164
	How to Make Matzah	180
	My Mother's Pesach	212
	Charlotte's Matzah Balls	213
	Hollandaise	219
	Mayonnaise	219
	Rugelach	225
	Tzimmes	265
	Crazy Cake	310
Io Epstein	Chocolate Mousse	287

F		
Sally-Ann Feldman	A Great Musician and a Great Cook: In Memory of Raph Gonley	60
	Cooking for the Wimbledon Night Shelter	96
	Crème au Chocolat	219
	Pea Soup	231
	Chicken Soup and Kneidlach	240
Albert Ferro	Greek Salad	249
Dani Freeman	Chocolate Mousse	287
Jo Freeman	Our Pesach "Plant"	210
	Halibut Sweet and Sour	211
	Grandma Dora's Borscht	233
G		
Gila Godsi	Easy Pizza	262
	Pantespanya (Pain d'Espagne)	311
	Kak B'milch (Salty Biscuits)	312
Miriam Goldman	Almond Macaroons	217
	Cinnamon Balls	217
Norma Golten	Pesach Lemon Cake	216
	Ratatouille Niçoise	259
Rosalind Gonley	Chill Con Carne for Fifty	63
	Tunisian Almond and Orange Cake	63
Ludmila Gorna	Polish Ryba Po Grecku ("Fish Greek Style")	40
H		
Cynthia Hipps	Honeycomb Ice Cream	287
	Tea Bread	303
	Healthy Carrot Cake	306
I		
Caroline Ingram	Orange-Carrot Spice Muffins	168
Hava Ish-Horowicz	Savta's Apple Cake	114
Judith Ish-Horowicz	Kiddushim at Wimbledon	30
	Judith's Hallah Dough Recipe	85
	Michael's Rice Recipe	274
Shoshi Ish-Horowicz	Recipe for a Streatham Friday Night	111
Liz Ison	Don't Say "Cheese"	21
	About the Wimshul Cooks Blog	27
	Apple Hallah	118
	Elucidating Latkes	138
	Traditional Potato Latkes	139
	Apple Latkes	144
	Easy Pressure Cooker Apple Sauce	145

	"Biblical" Hallah (Seven Species)	161
	Chocolate and Orange Matzah	197
	Matzah Granola	198
	Toffee Matzah Crunch	199
	Matzah Pudding: A Victorian Odyssey?	204
	Continental Plum Tart	310
Mindi Ison	Pesach Mornings by the Mersey	200
	Lemon Curd	200
	Matzah Pancakes	201
	Fried Matzah	201
	Compote	201
	Pavlova Made with Love and Dedication	289
J		
Marcelle Jay	The Cake for All Seasons	308
K		
Tal Kalderon	Tal's Falafel	246
	Sweet Potato Chips	247
	Israeli/Arabic Salad	247
Carra Kane	How to Break the Fast?	127
	Seven Biblical Species Muffins	163
	Hamantaschen - Texas Style	171
	Connie's Cream Cheese Cake	226
Alison Kelin	Time to Reinvent the Latke	141
	Corn Latkes	142
	Carrot Latkes	142
	Courgette Latkes	142
	Green Bean Latkes	142
	Cheese Latkes	142
	Banana and Raisin Loaf	168
	Old World Pesach Treats - Irish Style	208
	Imberlach – Carrot Candy	208
	Teiglach	208
Josie Knox	Fish Cakes	270
Lotte Kramer	Poems	18
Miriam Kramer	Oatmeal Chocolate Chip Cookies	314
Andres Kupfer	Warm Sweet Potato and Halloumi Salad	254
Kim Kushner	La Pasta (Orange Sponge Cake)	297

L		
Eleri Larkum	A Tallit Cake	43
	Abraham's Tent	49
	Bagels	69
	Twelve Tribes Cake	92
	Best Ever Biscuits for Icing (Gingerbread Biscuits)	135
	Eleri's Edible Sukkah	135
	Eleri's Gingerbread Dreidel	147
	A 1916 Plum Cake for Hanucah	150
	The House of Matzah	195
	Eleri's Mount Sinai Cake	228
	"Magic Red" Cake	301
	Sandwich Cookies	318
Adele Lazarus	Rosie's Fried Fish	268
Hilary Leek	Food and Community at Wimbledon & District Synagogue in the 1980s	103
	Cucumber and Cream Cheese Mousse	104
	Kneidlach	214
	Chocolate Torte	216
	Mushroom and Puy Lentil Soup	232
	Curried Nut Roast	262
	Passion Cake	307
Berlin Leiman	Cottage Cookies	315
Estelle Lerner	Gefilte Fish (Fish Cakes)	268
Michael Leventhal	Perfect Chocolate Brownies	294
Sara Levy	Rice Pudding	290
Wendy Levy	Easy Roasted Vegetables	266
Sally Lewis	Potato Bravas	255
	Sweet and Sour Meatballs	273
M		
Ruth Magnus	Leek and Watercress Soup	232
	Beef, Vegetable and Noodle Soup	241
Stella Mason	Very Quick Cake for Very Busy People	105
	Grandma Freda's Braised Chestnut and Mushroom Pie	264
Yvonne Mason, Orli Kendler-Rhodes & Sharon Cousins	The Original Biblical Superfoods!	159
Yvonne Mason	Grandma's Pesach Biscuits	216
	Winter Soup	242
Camilla McGill	How the Bagel Arrived in SW19	65
with Carra Kane	A Communal Seder	191

333

	Creamed Tomato and Pasta Soup	232
	Spanish Chicken Casserole	271
	Light Chocolate Cake	298
	Marion's Recipes	316
N		
Silvia Nacamulli	Pizza Romana (Candied Fruitcake)	295
O		
Hannah O'Keeffe	Hannah's Tzedakah Project	58
	Hannah's Most Dangerous Cake	58
Merav Oppenheimer	Harira Soup	236
P		
Adam Parker	Adam's Swiss Creamy Chestnut Soup	243
Nick Parish	Chicken Paprika	273
Carol Plummer	Blue Poppy Seed Cake	307
Nina Portugal	Flory Solomon's Indian Selection	280
	Tomato Bhaji	280
	Potato Bhaji	280
	Spicy Tuna Fish Cakes	281
	Spinach Bhaji	281
	Tuna Fish Curry	281
	Rice with Red Lentils (Khichdi)	282
	Curried Corn	282
	Fresh Green Masala	282
	Tandoori Chicken	282
	Curried Chicken	283
	Mince Koftas (Meatballs)	283
Victoria Prever	Plum and Ginger Ice Cream with Crumble Topping	288
	Roasted Nectarine Ice Cream	288
R		
Ella Raz Rhodes	Stuffed Aubergines	133
	Apple Cake	300
Claudia Roden	Bazargan	167
Rabbi Sylvia Rothschild	Hallah and Sermon Preparation Plaited Together	45
	Reflections on Tu B'Shevat	154
	Date and Walnut Bread	156
	What Would I Put Onto a Seder Plate?	188
	The Meaning of Matzah and a Short History of Bread	220
Jamie Ryvchin	Jamie's Apple and Honey Cake	124

S		
Emma Samuels-Lee	Red Velvet Cupcakes	309
	Gluten-Free Carrot and Cinnamon Cupcakes	309
Sandy Scher	Sandy's Famous Mushroom Almond Pate	249
Marion Schindler	Polly's Strudel (Layered Apple and Plum Pie)	120
Jackie Schmid	Wok Fried Honey Soy Chicken	271
	Yummy Sesame Chicken Schnitzel	272
Ellen Sheridan	Parsnip and Apple Soup	241
	Sweet Potato and Lentil Soup	242
	Chicken in Vegetable Sauce	272
Rabbi Sybil A. Sheridan	Bread From the Earth and From Heaven	41
	Baking Matzah in Ethiopia	182
	What to Eat on Pesach	183
	My Dinner with Heston Blumenthal	275
	Oma's Braised Beef	277
Amy Shocker	One Bowl Brownies	308
Lynne Sidkin	Cakes, Care and Respect	33
	Honey Cake	35
	Lemon Drizzle Cake	35
	Chocolate Fridge Biscuits	36
	Rocky Road	36
	Chocolate Orange Kiddush Loaf with Fudge Frosting	37
	Dutch Apple Cake	37
	Kiddush Chocolate Brownies	38
	Many Hands	39
	Almond Pudding	217
	Chocolate Orange Brownies	217
	No-Bake Chocolate Cheesecake	227
	Plaice Fillets with Smoked Salmon	266
	Chocolate Torte	305
Caroline Silver Lewis	Soup, Beautiful Soup	234
Victoria Silverlock	Baking a Biblical Story at Playshul	88
	Dreidel Cookies	149
Ludmilla Silverov	Blinis	285
Olin Sloan	Lekvár	178
Julia Stanton	My Friday Evening	115
	Lazy Chicken and Rice	116
Marion Style	Marion's Matzah Balls	215
	Marion's Ginger Biscuits	316
	Chocolate Chestnut Cake	317

T		
Nadine Tuffin	Nadine's Chopped Liver	248
Sharon Tyler	Banana Ginger Cake	303
U		
Josephine Urban	Egg and Onion	248
Jessica Urvicz	Gratin de Courgettes Au Chevre et Noisettes	255
V		
Aaron & Sophie Vallance	Kamish Broit	317
Veena Vohora	A Mosaic Stew	107
W		
Judy Weleminsky	Pesach Rolls	211
Renee Woolf	Welsh Cakes and Strudel: A Bar Mitzvah Baking Tale	50
	Strudel (My Way!)	56
	Scones	56
	Grandma's Welsh Cakes	56
Z		
Nicki Zisman	Chocolate Fridge Cake	315
Susan Zisman	Almond Cake	301

List of Recipe by Type

SOUPS	
Adam's Swiss Creamy Chestnut Soup	243
Barley Soup	165
Beef, Vegetable and Noodle Soup	241
Carrot and Lentil Soup	231
Chicken Soup and Kneidlach	240
Creamed Tomato and Pasta Soup	232
Dona Maria's Gazpacho	239
Grandma Dora's Borscht	233
Harira Soup	236
Leek and Watercress Soup	232
Mushroom and Puy Lentil Soup	232
Parsnip and Apple Soup	241
Parsnip Soup	231
Pea Soup	231
Sweet Potato and Lentil Soup	242
Winter Soup	242

STARTERS, SIDES AND SALADS	
Asparagus Salad with Sesame Seeds	253
Bazargan	167
Gratin de Courgettes Au Chevre et Noisettes	255
Israeli/Arabic Salad	247
Janet's Jewel Salad	252
Marinated Cucumber Salad	251
Nadine's Chopped Liver	248
Noodle Salad	252
Potato Bravas	255
Puy Lentil Salad	253
Tabbouleh	251
Tal's Falafel	246
Very Very Easy Coleslaw	252
Warm Sweet Potato and Halloumi Salad	254
Greek Salad	249
Egg and Onion	248
Sandy's Famous Mushroom Almond Pate	249
Sweet Potato Chips	247
Hummus Fit for Kings and Paupers	258

MAINS	
Vegetarian	
Amazing Spinach Casserole	259
Apple Latkes	144
Aromatic Stuffed Pepper	132
Baked Potato Latkes	144
Carrot Latkes	142
Cheese Latkes	142
Chris' Puff Pastry Rolls	259
Corn Latkes	142
Courgette Latkes	142
Courgette or Aubergine Gratin	260
Courgette Bake	263
Curried Corn	282
Curried Nut Roast	262
Easy Pizza	262
Easy Roasted Vegetables	266
Gluten-free Latkes	145
Grandma Freda's Braised Chestnut and Mushroom Pie	264
Green Bean Latkes	142
Michael's Rice Recipe	274
Mushroom Spelt Risotto	278
Persian Aubergines	165
Persian Latkes	144
Pesaj Spinach Minna Drizzled with Grape Syrup	203
Potato Bhaji	280
Quick Carrot and Courgette Pancakes	263
Ratatouille Niçoise	259
Rice with Red Lentils (Khichdi)	282
Seven Veg Tagine	265
Spinach Bhaji	281

Spinach Borrecas	224
Spinach Quiche	260
Tomato Bhaji	280
Traditional Potato Latkes	139
Tzimmes	265
Veggie Stew	108

Fish

Fish Cakes	270
Gefilte Fish (Fish Cakes)	268
Halibut Sweet and Sour	211
Lorna's Fish Pie	267
Mixed Ecuadorian Ceviche (Fish Marinated in Lemon and Lime Juice)	270
Plaice Fillets with Smoked Salmon	266
Polish Ryba Po Grecku ("Fish Greek Style")	40
Rosie's Fried Fish	268
Saumon Poche with Creamy Sauce	47
Spicy Tuna Fish Cakes	281
The Most Honest Recipe I Know: Arctic Chowder	257
Tuna Fish Curry	281
Yoghurt Coriander Fish	267

Meat

Bell Peppers Stuffed with Beef and Rice	274
Chicken in Vegetable Sauce	272
Chicken with Garlic Potatoes and Rosemary	279
Chicken Paprika	273
Chilli Con Carne for Fifty	63
Curried Chicken	283
Lazy Chicken and Rice	116
Mince Koftas (Meatballs)	283
Nadine's Chopped Liver	248
Oma's Braised Beef	277
Spanish Chicken Casserole	271
Sweet and Sour Meatballs	273
Tandoori Chicken	282
Wok Fried Honey Soy Chicken	271
Yummy Sesame Chicken Schnitzel	272

BREAD

"Biblical" Hallah (Seven Species)	161
Apple Hallah	118
Bagels	69
Rabbi Sylvia's Hallah	45
Judith's Hallah Dough Recipe	85

PUDDINGS

Betty's Lockshen Pudding	286
Blinis	285
Chani Smith's Avocado Dessert	287
Chocolate Mousse	287
Chocolate Mousse	287
Compote	201
Crème au Chocolat	219
Honeycomb Ice Cream	287
Iced Pomegranate Grains	169
Pavlova Made with Love and Dedication	289
Pears in Honey, White Wine and Cardamom	292
Plum and Ginger Ice Cream with Crumble Topping	288
Polly's Strudel (Layered Apple and Plum Pie)	120
Rhubarb Compote	292
Rice Pudding	290
Roasted Nectarine Ice Cream	288
Sam's Fruity Crumble	291
Tiramisu	290

CAKES

Alec Cake	302
Almond Cake	301
Almond Pudding	217
Almond, Honey and Whisky Lemon Cake	122
Apple Cake	300
Balawa	312
Banana Ginger Cake	303
Banana and Raisin Loaf	168
Blue Poppy Seed Cake	307
Cake for All Seasons	308
Chocolate Chestnut Cake	317
Chocolate Orange Brownies	217
Chocolate Orange Kiddush Loaf with Fudge Frosting	37
Chocolate Torte	216
Chocolate Torte	305
Connie's Cream Cheese Cake	226
Continental Plum Tart	310
Crazy Cake	310
Date and Walnut Bread	156
Dutch Apple Cake	37
Eleri's Mount Sinai Cake	228
"Emma's" Brownies	305
Fruit Cake	300
Gateau Lawrence	305
Gluten-free Carrot and Cinnamon Cupcakes	309
Grandma's Welsh Cakes	56
Hamantaschen - Texas Style	172
Hannah's Most Dangerous Cake	59
Healthy Carrot Cake	306
Honey Cake	35
Jamie's Apple and Honey Cake	124
Kiddush Chocolate Brownies	38
La Pasta (Orange Sponge Cake)	297
Lekach (Honey Cake)	121
Lemon Drizzle Cake	35
Light Chocolate Cake	298
"Magic Red" Cake	301
My Sultana Cheesecake	226
No-Bake Chocolate Cheesecake	227
One Bowl Brownies	308
Orange-Carrot Spice Muffins	168
Pantespanya (Pain dEspagne)	311
Passion Cake	307
Perfect Chocolate Brownies	294
Pesach Lemon Cake	216
Pizza Romana (Candied Fruitcake)	295
Red Velvet Cupcakes	309
Rugelach	225
Savta's Apple Cake	114
Scones	56
Seven Biblical Species Muffins	163
Strudel (My Way!)	56
Tea Bread	303
Tunisian Almond and Orange Cake	63
Very Quick Cake for Very Busy People	105
Yoghurt Cake	302

BISCUITS

Almond Macaroons	217
Best Ever Biscuits for Icing (Gingerbread Biscuits)	135
Chocolate Fridge Cake	315
Chocolate Fridge Biscuits	36
Cinnamon Balls	217
Cottage Cookies	315
Dreidel Cookies	149
Eleri's Edible Sukkah	135
Eleri's Gingerbread Dreidel	147
Grandma's Pesach Biscuits	216
Jason's Almond Citrus Macaroons	314
Joseph Biscuits	88
Kak B'milch (Salty Biscuits)	312
Kamish Broit	317
Marion's Ginger Biscuits	316
Oatmeal Chocolate Chip Cookies	314
Rocky Road	36
Sandwich Cookies	318
Seven Biblical Species Cookies	164

SUITABLE FOR PASSOVER

Almond Macaroons	217
Almond Pudding	217
Anne's Amazing Apple Sauce	145
Chani Smith's Avocado Dessert	287
Chicken Soup and Kneidlach	240
Chicken with Garlic Potatoes and Rosemary	279
Chocolate and Orange Matzah	197
Chocolate Mousse	287
Chocolate Mousse	287
Chocolate Orange Brownies	217
Chocolate Torte	216
Cinnamon Balls	217
Compote	201
Crème au Chocolat	219
Date Butter	162
Egg and Onion	248
Eingemachts (Beetroot Jam)	209
Fish Cakes	270
Fried Matzah	201
Gefilte Fish (Fish Cakes)	268
Grandma Dora's Borscht	233
Grandma's Pesach Biscuits	216
Halibut Sweet and Sour	211
Hollandaise	219
Matzah, How to Make	180
Iced Pomegranate Grains	169
Imberlach – Carrot Candy	208
Israeli/Arabic Salad	247
Jason's Almond Citrus Macaroons	314
Leek and Watercress Soup	232
Lekvár	178
Lemon Curd	200
Marinated Cucumber Salad	251
Matzah Granola	198
Matzah Pancakes	201
Matzah Pudding	205
Mayonnaise	219
Mixed Ecuadorian Ceviche (Fish Marinated in Lemon and Lime Juice)	270
Nadine's Chopped Liver	248
Persian Aubergines	165
Pesach Lemon Cake	216
Pesach Rolls	211
Pesaj Spinach Minna Drizzled with Grape Syrup	203
Ratatouille Niçoise	259
Rhubarb Compote	292
Rosie's Fried Fish	268
Teiglach	208
The House of Matzah	195
The Most Honest Recipe I Know: Arctic Chowder	257
Toffee Matzah Crunch	199
Traditional Potato Latkes	139
Sweet Potato Chips	247
Tzimmes	265

MATZAH BALLS

Kneidlach with Chicken Soup	240
Charlotte's Matzah Balls	213
Kneidlach	214
Marion's Matzah Balls	215
Matzah Balls	214
Passover Lochen	207

PASSOVER (KITNIYOT)

Aromatic Stuffed Pepper	132
Bell Peppers Stuffed with Beef and Rice	274
Chilli Con Carne for Fifty	63
Rice Pudding	290
Winter Soup	242

Index

A

Alec Cake 302
Almond
    Almond Cake 301
    Almond, Honey and Whisky Lemon Cake 122
    Almond Macaroons 217
    Almond Pudding 217
    Balawa 313
    Chocolate Torte 216
    Grandma's Pesach Biscuits 216
    Jason's Almond Citrus Macaroons 314
    Pesach Lemon Cake 216
    Sandy's Famous Mushroom Almond Pate 249
    Tunisian Almond and Orange Cake 63
Apple 190
    Anne's Amazing Apple Sauce 145
    Apple Cake 300
    Apple Hallah 118
    Apple Latkes 144
    Apple Sauce 99
    Apple Steffan 128
    Compote 201
    Dutch Apple Cake 37 339
    Jamie's Apple and Honey Cake 124
    Parsnip and Apple Soup 241
    Polly's 'Strudel' (Layered Apple and Plum Pie) 120
    Pressure Cooker Apple Sauce 145
    Savta's Apple Cake 114
    Strudel (My Way!) 56
Apples and Honey Nursery 72 112 173 311
Arctic Chowder 257
Asparagus Salad with Sesame Seeds 253
Aubergines
    Courgette or Aubergine Gratin 260
    Persian Aubergines 165
    Stuffed Aubergines 133
Avocado Dessert 287

B

Bagels
    How the Bagel Arrived in SW19 65
Balawa 313
Banana and Raisin Loaf 168
Banana Ginger Cake 303
Barley Soup 165
Barmitzvah 33
    Welsh Cakes and Strudel: A Bar Mitzvah Baking Tale 50
Bat Mitzvah 55 58
    Hannah O'Keeffe 58
Beef
    Beef, Vegetable and Noodle Soup 241
    Beef with Pickled Walnut 238
    Braised Beef, Oma's 277
    Chilli Con Carne for Fifty 63
Beer 220
Bell Peppers Stuffed with Beef and Rice 274
Bhaji
    Potato Bhaji 280
    Spinach Bhaji 281
    Tomato Bhaji 280
"Biblical" Hallah 161
Biscuits
    Almond Macaroons 217
    Chocolate Fridge Biscuits 36
    Cinnamon Balls 217
    Cottage Cookies 315
    Dreidel Cookies 149
    Ginger Biscuits, Marion's 316
    Jason's Almond Citrus Macaroons 314
    Joseph Biscuits 88
    Kak B'milch (Salty Biscuits) 312
    Kamish Broit 317
    Oatmeal Chocolate Chip Cookies 314
    Pizza Romana 295
    Rocky Road 36
    Sandwich Cookies 318
    Seven Biblical Species Cookies 164

Blinis 285

Blog 13 27 28 163 268 286

Blue Poppy Seed Cake 307

Blue, Rabbi Lionel 28 257

Blumenthal, Heston 28 268 275 278 • *See also* Celebrity chefs

    Mushroom Spelt Risotto 278

    My Dinner with Heston Blumenthal 275

Borscht, Grandma Dora's 233

Bread 41 • *See also* Hallah

    Bagels 69

    Short History of Bread 220

Brownies • *See* Chocolate brownies

C

Cake • *See also* Chocolate and Chocolate Brownies *See also* Cheesecake

    Alec Cake 302

    Almond Cake 301

    Apple Cake 300

    Banana and Raisin Loaf 168

    Banana Ginger Cake 303

    Blue Poppy Seed Cake 307

    Carrot and Cinnamon Cupcakes, Gluten-Free 309

    Carrot Cake, Healthy 306

    Continental Plum Tart 310

    Crazy Cake 310

    Date and Walnut Cake 306

    Fruit Cake 300

    Honey Cake

        Almond, Honey and Whisky Lemon Cake 122

        Honey Cake, Lynne's 35

        Jamie's Apple and Honey Cake 124

        Lekach (Honey Cake) 121

    Kiddush Cakes 105

        Chocolate Orange Loaf with Fudge Frosting 37

        Dutch Apple Cake 37

        Kiddush Chocolate Brownies 38

        Lemon Drizzle Cake 35

    Lemon Cake for Pesach 216

    "Magic Red" Cake 301

    My Mum's Date and Walnut Bread 156

    Orange-Carrot Spice Muffins 168

    Passion Cake 307

    Red Velvet Cupcakes 309

    Savta's Apple Cake 114

    Seven Biblical Species Muffins 163

    Tea Bread 303

    The Cake for All Seasons 308

    Very Quick Cake for Busy People 105

    Yoghurt Cake 302

Carrot

    Carrot and Cinnamon Cupcakes, Gluten-Free 309

    Carrot and Courgette Pancakes 263

    Carrot and Lentil Soup 231

    Carrot Cake, Healthy 306

Catering

    Catering Tips from Sally-Ann 62

    Many Hands 39

    Renee's Top Tips 55

Cheesecake 27 34 226

    Connie's Cream Cheese Cake 226

    My Sultana Cheesecake, Diane Barnett's 226

    No-Bake Chocolate Cheesecake 227

Chestnut

    Chestnut, Braised and Mushroom Pie, Grandma Freda's 264

    Chestnut Soup, Adam's Swiss Creamy 243

    Chocolate Chestnut Cake 317

Chicken

    Chicken in Vegetable Sauce 272

    Chicken Paprika 273

    Chicken Soup 240

    Chicken with Garlic Potatoes and Rosemary 279

    Curried Chicken 283

    Lazy Chicken and Rice 116

    Spanish Chicken Casserole 271

    Tandoori Chicken 282

Wok Fried Honey Soy Chicken 271
Yummy Sesame Chicken Schnitzel 272
Chilli Con Carne for Fifty 63
Chinese New Year 83
Chocolate
    Chocolate Brownies
        Chocolate Orange Brownies 217
        "Emma's" Brownies 305
        Kiddush Chocolate Brownies 38 339
        One Bowl Brownies 308
        Perfect Chocolate Brownies 294
    Chocolate Chestnut Cake 317
    Chocolate Fridge Biscuits 36
    Chocolate Fridge Cake 315
    Chocolate Mousse 287
    Chocolate Orange Loaf with Fudge Frosting 37
    Chocolate Torte 216 305
    Crème au Chocolat 219
    Gateau Lawrence (Chocolate Cake) 305
    Hannah's Most Dangerous Cake 59
    Light Chocolate Cake 298
    No-Bake Chocolate Cheesecake 227
Chocolate Torte 216
Christmas 40 100
Cinnamon Balls 217
Coleslaw, Very Very Easy 252
Compote 201
Continental Plum Tart 310
Cookies • *See* Biscuits
Corn, Curried 282
Cottage Cookies 315
Courgette
    Courgette Bake 263
    Courgette or Aubergine Gratin 260
    Gratin de Courgettes Au Chèvre et Noisettes 255
    Ratatouille Niçoise 259
Creamed Tomato and Pasta Soup 232
Crème au Chocolat 219
Crumble, Sam's Fruity 291

Cucumber and Cream Cheese Mousse 103
Cucumber Salad, Marinated 251
Curried Nut Roast 262

D

Dainty Dinners and Dishes for Jewish Families 204 206
Date and Walnut Bread, My Mum's 156
Date and Walnut Cake 306
Date Butter 162
Dreidel Cookies 149
Dutch Apple Cake 37 339

E

Eat with Us • *See* Ladies Guild
Egg and Onion 248
Eid-al Adha 83
Eingemachts (Beetroot Jam) 209
"Emma's" Brownies 305
Exodus 41 184

F

Fairtrade 95
Falafel, Tal's 246
Fish 100 • *See also* Sushi
    Arctic Chowder 257
    Cold Fried Fish 238
    Fish Cakes 270
    Fish Pie, Lorna's 267
    Gefilte Fish (Fish Cakes) 268
    Halibut Sweet and Sour 211
    Mixed Ecuadorian Ceviche (Fish Marinated in Lemon and Lime Juice) 270
    Plaice Fillets with Smoked Salmon 266
    Polish Ryba Po Grecku ("Fish Greek style") 40
    Rosie's Fried Fish 268
    Saumon Poche & Creamy Sauce 47
        Court Bouillon (fish stock) 47
    Spicy Tuna Fish Cakes 281
    Tuna Fish Curry 281

Yoghurt Coriander Fish 267

Fruit Cake 300

Fruitcake, Candied • *See* Pizza Romana

G

Gateau Lawrence (Chocolate Cake) 305

Gazpacho, Dona Maria's 239

Gefiltefest 294

Gefilte Fish • *See* Fish

Ginger Biscuits, Marion's 316

Gooseberry Bushes and Gazpacho: Reminiscences and a Recipe 237

Gospel of Matthew 42

Grandma's Pesach Biscuits 216

Grandma's Welsh Cakes • *See* Welsh Cakes

Granola, Matzah 198

Greek Salad 249

Greenberg, Florence 204 238

H

Hallah 45 73 85 118 161
    Apple Hallah 118
    "Biblical" Hallah 161
    Hallah and Sermon Preparation Plaited Together 45
    Judith's Hallah Dough Recipe 85

Hamantaschen
    Hamantaschen -Texas style! 171
    Hamantaschen - WimShul Style! 173

Hannah's Most Dangerous Cake 59

Hanukkah 80 99 • *See also* Latkes *See also* Apple Sauce
    Dreidel Cookies 149
    Plum Cake for Hanucah, 1916 150

Harira Soup 236

Havdalah 84

Heder 65 67 182

Henry, May & Halford, Kate 204

Honey Cake • *See* Rosh Hashanah *See also* Kiddush and Cake

Honeycomb Ice Cream 287

I

Iced Pomegranate Grains 169

Imberlach (Carrot Candy) 208

Israeli/Arabic Salad 247

J

Jam
    Eingemachts (Beetroot Jam) 227
    Lekvár 178

Jamie's Apple and Honey Cake 124

Janet's Jewel Salad 252

Jewish Chronicle 28 88

Joseph Biscuits 88

Juvenal 221

K

Kak B'milch (Salty Biscuits) 312

Kamish Broit 317

Kiddush
    Cakes, Care and Respect 33
    Kiddush Cakes 35
        Chocolate Fridge Biscuits 36
        Chocolate Orange Loaf with Fudge Frosting 38
        Kiddush Chocolate Brownies 38
        Lemon Drizzle Cake 35
        Rocky Road 36
    Kiddushim at Wimbledon 30

Kitniyot 184

Kneidlach • *See* Matzah Balls

Kramer, Lotte, Poems
    A Lettuce With Herbs 18
    An Old Woman Cooking Eggs 19
    Cherries 19

Kushner, Kim 297

L

Ladies Guild 15 30 103 106
    Eat with Us 103

Lag B'Omer 83

Larkum, Eleri - cakes 43

Abraham's Tent Confection 49
"Magic Red" Cake 301
Mount Sinai Cake 228
Plum Cake for Hanucah, 1916 150
Tallit Cake 43
The House of Matzah 195
Twelve Tribes Cake 92
Latkes 99
   Apple Latkes 144
   Baked Potato Latkes 144
   Carrot Latkes 142
   Cheese Latkes 142
   Corn Latkes 142
   Courgette Latkes 142
   Gluten-Free Latkes 145
   Green Bean Latkes 142
   Persian latkes 144
   Time to Reinvent the Latke? 141
   Traditional Potato Latkes 139
Lazy Chicken and Rice 116
Leek and Watercress Soup 232
Lekach (Honey Cake) 121
Lekvár 178
Lemon
   Lemon Curd 200
   Lemon Drizzle Cake 35 339
Lemon Cake for Pesach 216
Liver, Chopped, Nadine's 248
Lockshen Pudding 286

M

"Magic Red" Cake 301
Manna 41 42
Markison, Jerry, Limericks • See Limericks
   A Woman of Substance 140
   Bagelology 71
   Unleavened Bread 222
Masala, Fresh Green 282
Matzah • See also Passover
   Baking Matzah in Ethiopia 182
   Chocolate and Orange Matzah 197

Fried Matzah 201
How to Make Matzah 180
Matzah Granola 198
Matzah Pancakes 201
Matzah Pudding 204 205
   A Lady's Passover Pudding 205
   Florence Greenberg's Matzah Pudding 205
   Matzah Pudding: A Victorian Odyssey? 204
Pesaj Spinach Minna Drizzled with Grape Syrup 203
The House of Matzah 195
The Meaning of Matzah and a Short History of Bread 220
Toffee Matzah Crunch 199
Ways with Matzah 197
Matzah Balls 192
   Charlotte's Matzah Balls 213
   Kneidlach, Sally-Ann Feldman 240
   Marion's Matzah Balls 215
   Matzah Balls, Diane Barnett's 214
Mayonnaise 219
Measurements 16
Meatballs, Sweet and Sour 273
Mince Koftas (Meatballs) 283
Montefiore, Lady Judith 205
Mosaic Stew 107
Mushroom
   Mushroom Almond Pate, Sandy's Famous 249
   Mushroom and Puy Lentil Soup 232
   Mushroom Spelt Risotto 278

N

Nacamulli, Silvia 295
Nectarine, Roasted Ice Cream 288
New Year • See Rosh Hashanah
Night Shelter 15 96 97 99 231
Noodle Salad 252
Norooz, Persian New Year 83

O

Oatmeal Chocolate Chip Cookies 314

Orange
- Orange-Carrot Spice Muffins 168
- Tunisian Almond and Orange Cake 63

P

Parent Teacher Association (PTA) 65

Parsnip and Apple Soup 241

Parsnip Soup 231

Passion Cake 307

Passover 80 188 • *See also* Matzah *See also* Matzah Balls
- A Communal Seder 191
- Almond Macaroons 217
- Almond Pudding 217
- Chocolate Orange Brownies 217
- Chocolate Torte 216
- Cinnamon Balls 217
- Crème au Chocolat 219
- Grandma's Pesach Biscuits 216
- Kitniyot 184
- "Kosher for Passover" Baking Powder 217
- Mayonnaise 219
- Memories of an East Ham Pesach 207
- My Mother's Pesach 212
- Old World Pesach Treats – Irish Style 208
- Our Pesach "Plant" 210
- Passover Lochen 207
- Pesach Lemon Cake 216
- Pesach Mornings by the Mersey 200
- Pesaj Spinach Minna Drizzled with Grape Syrup 203
- Recollections of Chilean Pesaj (Pesach) 202
- Seder • *See* Passover
- What to Eat on Pesach 183
- What Would I Put onto a Seder Plate? 188

Pastry
- Balawa 313
- Chris' Puff Pastry Rolls 259
- Continental Plum Tart 310
- Grandma Freda's Braised Chestnut and Mushroom Pie 264
- Hamantaschen - Texas style! 171
- Polly's 'Strudel' (Layered Apple and Plum Pie) 120
- Rugelach 225
- Scones 56
- Spinach Borrecas 224
- Spinach Quiche 260

Pavlova Made with Love and Dedication 289

Pears in Honey, White Wine and Cardamom 292

Pea Soup 231

Persian Aubergines 165

Pesach • *See* Passover

Pesach Lemon Cake 216

Pirkei Avot 41

Pizza, Easy 262

Pizza Romana 295

Pliny the Elder 220

Plum
- Continental Plum Tart 310
- Plum and Ginger Ice Cream with Crumble Topping 288
- Plum Cake for Hanucah, 1916 150
- Polly's 'Strudel' (Layered Apple and Plum Pie) 120

Polish Ryba Po Grecku ("Fish Greek style") 40

Polly's 'Strudel' (Layered Apple and Plum Pie) 120

Pomegranate 188
- Iced Pomegranate Grains 169

Potato Bhaji 280

Potato Bravas 255

Pressure Cooker Apple Sauce 145

Puddings
- Almond Pudding 217
- Avocado Dessert 287
- Chocolate Mousse 287
- Crumble, Sam's Fruity 291

Honeycomb Ice Cream 287
Lockshen Pudding 286
Nectarine, Roasted Ice Cream 288
Pavlova Made with Love and Dedication 289
Pears in Honey, White Wine and Cardamom 292
Plum and Ginger Ice Cream with Crumble Topping 288
Polly's 'Strudel' (Layered Apple and Plum Pie) 120
Rhubarb Compote 292
Rice Pudding 290
Tiramisu 290

Puff Pastry Rolls, Chris' 259
Purim 80
   Hamantaschen -Texas style! 171
   Hamantaschen - WimShul Style! 173
   Purim bake-in 173
Puy Lentil Salad 253

R

Rabbi
   Rabbi Eleazar ben Azariah 41
   Rabbi Hillel 31
   Rabbi Lionel Blue • *See also* Blue, Rabbi Lionel
   Rabbi Shammai 31
   Rabbi Sybil A. Sheridan 33 191
      Baking Matzah in Ethiopia 182
      Bread from the Earth and from Heaven 41
      My Dinner with Heston Blumenthal 275
      What to Eat on Pesach 183
   Rabbi Sylvia Rothschild
      33 41 45 154 156 188 220
      Hallah and sermon preparation plaited together 45
      The Meaning of Matzah and a Short History of Bread 220
      What Would I Put onto a Seder Plate 188
   Rabbi Yehudah Arie Leib Alter 42

   Rav Kook 155
   S'fat Emet 42
Raph Gonley 60
Ratatouille Niçoise 259
Recipe for Preserving Children 106
Red Velvet Cupcakes 309
Reflections on Tu B'Shevat 154
Rhubarb Compote 292
Rice
   Rice, Michael's 274
   Rice Pudding 290
   Rice with Red Lentils (Khichdi) 282
Roasted Vegetables, Easy 266
Rocky Road 36 339
Roden, Claudia 28 167 238 • *See also* Celebrity chefs
Rose, Evelyn 275
Rosh Hashanah 27 79
Rothschild, Rabbi Sylvia • *See* Rabbi Sylvia Rothschild
Rugelach 225

S

Salads
   Asparagus Salad with Sesame Seed 253
   Bazargan, Bulgar Salad 167
   Coleslaw, Very Very Easy 252
   Cucumber Salad, Marinated 251
   Greek Salad 249
   Israeli/Arabic Salad 247
   Janet's Jewel Salad 252
   Noodle Salad 252
   Puy Lentil Salad 253
   Sweet Potato, Warm, and Halloumi Salad 254
   Tabbouleh 251
Sandwich Cookies 318
Sandy's Famous Mushroom Almond Pâté 249
Savta's Apple Cake 114
Scones 56 339
Seder • *See* Passover
Sephardi 184

Seven Biblical Species 157
    Seven Biblical Species Cookies 164
    Seven Biblical Species Muffins 163
    The Original Biblical Superfoods! 159

Shabbat
    Recipe for a Streatham Friday Night 111
    Shabbat Club 34
    Shabbat Lunch with a French Twist 47
    Welcome Shabbat 49

Shavuot 83 223

Sheridan, Rabbi Sybil • *See* Rabbi Sybil Sheridan

Simcha 30

Simchat Torah 31 73 80 104

Soup
    Adam's Swiss Creamy Chestnut Soup 243
    Barley Soup 165
    Beef, Vegetable and Noodle Soup 241
    Borscht, Grandma Dora's 233
    Borsht 100
    Carrot and Lentil Soup 231
    Chicken Soup 240
    Creamed Tomato and Pasta Soup 232
    Gazpacho, Dona Maria's 239
    Harira Soup 236
    Leek and Watercress Soup 232
    Mushroom and Puy Lentil Soup 232
    Parsnip and Apple Soup 241
    Parsnip Soup 231
    Pea Soup 231
    Soup, Beautiful Soup 234
    Sweet Potato and Lentil Soup 242
    Winter Soup 242

Spinach
    Amazing Spinach Casserole 259
    Pesaj Spinach Minna Drizzled with Grape Syrup 203
    Spinach Bhaji 281
    Spinach Borrecas 224
    Spinach Quiche 260

Stanton, Julia, My Friday Evening 115

Strudel 56 339

Sukkot 80
    Aromatic Stuffed Peppers 132
    Dutch Apple Cake 37 339
    Stuffed Aubergines 133

Sushi 28 30 34

Sweet Potato
    Sweet Potato and Lentil Soup 242
    Sweet Potato Chips 247
    Sweet Potato, Warm, and Halloumi Salad 254

T

Tabbouleh 251

Tagine, Seven Veg 265

Tea Bread 303

Teiglach 208

Tiramisu 290

Toffee Matzah Crunch 199

Tomato Bhaji 280

Torah 31 41 42 49 73 80 104 157 222
    Bible Stories 83
        Baking a Biblical Story at Playshul 88

Tu B'Shevat 27 80 153 154 156 160 161 165
    "Biblical" Hallah 161
    My Mum's Date and Walnut Bread 156
    Reflections on Tu B'Shevat 154

Tunisian Almond and Orange Cake 63

Twelve Tribes Cake 92

Tzimmes 265

V

Veggie Stew 108

Very Quick Cake for Busy People 105

W

Welsh Cakes
    Grandma's Welsh Cakes 56 339

Wimbledon Night Shelter 96
    Merton Winter Night Shelter 97

Wimshul Cooks 4 13 27 28 50 144 173 268 276 294

Winter Soup 242

Y

Yoghurt Cake 302
Yom Ha'Atzmaut 80